*For Aurora Martínez Ramos,
with gratitude for her dedication to
English learners, and her commitment
to the SIOP® Model.*

        —mev & je

*To my family: Ken, Katie, and Luke,
for their support and love.*

        —maw

99 MORE Ideas and Activities for Teaching English Learners with the SIOP® Model

MaryEllen Vogt

California State University, Long Beach

Jana Echevarría

California State University, Long Beach

Marilyn Amy Washham

Pearson Education

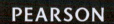

Boston • Columbus • Indianapolis • New York • San Francisco • Upper Saddle River
Amsterdam • Cape Town • Dubai • London • Madrid • Milan • Munich • Paris • Montréal • Toronto
Delhi • Mexico City • São Paulo • Sydney • Hong Kong • Seoul • Singapore • Taipei • Tokyo

Vice President, Editor in Chief: Jeffery W. Johnston
Senior Acquisitions Editor: Julie Peters
Editorial Assistant: Andrea Hall
Director of Marketing: Margaret Waples
Executive Marketing Manager: Krista Clark
Project Manager: Annette Joseph
Project Coordination and Text Design: Electronic Publishing Services Inc., NYC
Photo Researcher: Electronic Publishing Services Inc., NYC
Operations Specialist: Linda Sager
Electronic Composition: Jouve
Cover Design: Suzanne Behnke
Cover Images: KidStock/Blend Images/Corbis and Reflektastudios/Fotolia

Credits and acknowledgments borrowed from other sources and reproduced, with permission, in this textbook appear on the appropriate page within text.

Library of Congress Cataloging-in-Publication Data
Vogt, MaryEllen.
   99 more ideas and activities for teaching English learners with the SIOP® model / MaryEllen Vogt, Jana Echevarría, Marilyn Amy Washam.
      pages cm. — (SIOP series)
   Includes bibliographical references.
   ISBN 978-0-13-343106-3
   1. English language—Study and teaching—Foreign speakers.   2. English language—Study and teaching—Activities.   3. Language arts—Correlation with content subjects.   I. Echevarria, Jana.   II. Washam, Marilyn Amy.
III. Title.   IV. Title: Ninety-nine more ideas and activities for teaching English learners with the SIOP® model.
   PE1128.A2V64 2014
   428.0071—dc23
                                                                            2013039198

28 17

ISBN 10: 0-13-343106-1
ISBN 13: 978-0-13-343106-3

MaryEllen Vogt is Professor Emerita of Education at California State University, Long Beach. Dr. Vogt has been a classroom teacher, reading specialist, special education specialist, curriculum coordinator, and teacher educator. She received a doctorate in Language and Literacy from the University of California, Berkeley. Dr. Vogt is an author of over 60 articles and chapters, and is co-author of sixteen books for teachers and administrators, including *Making Content Comprehensible for English Learners: The SIOP® Model* (2013), and the other books in the SIOP series. Her research interests include improving comprehension in the content areas, teacher change and development, and content literacy and language acquisition for English learners. Dr. Vogt has provided professional development in all fifty states and in several other countries, including Germany, where she served as a Visiting Scholar at the University of Cologne. She was inducted into the California Reading Hall of Fame, received her university's Distinguished Faculty Teaching Award, and served as President of the International Reading Association.

Jana Echevarría is Professor Emerita of Education at California State University, Long Beach, where she was selected as Outstanding Professor. She has taught in elementary, middle, and high school in general education, special education, ESL, and bilingual programs. She has lived in Taiwan, Spain, and Mexico and is an internationally known expert on second language learners. Her research and publications focus on effective instruction for English learners, including those with learning disabilities. She has presented her research across the U.S. and internationally including Oxford University (England), Wits University (South Africa), Harvard University (U.S.), South East Europe University (Macedonia), and University of Barcelona (Spain). Publications include the popular SIOP book series and over 50 books, book chapters, and journal articles.

Marilyn Amy Washam is an Education Specialist for Pearson. She has taught elementary ESL, junior high ESL, and high school sheltered English Language Arts. She has also worked as a Recent Immigrant Specialist and ESL Coordinator at the district level where she worked with teachers and administrators to implement the SIOP® Model. For the past ten years, Amy has worked with educators in over 25 states, Puerto Rico, St. Croix, and Canada on SIOP implementation. She thanks her husband, Ken, and her children, Katie and Luke, for their support and love.

Contents

4   Comprehensible Input   60

Alphabetical Listing of Ideas and Activities

FIGURES

Welcome to *99 MORE Ideas and Activities for Teaching English Learners with the SIOP® Model!* This book is intended to provide "SIOPers" everywhere with an additional resource to use during your planning and implementation of effective SIOP lessons.

It has been nearly two decades since we began conceptualizing and researching what effective content and language instruction for English learners must be if students are to achieve English proficiency and academic success in school. During this time, we have learned a great deal from the thousands of classroom teachers, ESL specialists, administrators, professors, researchers, and students with whom we have collaborated and worked. From these people, young and not-so-young, we have learned that:

- The SIOP® Model is a lesson planning and delivery system that teachers can learn to implement consistently and to a high degree with professional development and coaching.

- The SIOP® Model, when implemented to a high degree, has been found to bring about significant academic and language gains not only for English learners, but for all students, as measured on standardized tests (Echevarria, 2012; Echevarria, Richards-Tutor, Canges, & Francis, 2011; Echevarria & Short, 2010; Echevarria & Short, 2011; Echevarria, Short, Richards-Tutor, & Himmel, 2011). For a full discussion of what constitutes high implementation of the SIOP® Model, see Chapter 11 in Echevarria, Vogt, and Short, 2013; 2014a; 2014b; and Echevarria, Short, Richards-Tutor, Chinn, and Ratleff, 2011.

- Effective SIOP teachers who consistently implement the Model's eight components and thirty features do so throughout the day, rather than using the instructional framework for some students and not for others, or for some subject areas (or periods) and not for others. These teachers believe and demonstrate through their teaching that the SIOP® Model is "the way I teach," every day and during all instructional periods.

What follows is a brief overview of the SIOP® Model's eight components. Grouped within the components are the thirty instructional features. This complex instructional framework that is elaborated in the SIOP protocol provides teachers of English learners and native speakers alike with the means to plan, teach, and assess effective, comprehensible, and appropriate instruction. See Appendix A for the complete Sheltered Instruction Observation Protocol (SIOP).

The SIOP® Model includes the following eight components:

1. **Lesson Preparation**   Teachers plan lessons carefully, paying particular attention to language and content objectives, appropriate content concepts, the use of supplemental materials, adaptation of content, and meaningful activities.

2. **Building Background**   Teachers make explicit links to their students' background experiences and knowledge, and past learning, and teach and emphasize key vocabulary.

3. **Comprehensible Input**   Teachers use a variety of techniques to make instruction understandable, including speech appropriate to students' English proficiency, clear

academic tasks, modeling, and the use of a variety of techniques, including visuals, hands-on activities, demonstrations, gestures, and body language.

4. **Strategies**　Teachers provide students with instruction in and practice with a variety of learning strategies, scaffolding their teaching with techniques such as think-alouds, and they promote higher-order thinking through questions and tasks at a variety of levels.

5. **Interaction**　Teachers provide students with frequent opportunities for interaction and discussion, group students to support content and language objectives, provide sufficient wait-time for student responses, and appropriately clarify concepts in the student's first language, if possible and as necessary.

6. **Practice & Application**　Teachers provide hands-on materials and/or manipulatives, and include activities for students to apply their content and language knowledge through all language skills (reading, writing, listening, and speaking).

7. **Lesson Delivery**　Teachers implement lessons that clearly support content and language objectives, use appropriate pacing, and have high levels of student engagement.

8. **Review & Assessment**　Teachers provide a comprehensive review of key vocabulary and content concepts, regularly give specific, academic feedback to students, and conduct assessment of student comprehension and learning throughout the lesson.

Overview of This Book

This title responds to frequent requests from educators for additional SIOP resources that will help make lesson planning and delivery more effective, more interactive, and less time-consuming. We've responded to your requests with this book that has a variety of ideas and activities that you can add to your teaching repertoire.

- **Chapter 1. Getting Started**　This chapter serves as your "owner's manual" for the book. We ask that you read it before you begin discovering all the ideas and activities so that you can streamline the SIOP lesson planning process while making your lessons more effective.

- **Chapters 2–9. The SIOP Components and Features**　In each of these chapters, you will find a brief description of each of the SIOP components and features, along with ideas and activities that are particularly effective for attending to particular SIOP features.

- **Chapter 10. Putting It All Together**　In this chapter, we discuss the SIOP lesson planning process and include a SIOP lesson plan template with suggestions for how and where to implement the thirty features in your lessons. The chapter also includes lesson plans created by SIOP teachers at a variety of grade levels and subject areas.

- **Appendixes**
  - **Appendix A**　The SIOP Protocol (for specific guidance on how to use the Protocol for observations, see Echevarria, Vogt, & Short, 2013; 2014a; 2014b).

- **Appendix B**   The process and product verbs listed on this chart are organized by the levels of the Revised Bloom's Taxonomy (Anderson & Krathwohl, 2001). They can be used when writing objectives to ensure that your content and language goals represent a variety of cognitive levels.
- **Multi-Layered Table of Contents**   You may have already noticed that you can pick and choose which table of contents works best for you: (1) the standard, chapter-by-chapter table of contents or (2) the table of contents that lists all of the ideas and activities alphabetically and by feature. We hope this helps you find what you need when you need it!
- **i** **dea and** **a** **ctivity Icons**   Throughout the book, for each of the 99 ideas or activities, you will find an icon that identifies whether it is a teaching idea or an instructional activity. Use these icons to guide you as you're planning SIOP lessons.

Acknowledgments

First, we wish to acknowledge and heartily thank all the SIOP teachers who have contributed their ideas, activities, and lesson plans for this book. You amaze us with your creativity, informed approach to lesson design, and commitment to using instructional activities in a truly meaningful way. We wanted this book to be authentic, for you our reader, and these teachers' ideas and deep understandings of the SIOP® Model have made it so. In this book, you will find the ideas, activities, and lesson plans of real teachers in real classrooms with real kids—English learners and native English speakers, alike. We have made every attempt to correctly identify the originators. If you know of any activity that is not correctly attributed, please let us know.

We also thank the SIOP teachers who shared their thoughts for the Teacher Reflections that begin each chapter. Their collective voices articulate the power of the SIOP Model and we appreciate their insights and wisdom. Their Teacher Reflections about using SIOP are sprinkled throughout the book, and we thank them for contributing their insights to our book. We also enthusiastically acknowledge our reviewers, whose helpful suggestions and thoughtful ideas are greatly appreciated. They include: Julia López-Roberston, University of South Carolina; Lorraine Smith, District School Board of Collier County; and Susan Seay, University of Alabama at Birmingham.

Without our Pearson editorial staff, there would be no SIOP books. We especially appreciate the assistance of our copy editor, Kathy Smith, and our editor, Julie Peters, for their support and expertise during the publication of this book. As always, we express our thanks to our SIOP colleague and friend, Deborah Short, for her ideas and collegiality; and to Keith Vogt for his creative illustrations that appear throughout the book. And finally, to our families who lovingly (and with great patience) support our work, we thank you.

mev
je
maw

1 Getting Started: Activities and SIOP Lessons

Monkey Business/Fotolia

A Teacher's Reflection

My impression from my first SIOP Institute was WOW! This is something different from all of the gimmicky workshops I have been to in the last 14 years. (Not all were gimmicky, but too many were a waste of time.) In my role as a district ESL specialist, I felt that the activities I used to help my students learn were not enough to help me coach the entire district. SIOP gave me the tools to coach . . . >>>

Shortly after attending the SIOP Institute, I attended a SIOP session at a convention in Texas. I was so excited about it, but equally disappointed when the entire session was about activities with no mention of the SIOP features. At what point do we lose SIOP when we begin focusing exclusively on various activities? Once I became a SIOP trainer, I found that teachers want lots of activities during the trainings. So, I started giving each activity a name, writing the directions for each on the slides, and keeping track of the activities on chart paper. And then it happened: With so much focus on activities, some participants in a training starting spoofing how I introduced the activities. They said they made up a new activity called "Stop, Talk, and Gawk." I got the point that teachers need more than just activities with cute names, and quickly readjusted. Although all of our SIOP trainings include activities, techniques, and teaching methods, there is <u>no</u> SIOP without an understanding of its features. We have to keep in mind that the activities are not the end goal.

—Amy Washam, Former ESL Specialist, Lewisville Independent
School District; Pearson SIOP Education Specialist, Texas

This chapter is all about getting started with this new volume of SIOP ideas and activities. You may be just getting started with planning SIOP lessons, or you may be a SIOP veteran who is eager to implement new ideas and activities into your SIOP lesson plans. Either way, this book will help you accomplish the goal of writing effective SIOP lessons and units.

You may be wondering what this book's relationship is to the core text, *Making Content Comprehensible for English Learners: The SIOP® Model* (Echevarria, Vogt, & Short, 2013; Echevarria, Vogt, & Short, 2014a, elementary; 2014b, secondary). It is our expectation that anyone who is reading this book has already read one of the core SIOP texts. From our experience (and that of most, if not all, high-implementing SIOP teachers), reading one of these books and reflecting on its content is essential for a thorough understanding of the SIOP® Model. *Please don't attempt to do a short-cut* and assume that you'll gain deep understandings of the SIOP® Model by reading this book. To use effectively the ideas and activities included in this book, you need to first understand the SIOP® Model's features thoroughly, and that takes more study than is provided in this text.

To make best use of this book, we've included the following highlights that we hope will make for more interesting reading, as well as assist in streamlining your SIOP lesson planning.

- **A Teacher's Reflection** Each chapter begins with a SIOP teacher's thoughts about a particular SIOP component. These set the stage for the information and activities that follow. You'll note that this chapter begins with reflections from a teacher who is also a SIOP trainer.

- **Criteria for Selecting the Ideas and Activities** As you peruse the book, you may recognize a couple of the ideas and activities that you already use, or they be a modification of a familiar activity. It's important to remember that in the SIOP® Model, any and all activities may be appropriate, if they:

  - Provide practice and application of your lesson's key content and language concepts, and thus your content and language objectives (the *most important* criterion).

- Are meaningful.
- Enable you to attend to SIOP features.

All of the ideas and activities in this book have been used by SIOP teachers. You will notice their names and schools after the name of an activity. What distinguishes this book from other "activity books" is that all of the teachers who have recommended the activities use the SIOP® Model to teach English learners and other students. We authors created and have used the activities that don't have any attribution (name, school, town), and we include them because they're effective in SIOP classrooms.

- **Organization of Ideas and Activities**   In the first volume of *99 Ideas,* we organized the ideas and activities by SIOP *component* (see Vogt & Echevarria, 2008). In this book, we have organized the new ideas and activities by each of the thirty SIOP *features*, with each chapter focusing on one of the eight SIOP components. Our reasons for this structure are twofold:

  1. We want you to remember that all thirty features are of equal importance, and each should be considered when planning SIOP lessons.

  2. We hope you will see the interrelatedness of the thirty features, where they overlap and support one another, and where they might stand alone.

- **Identifying SIOP Features for the Ideas and Activities**   All of the ideas and activities in the book include a specific SIOP feature that you may want to focus on when using the activity. This is not meant to imply that you must select thirty activities in order to include all SIOP features in your lessons! Rather, the feature numbers are simply suggestions that a particular activity may be a good one to use when focusing on a particular feature.

  As the book's title indicates, there are also "ideas" provided for some of the SIOP features. For example, consider Feature 18 in Interaction: *Sufficient wait time for student responses consistently provided.* While an "activity" may not be necessary or appropriate for increasing your wait time after you pose a question, there are particular techniques you can use to make sure you are allowing English learners and other students sufficient time to process an answer to a question, perhaps in a language other than English. Therefore, ideas rather than activities are provided for this SIOP feature.

- **Additional SIOP Features**   As mentioned, each idea or activity targets one particular SIOP feature, but because of the interrelatedness of the features, we suggest other alternatives in "Additional SIOP Features."

- **Content and Language Objectives**   Of all the SIOP features, planning for content and language objectives in each and every lesson is the most challenging. Therefore, we have provided you with numerous examples that you can use as models for writing your own content and language objectives. We've also provided student friendly options for writing and orally conveying objectives for young children. We've written the content and language objectives that you'll find throughout the book with various subject areas and grade levels in mind.

  Most important: Remember that objectives are not written for "activities," per se. Keep this in mind and use the following principles to help focus your writing of SIOP objectives and lessons:

  - Content and language standards guide your choice of content and language objectives for all lessons.

- Once you decide on your objectives, select a meaningful activity that will best help your students practice and apply the content and language skills identified by the objectives.

- The purpose of a lesson is having students learn content concepts, information, and/or skills as reflected in the content objectives; while at the same time, students are developing English language proficiency, as indicated by the language objectives.

Resist the temptation to select an activity first—and then write objectives that "match." The activities in this book are intended to be the _means_ to the end (that is, students meeting the objectives), not _the end_. The _end_ is when your students successfully meet the content and language objectives of your lesson, in part because they have had practice and application with a meaningful, relevant activity.

● **Grade Levels for Ideas and Activities** Most of the grade levels that are indicated for the book's ideas and activities are K–12. While we know that may be a little frustrating since you want activities for the specific grade you're teaching this year, the reality is that we selected activities that really do span grade levels, given appropriate modifications, such as easier or more challenging texts or a range of difficulty of key vocabulary, and so forth. That said, you'll notice that there are some activities that just work better with older students, or younger ones, and we've identified these as such. Don't be afraid to select and modify activities for your students as needed.

● **Matching Activities to Your Subject Area(s)** As we began working on this book by observing classroom lessons, gathering activities, and collecting lesson plans, we discussed having a spot for each activity where we would recommend subject areas that would be a good match for that particular activity. We quickly realized that nearly all of the ideas and activities in this book are appropriate and can be adapted for virtually any subject area. If you read an activity and decide it won't work for the content you teach, move to the next one—but before you do so, if your reason for moving is that the activity seems to focus too much on language arts, then consider that you may need to include more language practice in your classroom. Our hope is that you will find nearly all of these activities to be useful and adaptable, except perhaps those that are targeted for a different grade level than the one(s) you teach.

● **Step-by-Step Directions for Each Idea or Activity** To assist you in planning, each activity's directions are included in easily followed, numbered steps. You will also find photographs of students' work for some activities, as well as bulletin board displays and illustrations. We hope these visuals will bring the activities "to life" for you and provide additional context. Further, a list of materials needed for each activity is included.

● **SIOP Protocol** You will find the SIOP protocol in Appendix A. This is included so you can use it to check the degree to which you're including each feature as you plan your lessons. Keep in mind that in the elementary grades, your goal should be to include all thirty SIOP features in your lessons that occur throughout the day. Of course, it's unreasonable to assume that you will include thirty instructional features in a 10-minute phonics or spelling lesson. However, it is reasonable to assume that all thirty can be implemented in a grade 5, two-day social studies lesson, where you have a 40-minute instructional block each day. Similarly, if you teach grades 6–12, a lesson may extend over a few days (2–3), and your goal will be to implement all thirty features during that time period. It is important to remember that the more consistently you implement SIOP's thirty features in your lessons, the more likely it will be that your students will make significant academic and language growth.

● **SIOP Lesson Plans**   In Chapter 10, you will find six detailed SIOP lesson plans that were written by SIOP teachers. There are three reasons for the level of detail in these lessons:

- We wanted to include as much detail as possible so you can easily follow and picture the instructional sequence.

- We wanted you to see how all the SIOP features are woven together throughout a lesson.

- We wanted to admit to you that lesson planning in the early stages of learning the SIOP® Model may remind you of when you were a student teacher!

We're sure you remember those long, detailed lesson plans you wrote as a preservice teacher. We have found that the thinking processes of preservice teachers who try to include all the "parts of a lesson" are similar to those of new SIOP teachers as they attempt to write lessons with all "the parts of SIOP." The good news, for student teachers and SIOP teachers alike, is that with practice, both the time it takes to plan and the length of the actual lesson plan are greatly reduced. Before long, SIOP's thirty features will be etched in your brain and you can plan a strong, effective SIOP lesson in much less time with much less work. To view additional SIOP teachers' lesson plans, along with unit plans and other ideas and activities, see Echevarria, Vogt, and Short, 2010 (mathematics); Short, Vogt, & Echevarria, 2011a (history/social studies); and 2011b (science); and Vogt, Echevarria, and Short, 2010 (English language arts). These SIOP content books focus on lesson planning for grades K–2, 3–5, 6–8, and 9–12.

We have one more suggestion before you begin digging into the 99 ideas and activities in the chapters that follow. Previously, we have mentioned the interrelatedness of the thirty SIOP features. It's also important to remember that the eight SIOP components are not only *interrelated* but also *interdependent*. Together, they make up the whole that is the SIOP® Model. In the SIOP research studies, the greatest academic gains have been found when teachers use the entire SIOP® Model consistently, not just activities here and there in lessons. We hope you enjoy this book and that your students will benefit from the lessons you design using the ideas and activities herein!

Thinking about Activities and Lesson Planning

1. In this chapter, we make a strong point for selecting activities that provide practice and application of a lesson's content and language objectives. Amy suggests in the Teacher's Reflection segment that teachers often just want activities, and they don't think much about how or why to select them. Why do you think this often happens? Reflect on the commercial teacher's guides that accompany the texts your district has adopted. Do the activities suggested in the lesson plans provide practice and application of the learning goals or standards that are identified for that lesson? What are the implications for planning your own lessons from the teacher's guides?

2. Make a list of the activities you currently use that are your students' favorites because they're fun and engaging. If you begin to more consistently select activities based on your content and language objectives, which of the fun activities will you continue to use? Are there any that you may need to reconsider before you use them again, because while they're fun, they may not be particularly meaningful? How will you know the difference?

2 Lesson Preparation

A Teacher's Reflection

The shift in my thinking to ensure students are given the opportunity to read, write, listen, and speak throughout a lesson has greatly increased positive student responses. Students feel energized when the task is measurable and can be accomplished within one class period instead of over a series of days.

—Molly Richardson, 6–8 Resource Room Math Teacher,
Olympic Middle School, Auburn, Washington

People frequently ask us which is the most important of the SIOP components. We always respond that our research has shown that the eight components are of equal importance. Picking and choosing components or features isn't possible because if one or more is overlooked or omitted, you can't expect the academic gains for English learners and other students that have consistently been found during the 15 years of research on the SIOP® Model.

Because academic achievement is the ultimate goal, the way SIOP lessons are planned and delivered is incredibly important. The Lesson Preparation component is about preparing lessons that are:

- Focused on both content concepts and language development.

- Comprehensible to all students.

- Targeted to students' academic and language strengths and needs.

- Differentiated as needed.

I'm sure that no reader of this book has *ever* done this, but figuring out what you're going to teach while waiting in line at the coffee drive-through on the way to school doesn't constitute effective planning for any student—but it's especially inappropriate for English learners. In contrast, during SIOP lesson planning, when each of the six features in Lesson Preparation is considered carefully, individually, and in combination with the others, all students benefit.

SIOP teachers sometimes complain that it takes longer to create a SIOP lesson, especially in the beginning stages of learning the Model. We're not surprised to hear this because SIOP planning requires attention to each of the thirty features. However, the more lesson plans you create, the more automatic the planning becomes. The ideas and meaningful activities that are included in this book are intended to make your lesson planning not only more effective but also more expedient.

We begin with the six features of Lesson Preparation, each of which is equally important. During effective SIOP lessons with Lesson Preparation, you will discover:

- Your students know what is expected of them during each lesson related to the content and academic language that is being taught (Features 1 & 2).

- Your students are able to grapple with and learn grade-level content information (Feature 3).

- Your students use supplementary materials and adapted content to comprehend challenging content and language concepts (Features 4 & 5).

- Your students engage in meaningful activities to practice and apply the content and academic language concepts they are being taught (Feature 6).

Feature 1 Content Objectives Clearly Defined, Displayed, and Reviewed with Students

"Arguably the most basic issue a teacher can consider is what he or she will do to establish and communicate learning goals, track student progress, and celebrate success . . . for learning to be effective, clear targets in terms of information and skill must be established . . . once goals have been set it is natural and necessary to track progress" (Marzano, 2007, 9).

Many teachers tell us that objectives are important because students need to know what they are going to do during a lesson, but we only partially agree with that statement. Students may appreciate knowing what they are going to be doing during class, but they will benefit more when they know what they are responsible for learning. It's important to remember that objectives are more than just an agenda of activities (Echevarria, Vogt, & Short, 2013, p. 30). Rather, clear lesson objectives enable students and teachers alike to track progress in meeting learning goals. If we only post an agenda or list of activities to complete, students simply check off what they finish rather than monitor what they are learning.

Another important distinction to remember is that content and language objectives are different from activities. *Objectives* stem from content and language standards, including the Common Core State Standards or your state content standards, the WIDA language standards (WIDA Consortium, 2007), or your state's ELD or ELP language standards. Clearly written objectives focus on what students are supposed to know and be able to do at the end of a lesson. We often tell teachers that objectives are *non-negotiable* because they are derived from standards that delineate what students must learn at various grade levels.

In contrast, *activities* provide the means for students to practice and apply content and language learning that is the focus of objectives. Activities are *flexible* and *negotiable,* and there is a wide variety of activities and techniques teachers can employ to help students meet objectives. While the same objectives are often written for all students, the way students practice, apply, and ultimately master those objectives may differ depending on students' strengths and needs. That is, while it is most often unnecessary to differentiate content objectives, it is frequently necessary to differentiate the activities that enable students to meet them. It is sometimes necessary to differentiate language objectives because of students' varying English proficiency levels, but it's also possible to have a language objective for all students, such as: *Summarize the main point of a letter written to the editor of a magazine.* The activity students do to meet that objective could differ greatly based upon students' language needs: oral presentation, a drawing with key points illustrated, a written summary, a role play, or a Concept Definition Map (Echevarria, Vogt, & Short, 2013, p. 81) are just a few possibilities.

So, we hope you see that it is imperative not to confuse objectives with activities. As a final example of this axiom, think about when your students must learn new vocabulary words, define what they mean in a text, and use the new words to construct meaning. Not all students need to make a flip-book in order to learn the vocabulary. Mastering the new vocabulary is the objective, while making the flip-book is the activity. It is the means for helping students who need extra scaffolding to learn the targeted words.

As you look through the items listed below, think about which represent a well-written objective, the knowledge and/or skill students will learn, or an activity that teachers use to scaffold instruction.

1. Make a flip-book.[*]

2. Read a passage with comprehension.

3. Identify the characteristics of a quadrilateral.

4. Summarize a passage.

5. Complete a graphic organizer.

6. Solve equations.

7. Use key vocabulary to describe two events in the news that occurred this week.

8. Use Newton's Laws of Motion to explain what you saw in the experiment.

9. Determine key events that led to the start of World War II.

10. Watch a video.

As we move to some activities and techniques for writing and presenting effective content objectives, please keep in mind Rick Stiggins's recommendation: "In addition to beginning with a purpose in mind, we must also have a clear sense of the achievement expectations we wish our students to master . . . Understanding learning targets is the essential foundation of sound assessment, and of good teaching too." (Stiggins et al., 2006, p. 15) And good teaching is what the remainder of this book is all about!

---

[*] Answers: (1) activity; (2) learning or skill; (3) content objective; (4) learning or skill; also could be a language objective; (5) activity; (6) learning or skill; (7) language objective; (8) language objective; (9) content objective; (10) activity

Ideas & Activities for Content Objectives

Ideas for Communicating Objectives

It is important that students understand a lesson's learning goals or objectives. Sharing a lesson's objectives can be accomplished by using various activities or techniques, depending on the age of your students. For very young children, state objectives in "student-friendly" terms so that the children fully understand a lesson's content and language goals. Throughout this book, you will find student-friendly objectives for all ideas and activities that are recommended as appropriate for young children (grades K–2)[*].

SIOP Feature 1: Content objectives clearly defined, displayed, and reviewed with students

Additional SIOP Features: 2, 23, 24

Grade Level: K–12

Materials: Objectives should be posted where students can refer to them throughout the lesson. It is helpful to have a place designated for objectives on the board, but objectives can also be written on chart paper, posted on sentence strips in Pocket Charts, written on small dry-erase boards, displayed on a classroom monitor via PowerPoint®, and so forth. Some of the ideas that follow require student journals or other paper to write on.

Objectives: Not applicable

Grouping Configurations: Partners, small groups

Options and Directions:

 Choral Reading of Objectives

Students repeat, chorally as a whole class, after you read the objectives.

 Predict Learning Outcomes Using Sentence Frames

   a. Under the posted objectives, list the following sentence frames:

- I predict that the objective _____ will be easy for me to learn because _____.

- I predict that the objective _____ will be difficult for me to learn because _____.

   b. Save these sentence frames for review of the objectives at the end of the lesson.

Record the Objectives in Journals
submitted by Leslie M. Middleton, Instructional Coach, Rochester City School District, NY

   a. Post objectives and read them aloud.

   b. Ask students to record the objectives in their notebooks or journals.

---

[*] For teaching young children in pre-K and kindergarten, see Echevarria, Short, & Peterson (2012) for specific information about preparing their SIOP lessons.

c. Students rephrase the objectives in their own words in their journals.

d. Students refer to the objectives throughout the lesson, as needed.

Repeat Objectives to a Neighbor

a. After you present the objectives, ask students to repeat, rephrase, or summarize the objectives to their table partners.

b. For younger students, this can be done while students are actively engaged in centers (Echevarria, Short, & Peterson, 2012).

Think-Pair-Share the Objectives

a. Present the objectives and ask students to take about 30 seconds to think about how to rephrase the objectives in their own words.

b. Students share their thoughts on how to rephrase their objectives with their table partners.

c. Call on two or three students to restate a neighbor's revised objective.

Feature 2 Language Objectives Clearly Defined, Displayed, and Reviewed with Students

What is the difference between Feature 2 (*Language objectives clearly defined, displayed, and reviewed with students*), and Feature 6 (*Meaningful activities that integrate lesson concepts with language practice opportunities*)? One answer to this question is that objectives are what we are teaching (content and language) and activities are the ways students practice the objectives. Sometimes teachers mistakenly think that content objectives represent the "what" and language objectives represent the "how." This is incorrect. Language objectives focus on the language we're teaching and the language students are using, but they are not the activities we choose for students to practice and apply a lesson's content and language concepts.

Many teachers with whom we have worked have identified Feature 2 (Language Objectives) as the most challenging feature of the SIOP® Model primarily because in the past, language development wasn't a concern of content teachers other than those who teach English, language arts, and ESL. Writing objectives for students' language use wasn't even considered. However, we now know that it's important to create learning goals that focus on the academic language that students need to know and be able to use during a content lesson, and on other elements of language that they need to learn to succeed with all academic disciplines. Language objectives often need to be scaffolded for English learners through explicit instruction on how to achieve them.

As with content objectives, student progress toward meeting language objectives should be tracked throughout a lesson by you and your students. Figure 2.1 lists some teachers' language objectives taken from lesson plans. Which of these would be difficult for a student to use to track his or her progress? One way to answer this question is to consider whether the objective would make a good test question. Test questions are observable and measurable and have criteria for success. Similarly, with objectives, we should be able to watch student performance during a lesson (observable) and know the degree to which students have met or are close to meeting the objective (measurable). Note the following language objectives that are measurable. If they're not measurable, how could they be rewritten so that you'll know the degree to which students are meeting or not meeting them? The goal is to have criteria-specific objectives that can be easily measured. See the first example, and then try to figure out the others by yourself without reading our explanation. Do you agree with our suggested modifications? Also, what are characteristics that make these objectives difficult to measure? How might you need to scaffold these objectives for your students?

Figure 2.1   Non-Specific and Criteria-Specific Language Objectives

1. <u>Write a letter to a classmate and share it with him or her</u>. This is an activity; it is not specific, nor is it criteria-based. A better language objective is: *You will write a friendly letter, in the proper format, that describes something funny that happened to you this week.* This may sound like an activity, but as an objective, note that it is specific and it's measurable. As usually stated, an activity isn't specific, measurable, or observable. With the revised language objective, you can assess the friendly letter format and the student's description of a funny incident and his or her use of descriptive adjectives. Another measurable language objective could be included: *You will orally share the letter with a classmate.* This is also observable and measurable; the assessment can take place as you walk around

(continued)

Figure 2.1   Continued.

listening to the letters being read aloud. Was the oral reading clear? Was pronunciation accurate? Did the classmate laugh at the incidents that were described?

2. <u>Repeat each vocabulary word, act it out, write it down, and draw a picture to match</u>. This language objective says what students will do (activity), but it is also observable, measurable, and criteria specific (the picture must match). You can readily assess if students know the meanings of the key vocabulary words.

3. <u>Use math vocabulary (*double, one more*) to orally explain to a partner how to solve a double-plus-one addition problem</u>. This language objective is specific, measurable, and criteria specific (solving the math problem).

4. <u>Students will be able to write a story problem and share it with another student to solve. The person solving will be expected to answer using the sentence starter: *The difference* is _____</u>. This language objective is specific, measurable, and criteria specific in two ways: first for the person writing the story problem (it must be understandable), and second for the partner who must correctly use the sentence starter to solve the problem.

5. <u>In pairs, students will create a Venn Diagram to compare/contrast the different media coverage, write a paragraph, and share by reading it to another group</u>. This is an overloaded activity, not an objective. It's not specific because other than comparing/contrasting, there are no learning behaviors expressed. It would be better to take it apart. Content objective: "Students will compare and contrast the *NBC News* and *Boston Globe* coverage of the Marathon bombings." Language objective: "Students will write an analysis of the perspectives of the two media sources and will orally share it with peers." The use of the Venn diagram is irrelevant; some students may need it to organize their thoughts, but the graphic organizer should not be the focus here. The analysis is.

6. <u>Students will be able to categorize items under the appropriate linear metric unit of measurement on a 3-column chart and defend their choices to a partner</u>. This is specific and measurable, but it should be split into two objectives: one content (categorize) and one language (oral defense). The mention of the 3-column chart isn't necessary because you might wish to differentiate how students categorize. Including it in the objective isn't wrong; it's just not needed.

7. <u>Students will be able to explain the functions of cell parts through their writing</u>. This is somewhat specific and measurable, but requiring students to use specific vocabulary would help them develop their academic language and provide even more specific criteria.

8. <u>Students will comprehend content vocabulary</u>. This is not measurable because there are no criteria for determining whether or not students really do comprehend the content vocabulary. You could add that students would define content vocabulary or use content vocabulary to describe or summarize a concept, which would add specific, measurable criteria. It would also be better to list the specific vocabulary students are to describe or summarize.

9. <u>Students will identify the main characters, protagonist and antagonist, in the story</u>. This is measurable and specific as far as what students should identify. The objective also develops academic vocabulary because students are identifying the *protagonist* and *antagonist*, but the objective could be written with the additional criteria that students justify their answers using the word *because* or using a complex sentence.

10. <u>Students will take turns reading the story aloud</u>. This seems like a legitimate language objective, but there are no criteria for how students will learn to read aloud better than they already know how to do. Objectives should include knowledge or skills students need to learn, not knowledge and skills they already know. You could add criteria like pronunciation, fluency, and phrasing, which would require some instruction and would help students learn to read aloud more fluently.

Ideas & Activities for Language Objectives

ⓘ Three Questions to Ask About Language Objectives

We haven't met a teacher yet who doesn't initially struggle with writing language objectives—and that includes us, as well! For one thing, language objectives are foreign to most teachers and as a result, they can be daunting. In addition, many teachers don't feel comfortable being responsible for "teaching English" because they lack knowledge of grammar, sentence structure, figurative language (metaphors, similes, idioms), and other aspects of language that students need to know. We've heard many reasons for *not* teaching language objectives, including:

- "I'm *not* an English teacher!"
- "This is the job of the ESL teacher!"
- "My responsibility is to teach (insert subject area), not language."
- "I don't know what language to teach!"
- "If I try to teach English, I'll never cover my content standards!"
- "Most of my students already know English!"

You get the picture—and you might have said (or thought) one or more of these reasons yourself!

To help you figure out what academic language needs to be included in your content lessons, we came up with three important questions to consider when creating language objectives. We urge you to think about these questions as you're writing language objectives:

- **What academic language related to my lesson's topic do my students need to know and be able to use to meet the lesson's content objective(s)?** Each subject area you teach has its own academic language and it's important that you know it. Academic language includes specialized terms, phrases, and words that have multiple meanings: *product* (think math and the grocery store); *plot* (think a short story and the cemetery); *characters* (think again of a short story and writing on the computer); *rocks* (think igneous and dancing); *cell* (think organelle and jail). Academic language in varied subject areas also involves different sentence structures in text: compare reading a history chapter to reading a math chapter or a science or health chapter. As you prepare a lesson, look carefully through a text you expect students to read and identify the academic language students will need to know to be successful.

- **What would I like to hear my students say when they talk in class about the topic of this lesson?** Think about how you would answer this question for any given lesson. What words and terms do you want the students to use? How should your students' academic conversations sound? What academic phrases do you want students to use? Your answers indicate the academic language you need to teach and that your students need to practice.

- **What language can I teach and reinforce to move my students' language proficiency forward?** For English learners in particular, this is a very important question to consider because each day, they should be increasing their English knowledge and proficiency. You don't have to be an expert to consider this—just think carefully about the content you'll be teaching and see if there are opportunities to point something out. For example, in a history or social studies lesson, your speech and the text's writing will undoubtedly be in the past tense. Take a moment and remind students how past tense is created in most verbs (add *–ed*). Students can highlight or note the past tense words they find while reading. Or, point out that there are many words for *said* that are far more interesting to use when writing: *expressed, questioned, exclaimed, mentioned, told, laughed, whispered,* and so forth. Put these and other words in a list and remind students to use them. Moving students' language knowledge forward can be as simple as this! Just be aware of these teachable moments.

It might help you to review in detail the types of language that are regularly included in language objectives (see pages 32–37 in Echevarria, Vogt, & Short, 2013). As a quick overview, the types include:

1. **Academic vocabulary:** Key words needed to discuss, read, or write about the topic of the lesson. Within this category are:

   • *Content vocabulary:* Words or phrases that are names of people, places, events; scientific or mathematical terms, and so forth.

   • *General academic vocabulary:* Cross-curricular words and terms that are encountered in subject areas, such as *describe, explain, define, compare, persuade, support your answer, share with a partner, summarize.*

   • *Word parts:* Refers to roots, prefixes, and suffixes; for a list of common word roots and examples of words with them, see Echevarria, Vogt, and Short, 2013, pp. 72–73. Remember this important adage: *English words that are related in structure are almost always related in meaning* (Bear, Helman, Invernizzi, Templeton, & Johnston, 2011).

2. **Language skills and functions:** These words reflect the ways students use language in a lesson: reading, writing, listening, and speaking. Examples include: *finding evidence in a text while reading, recording observations during an experiment, listening to a speaker, asking questions,* and so forth.

3. **Language structures or grammar:** Focuses on the language structures used in your content, such as if–then sentences, the passive voice (common in science texts), past tense used in history, and so forth.

4. **Language learning strategies:** Teach your students how to learn on their own, through practice with corrective strategies, self-monitoring strategies, pre-reading strategies, and language practice strategies.

If this is all new information to you, please refer to *Making Content Comprehensible for English Learners: The SIOP® Model* (Echevarria, Vogt, & Short, 2013, pp. 33–37), for much more information about the types of academic language that are the focus of language objectives.

Feature 3 Content Concepts Appropriate for Age and Educational Background Level of Students

Because content and language objectives are derived from grade-level content and language standards, it is relatively easy to make sure that the content concepts you're teaching are appropriate for your students. Even though standards represent the academic goals teachers and students strive for, the educational backgrounds of some English learners may necessitate modifications. Consider the following three scenarios in terms of whether or not the modifications that are described are "appropriate," given this particular SIOP feature.

1. You teach a grade 9 physical science class. All of your students are in grade 9, except for five students (ages 16 and 17), who are taking your class because they are recent immigrants who have not had basic science and they must have the course units to graduate from high school.

2. You teach eighth grade American History, but because of many students' low reading and English proficiency levels, you decide to use the district-adopted grade 5 American History text for this particular class.

3. You teach grade 3, and your heterogeneous class of 28 includes eight English learners, five students who receive Special Education services, and four students who are designated as Gifted and Talented. You decide to teach students to do close readings of complex texts by using well-written, leveled texts that are written for students below, at, and above grade level. Your plan is to gradually increase the difficulty and complexity of the texts as students improve in their ability to read closely.

If you decided that the first and third scenarios constitute "appropriate" content concepts for students' age and educational backgrounds, you're right! The teachers are modifying their instruction and materials based on their students' language and content needs. In the case of the grade 9 class, which includes older English learners, the students' educational backgrounds have been considered in that they haven't had a basic science class in high school; thus, they are enrolled in the class, despite their age.

However, the teacher in the second scenario is not making a wise or appropriate choice for her grade 8 students. The content standards for grade 5 and grade 8 American History are obviously different, and so is the content in the respective textbooks. The teacher needs to teach to the grade 8 content standards, and instead of using the lower-level text, she should make appropriate adaptations and modifications as suggested by many of the SIOP features, and especially Feature 5 (Adaptation of Content to All Levels of Student Proficiency).

Ideas & Activities for Selecting Appropriate Content Concepts

ⓘ Know Your Students!

You're probably thinking, "This is a NEW teaching idea?" Nope, it's been around as long as there have been teachers and students. However, within the SIOP® Model, this is an idea whose time has come. If you have only one English learner or struggling student in your class, you must know his or her academic and language strengths and needs in order to plan appropriate instruction for that student. If you have several English learners, you need to know each of your students' educational backgrounds.

SIOP Feature 3: Content concepts appropriate to age and educational background

Additional SIOP Features: 5, 7, 8, 19, 25

Materials: File folder to gather assessment and interview data; summary sheet for educational background information

Objectives: Not applicable

Directions: If you have an ESL teacher or specialist in your school, enlist his or her assistance with gathering background data about your students who are English learners. If you don't have this help, you'll need to do some detective work yourself. The following information is essential to understanding English learners' (and other students') academic and language backgrounds as well as their current language and literacy proficiency. Keep in mind that a couple of these assessments can be done with the whole class (writing samples, interest inventory)—it's great to have this information for all of your students! For purposes of discussion in the points that follow, we consider a fictional English learner, Almasd, who is a second-generation immigrant from Armenia.

- **Educational History**   Depending on the age of a student, you may be able to gain this information from the student herself. For immigrant students, it is unlikely that a cumulative file will provide much information, so interviewing a family member or community liaison who speaks the student's L1 and English will be helpful. Ask about how much schooling the student has had; whether it's been continuous or interrupted; and whether there are work or other experiences the student has had that may have educational value (e.g., working in a shop, working in the fields, caring for children, living in a variety of places and settings, etc.). Remember that students may have been educated in non-traditional ways. Our student, Almasd, as a second-generation immigrant, has been educated exclusively in the United States. Therefore, be sure to check her cumulative file for any information that will be helpful to your planning.

- **Parent or Guardian Interview**   You may need to have an interpreter present for an interview of a parentor guardian. An interview is worth the expenditure of time because of the amount of information you can gather about your student. Some parents, depending on their own educational experiences, may be reluctant to come to school. In this case, some teachers make home visits. If you are a secondary teacher with more than a hundred students, home visits may not be possible, but talking with a community member who speaks the same home language as your student may be. If you are able to schedule an interview with a parent, please remember to keep the student as the focus of your conversation. Most parents are eager and proud to talk about their children. Our co-author, Amy, recently spoke to a SIOP teacher at PS 58 in the Bronx in New York City, and they talked about parent involvement in her classroom. New York City teachers are required to communicate effectively with parents, and this teacher asks her students to share the daily language objectives with their parents each day. Think of the parent–child discussions of academic language and vocabulary that go on in these homes in the evenings! This topic would be a great kick-off for a parent inventory.

- **Writing Sample in L1**   Once again, think of our fictional student, Almasd. Ask her to write in her home language, Armenian, about something she enjoys doing. If you don't speak Armenian, you can still gather a lot of information by observing how she writes her response. Does she write fluidly and comfortably? Are there several sentences that appear to include punctuation (for alphabetic languages)? Or does she seem strained and uncomfortable as she thinks about words and what to say? Is she able to produce very few sentences or words in Armenian? If possible, have a parent, guardian, other family member, community liaison, other student, or Armenian interpreter translate the writing sample so you can get a glimpse of the student's language and literacy development in her first language.

- **Writing Sample in English**   At a different time, ask Almasd to write about the same topic in English. Look for similar things in this sample as you did when the student wrote in her home language: fluidity, comfort, sentence structure, vocabulary, and so forth. You might discover that your student is fully literate in her first language, but struggles with English. Or you might find that she does not appear to be literate in either language. The implications for each of these findings regarding Almasd's language and literacy development and her content instruction are significant.

- **Reading Sample in L1**   If possible, ask your student to read some text aloud (at an appropriate grade level) in the home language. This text can be anything—a newspaper column, magazine article, recipe, or menu. Your purpose is hearing the student reading in her own language, so that you can assess her fluency (does she read effortlessly or does she struggle to identify words?); word recognition (does she stumble to identify words or are they easy for her to read?); and comprehension (is she able to tell you or an interpreter what she just read?). Research clearly shows that students are able to transfer their knowledge of literacy processes from one language to another, especially if they are fluent readers of their L1.

- **Reading Sample in English**   At a different time, ask your student to read aloud in English. If the text appears too difficult, be prepared to move to an easier text until she can read aloud somewhat comfortably. Is there a notable difference between the reading skills she displays when reading in Armenian and when reading English? In other words, do reading difficulties appear in both languages or only in English? Since Almasd has been in a U.S. school since kindergarten, it's important to know whether she knows how to read in Armenian. If so, who taught her?

- **Student Test Results in English**   Include here any information about the student's performance on standardized tests. What are Almasd's assessed strengths and needs according to your state test results?

- **Student Test Results in L1**   Depending on the language your students speak, there may be test data available in the home language, especially if it's Spanish. Check with your ESL specialist to see if a home language assessment has been done and if results are available.

This is required in many states for limited English proficient students, so it's important to know where the test results are located.

● **Interest Inventory** This is a great assessment idea for all your students, not just English learners. You can gain a great deal of information about your students' interests, activities, home life, friends, siblings, and so forth. This information can be used when you're planning lessons and selecting instructional materials. The following is an example of questions for an interest inventory.

Sample Interest Inventory

1. How old are you? _____
    What grade are you in? _____

2. Who lives in your home with you?* _____
    Do you like school?_____ Why or why not?_____

3. What subject(s) do you like best in school? _____

4. What books have you enjoyed reading? _____

5. What kind of books would you like to read in the future? _____

6. Do you like to play sports? _____
    What sports do you like to play? _____

7. What do you like to do at recess? _____

8. Do you like to play games? _____
    What games do you like to play? _____

9. What do you like to do when you are at home? _____

10. Do you like to watch TV? _____
    What is/are your favorite TV show(s)? _____

11. Do you like to listen to music? _____
    Do you like to sing? _____
    What is your favorite song(s)? _____

12. What do you like to eat? _____

13. What do you like to do with your friends after school? _____

14. What do you like to do on the weekend? _____

15. What things in life bother you most? _____

16. Who is your favorite person? _____
    Why? _____

17. Who do you think is the greatest person? _____
    Why? _____

18. What kind of person would you like to be when you are older? ___

---

*   Note the wording in this question. As you know, we cannot presume anything about what constitutes a "family" and where students might live. If you have students who are homeless (or you suspect they are), be sensitive in how you phrase questions on an interest inventory.

Feature 4 Supplementary Materials Used to a High Degree, Making the Lesson Clear and Meaningful (e.g., Computer Programs, Graphs, Models, Visuals)

Some teachers who are new to the SIOP® Model believe that this feature is all about including a lot of "bells and whistles" in their lessons. However, bells and whistles aren't what English learners and other students need. Instead, what will benefit them are supplementary materials that:

1. Provide context for new concepts.
2. Make abstract concepts concrete.
3. Enable students to make connections between what they have experienced, what they know, and what you're teaching.

Anything that can accomplish these goals is fair game as a "supplementary material." This includes models, illustrations, photographs, simple drawings, acting out, gestures, videos, something applicable from the Internet, an article, a piece of literature, a guest speaker, realia (real and authentic, including primary sources, such as a copy of an original document; or an actual letter to the editor in a newspaper)—and the list goes on.

The best way to understand why supplementary materials are so important for your students is to think back on the worst course you had in college. We bet there were NO supplementary materials—only a boring instructor with a large marker that he seldom used for anything that was helpful or interesting. Don't be that teacher . . .

Ideas & Activities for Supplementary Materials

ⓐ Personal White Board Think-Pair-Share

submitted by Carreba Williams, First Grade Teacher, Dodd Elementary, Little Rock Schools, AR

As you know, small white boards are used for a variety of reasons in classrooms. This activity provides students with a chance to jot down an answer to a teacher's question and then share it with a partner. As the partners hear each other's responses, they negotiate and decide upon what they think is the best answer to the question. Partners revise their original responses, as necessary, on the personal write boards. This activity provides students with time to think, along with the opportunity to read, write, listen, and speak.

SIOP Feature 4: Supplementary materials used to a high degree, making the lesson clear and meaningful

Additional SIOP Features: 14, 16, 17, 18, 20, 22

Grade Level: 2–12

Materials: Individual white boards, markers, erasers (or cloth)

Objectives:

- *Content:* Students will decide together on the best answer to a teacher-generated question.
- *Language:*
  1. Students will write an answer to a question on a white board.
  2. Students will read their answers to their partner.
- *Student Friendly:*
  - *Content:* I can think of an answer to my teacher's question and write it on my white board.
  - *Language:* I can read my answer to my partner and listen to his answers.

Grouping Configuration: Partners

Directions:

1. All students sit facing one another, each with an individual white board.
2. Following instruction and/or reading, ask students a question. Be sure the question is also written so students can read it themselves. For older students, you might provide a study guide or list of pertinent questions.
3. Allow wait time for processing.
4. Each student writes a response on his or her white board.
5. On your cue, students turn to their assigned partners and share what they wrote on their white boards. Depending on your students' ages and English proficiency levels, model this sharing process beforehand so students know exactly what to do. Remember to review the "ground rules" for the activity each time you assign it until it has become a routine.

6. Remind students to negotiate (again, you may need to model this) their answers until they both agree on the best answer or come up with a new one that they can agree on.

7. Students make revisions, as needed, on their own white boards.

8. On cue ("Show Me!"), all students hold up their white boards so you can see them and respond to their answers.

ⓐ Rotating Graffiti*

submitted by Pam Dutter, Dodson Elementary School, Washoe County School District, NV

We have all seen graffiti on the walls of buildings, on freeway overpasses, and on fences where graffiti "artists" have left their mark. Usually, the graffiti designs that include scribbles, pictures, and stylized words have been left illicitly, most often in a public place. Although graffiti is often seen as simply vandalism when space is used without permission from the owner, graffiti has an underlying message. The writings, drawings, and scribbles mean something.

For many students, the opportunity to share what they know using artistic expression is very appealing, and for English learners it is a chance to share what they have learned without worrying about making grammatical errors or missing a word or two. Pam Dutter uses a Rotating Graffiti activity in her classroom to help her students demonstrate their learning. Her students use their science logs as a reference for the graffiti art they will create about the science concepts they are studying.

SIOP Feature 4: Supplementary materials used to a high degree, making lesson clear and meaningful

Additional SIOP Features: 6, 14, 27, 28, 30

Grade Level: 4–10

Materials: Student notebooks or journals, large dry-erase boards or large pieces of chart paper, colored markers

Objectives:

- *Content:* Students will create a graffiti-like representation of the concepts studied using phrases and drawings.
- *Language:* Students will incorporate key vocabulary when drawing lesson concepts.

Grouping Configuration: Small groups (pairs, triads, or groups of four)

Directions:

1. Students will work in teacher-created small groups using their texts and notebooks as references.

2. Each white board or piece of chart paper has a different term or concept listed at the top. As an example, there might be 4–6 different boards placed around the room on

---

* You may be uncomfortable about using the term *graffiti* in your classroom, especially if your community has strong feelings (and laws) about gangs, taggers, and tagging. If you wish, this activity can been be renamed "Rotating Doodles," since *doodle* is a synonym for graffiti.

table top surfaces. (If large white boards are not available, chart paper can be posted on tables or the walls.)

3. Students work with their partners to negotiate how they will graphically represent the concept that is on the white board or chart paper.

4. Each set of partners uses a different color marker to demonstrate their learning on each board.

5. Model for students how they are to move from board to board adding information to another pair's drawings. They should demonstrate what they know about the topic and read what has been written on the white board or chart paper. They should not duplicate other partners' responses.

6. All student groups rotate to all boards.

7. Monitor the amount of time each pair is at each board before moving the students to the next one.

8. After all groups have had a chance to read and contribute to all white boards or charts, discuss and celebrate the students' work. What contributes to effective communication through graffiti? Why do you think it is now viewed in many places as a legitimate art form?

MaryEllen Vogt

MaryEllen Vogt

ⓐ Switching Ladders

submitted by Kimberly Howland, SIOP Trainer, Washoe County School District, NV

Too often, beginning English learners are relegated to lower level questions that only allow them to recall information. English learners, even newcomers with little English proficiency, have the ability to think critically if they are provided with effective scaffolding. Kimberly Howland uses a graphic organizer called a Concept Ladder (Allen, 2007, p. 19; Gillet & Temple, 1998) to provide English learners with the scaffolding they need to grapple with the content concepts they are learning.

SIOP Feature 6: Meaningful activities that integrate lesson concepts with language practice opportunities for reading, writing, listening, and speaking

Additional SIOP Features: 13, 14, 15, 16

Grade Level: 3–12

Materials: Concept Ladder template, access to the Process Verbs (see Appendix B). Depending on the age of students, the list of verbs may need to be shortened and modified before they receive it.

Objectives:

- *Content:* Students will answer various questions about (concept or topic).
- *Language:* Students will write questions at various levels of cognition.
- *Student Friendly:*
  - *Content:* I will answer questions about (concept or topic).
  - *Language:* I will ask different types of questions to students in my group.

Grouping Configuration: Small groups or individuals

Directions:

1. Provide students with a template for the Concept Ladder after they have read a text or been introduced to a new concept.

2. Review question types and ask students what they remember about the different levels of questions that have been discussed previously. You may wish to use either the revised Bloom's Taxonomy (see Echevarria, Vogt, & Short, 2013, pp. 124–125) or Question-Answer-Relationships (QAR) (see Vogt & Echevarria, 2008, p. 79) to teach different levels of questioning.

3. Explain and model how to use the verbs from the various levels to write a question about the text or concept they are studying (see Appendix B). For example, from the Remember category, the teacher might model the sentence, "Define a quantitative observation." And from the Analyze category, the teacher might model the sentence, "Compare a quantitative observation to a qualitative observation." Students who are new to English can copy the sentence structure, swapping out the concepts being defined and compared.

4. Working individually or in pairs, students write questions for each category using the verbs provided on their copy of the Process Verbs (Appendix B).

5. This activity can be differentiated for students of various English proficiency levels. Students with little English may use the same verbs that you modeled, replacing the concepts, or they may write only a few questions. Students with more English proficiency can try to use different verbs and may be able to create more questions. As long as each group writes two or three questions, everyone can participate in switching the ladders.

6. Once all students have their questions written on their "Ladder," the whole class will engage in an interactive process of "Switching Ladders" with other students.

7. Tell students to find another group and switch ladders.

8. Using their learning logs as a resource, the students will answer one question and then return the "Ladder" to the author and move on until all questions are answered.

ⓐ Whole Class Word Sort or Time Line Word Wall

submitted by Jose Ruiz, Solis Middle School, Donna, TX

English learners and other students benefit from having new vocabulary posted for them to refer to during a lesson. Jose Ruiz engages his students with word sorts that help them make thematic connections between the events they are studying in American History. Mr. Ruiz uses a large piece of chart paper (8 feet long), and sticky notes to create a class-sized word sort for his students to review at the end of a unit. This activity promotes student independence in making connections. In the first phase of the activity, the teacher recalls the topic details and models thematic connections. In the second phase, the students recall the details, with the teacher assisting them with the thematic connections. In the third phase, the students work more independently to make their own connections between the various topics studied.

SIOP Feature 4: Supplementary materials used to a high degree, making the lesson clear and meaningful

Additional SIOP Features: 6, 8, 9, 12, 14, 15, 27, 28, 29, 30

Grade Level: 4–12

Materials: Large piece of chart paper, at least 8 feet long; sticky notes (10 for each student); prepared list of words, terms, phrases, and/or dates to describe a topic

Objectives:

- *Content:*

  1. Students will determine central ideas or themes of (a topic).

  2. Students will analyze the development of the chosen central ideas or themes.

- *Language:* Students will write an explanation of how various topics are thematically connected, using a cause and effect sentence.

Grouping Configuration: Whole group, small group, individual

Directions:

Phase I:

1. Ask the class to brainstorm themes, topics, dates, or events that they have recently studied. As another option, prepare the topics or dates ahead of time and present them to the class.

2. Post the topics or dates near the top of an 8-foot piece of chart paper hung horizontally (like a timeline without the line).

3. Stand under or by the long piece of chart paper.

4. Ask students to stand facing the chart paper so they can see the dates or topics.

5. Call out several words, phrases, or dates that refer to one or more of the topics on the chart. The students look at each of the topics listed on the chart and try to decide which is best connected to the word or phrase the teacher just called out. For example, if the teacher says the word *independence,* the students would look on the chart and identify the topic *Revolutionary War* or the date *1776.* Scaffold this step, as needed, by having the words you're calling out written on sentence strips or large cards so students can hear and see them.

6. Give students clues if they are struggling with the answers, or ask follow-up questions to extend their responses.

Phase II:

7. Give students ten sticky notes each and ask them to write a word or phrase they remember from Phase I on each sticky note. Each student should be able to recall ten words or phrases from Phase I. The students might remember the word *independence* and write it on a sticky note. To scaffold this step, students can work with partners.

8. Once the students have completed their sticky notes, tell them to go, as a whole group, to post their sticky notes under the correct topics or dates. For example, the word *independence* could be posted under the topics of *1776* or *Revolutionary War.* Have all of the students post their sticky notes at the same time—bumping into each other is half the fun! This is also the reason the chart paper must be long.

9. Once all of the sticky notes are posted under the topics on the chart paper, read each one and ask the class if it is placed correctly. This is an opportunity for students to elaborate on the concepts and the teacher to clarify any misconceptions.

10. Model how to make thematic connections between the topics using the words written on the sticky notes.

Phase III:

11. Have students work in small groups to make at least one thematic connection between topics.

12. As each group shares its thematic connection, ask for clarifying questions and point to the large chart to help other students comprehend the connection.

13. Ask students to work independently to make at least one thematic connection between the topics listed on the large chart paper. This connection can be written in a journal and later shared with the class.

14. To meet the language objective, each student should be able to articulate in writing how the topics are thematically connected.

Feature 5 Adaptation of Content (e.g., Text, Assignment) to All Levels of Student Proficiency

Sometimes, teachers misunderstand this SIOP feature and think it means that all difficult texts must be rewritten for English learners and struggling readers, or that only easy texts can be provided for them. Another misconception is that abstract concepts should be avoided for this group of students, and the focus should be on more concrete ideas that can be readily understood.

When you consider that our goal as teachers is for ALL students to meet grade-level content and language standards, then we must plan lessons according to these standards, but modify instruction so that students have a chance to meet them. In *Making Content Comprehensible for English Learners: The SIOP® Model* (Echevarria, Vogt, & Short, 2013, Chapter 2), you will find a variety of ways to appropriately modify content and texts for English learners and other students. What these ideas and the ones that follow have in common is that they provide students with *access* to challenging texts and abstract concepts. With these types of modifications, your students have a far better chance of meeting their grade-level standards.

Ideas & Activities for Adapting Content and Texts

Adapted Graphic Organizer

submitted by Pam Dutter, Dodson Elementary School, Washoe County School District, NV

Research has found that graphic organizers (GOs), visual representations of ideas, benefit English learners and other students because information is organized into manageable and understandable units. GOs assist students in seeing how pieces of information about a particular topic are related, and they enable students to classify the key concepts. To further scaffold language and content for students who need extra support, you can partially complete a graphic organizer prior to distributing it to the class. It's a great way to differentiate within your class: some students work from a blank GO; others have 1–2 boxes completed; a few students may require several of the boxes to be completed. GOs also provide context for generating student conversations, discussion, and writing about the key concepts and vocabulary.

SIOP Feature 5: Adaptation of content to all levels of student proficiency

Additional SIOP Feature: 14

Grade Level: 2–12

Materials: Various copies of a graphic organizer that are appropriate for the lesson you are teaching; chart paper, document camera, or interactive white board for projecting the blank graphic organizer

Objectives:

- *Content:* Students will organize (or classify, list, etc.) information about (topic).*
- *Language:* Students will use the following words to organize the (topic) on a graphic organizer (insert vocabulary list).

Grouping Configuration: Individuals, pairs, whole group

Directions:

1. Choose a graphic organizer that suits the lesson's concept and language objectives.
2. Partially complete the graphic organizer with labels, sentence frames, or words. Students with less English proficiency may need more sentence frames, while students with more language proficiency may only need a few words here and there. Newcomer students might benefit from pictures on the graphic organizer that explain the concepts.
3. At the beginning of the lesson, present a blank graphic organizer to the entire class. This can be presented on a chart, using a document camera, or on an interactive white board.
4. It might be appropriate to tie the graphic organizer into the objectives, explaining how the lesson's concepts will be organized using the language objectives.

---

*   Note: The type of GO you are using determines how you write the content objective. Consider the learning you want students engaged in. See Appendix B to guide you.

5. Throughout the lesson, students complete the graphic organizer. When necessary, model where to add information on the blank graphic organizer.

6. The graphic organizers can be used to encourage interaction by having students share or compare their answers.

7. At the end of the lesson, students have the language and content of the lesson incorporated into a graphic organizer they can use as a reference for continued practice of the lesson's concepts and language.

ⓐ Adapted Text Guided Reading Questions

submitted by Isabel Ramirez & Lois Hardaway, Sheltered ELA Teachers, Lewisville High School, TX

This technique helps English learners and other students dissect the plot of complex texts using guided questions and a comprehensible outline of the original text. First, create an extremely detailed list of questions about the basic plot of the story. You can use either the original text or an adapted text with some of the key details omitted to write the guided questions. The list of unanswered guided reading questions becomes a form of adapted text for students. They must read the original text to find the answer to the questions or to locate information that is missing in the adapted text. The Adapted Text Guided Reading Questions assist students in understanding the basic plot of the story, while the more complex inferences and themes will be discussed after students are more acquainted with the plot of the original text.

SIOP Feature 5: Adaptation of content (e.g., text, assignment) to all levels of student proficiency

Additional SIOP Features: 12, 13, 14, 15, 16, 20, 22

Grade Level: 6–12

Materials: Copy of the Adapted Text Guided Reading Questions for each student, copies of the original text, copies of the sentence frames, highlighters if text can be marked up

Objectives:

- *Content:* Students will read the original text to dissect the plot.
- *Language:*
  1. Students will discuss the details from the text using text evidence to support their statements.
  2. Students will define the word *dissect* and explain how it applies to the plot of a short story.

Grouping Configuration: Individual, partners, whole class

Directions:

1. Provide background information on the text students will read.

2. Ask students to scan the first few lines of the text.

3. Encourage students to talk about the text and discuss what they think might be difficult to comprehend.

4. Hand out the Adapted Text Guided Reading Questions (sample questions follow).

5. Explain that students will find the answers to the guided reading questions in the text.

6. Read the first guided reading question together, and then allow students time to look for the answer. Students can work in pairs or on their own.

7. After students have had time to look for the first answer, ask several students how they found it. There should be discussion about using context clues, reading a sentence more than once, and looking up unknown words.

8. Students complete the Adapted Text Guided Reading Questions in pairs. Eventually, if students have ample reading and language proficiency, and as they become familiar with the guided questions, they can complete the questions for homework.

9. After students complete the guided reading questions, discuss answers and questions that weren't answered.

10. Use, as needed, the following sentence frames to initiate class discussion:

    • For this question, I found the following answer _____.

    • My answer is different. I found _____.

    • That answer is similar to mine. Here's my answer _____.

    • My answer is different. I found this answer _____.

    • I think this answer is correct because _____.

    • I figured out the answer to this question by _____.

    • Another way to answer the question is _____.

    • This question was really hard to answer because _____.

    • This question was really easy to answer because _____.

11. When the guided reading questions sheet is completed, it reads like an adapted version of the text with the basic plot summarized. You can encourage students to complete the guided reading questions by allowing them to use the completed guided questions on a subsequent quiz or test.

Examples of Adapted Text Reading Questions for "A Rose for Emily"
(*see Chapter 10 for the lesson plan and complete list of questions*)

1. Who went to Miss Emily's funeral?

2. What did the women want to see?

3. Who were the only people to see it in the past ten years?

4. What surrounded Miss Emily's house?

5. What does Faulkner mean when he says, "[Insert a quote from the text]"?

6. Why did Colonel Sartoris remit Miss Emily's taxes?

7. What happened when the next generation mailed her tax notices?

8. When the men went to her house to discuss the taxes,

   a. how did the house smell?

   b. how did the house look?

9. Describe Emily at this point in her life (when the men come to visit).

10. What do the words "[Insert a quote from the text]" suggest?

ⓘ Using Adapted Text to Provide Access to Complex Texts
submitted by Isabel Ramirez, Sheltered ELA III Teacher, Lewisville High School, TX

Isabel Ramirez explains why she helps her high school English learners understand the basic plot of a short story before having them read the actual text. She states, "I don't want students to be bogged down by what is happening in the story; rather, I want them to figure out how the author creates what is happening." After the students learn the basic plot of the story, the teacher can bring in the original text for students to read more deeply, such as how the author creates mood and tone, uses references and analogies, and tells a story using chronology. Isabel explains that "Vocabulary is rarely the biggest hurdle to accessing complex text. It is usually the concepts involved within the text, or the text structure, or textual constructs that makes it difficult, like a story not in chronological order." Once students know the plot of a story, they can study the original text in order to determine how the author tells the story.

SIOP Feature 5: Adaptation of content (e.g., text, assignment) to all levels of student proficiency

Additional SIOP Features: 13, 14

Grade Level: 5–12

Materials: Two texts: one adapted and one complex

Authors' Note: Some English teachers may question this process because they think it provides too much scaffolding. The Common Core State Standards require that students be able to independently do *close readings* of *complex texts*. To accomplish this, reading expert Dr. Tim Shanahan suggests that some students will benefit from having what he calls "apprentice texts" (Shanahan, 2011). These provide a stair-step to more challenging texts and they enable students to learn how to do a close reading in texts they can comfortably read. As teachers provide increasingly complex texts, these students can then practice and apply their close reading skills and strategies to these new texts. This is precisely what this activity provides—an apprentice "text" before English learners and other students grapple with the more complex text.

Feature 6 Meaningful Activities that Integrate Lesson Concepts with Language Practice Opportunities for Reading, Writing, Listening, and/or Speaking (e.g., Surveys, Letter Writing, Simulations, Constructing Models)

We're sometimes asked what is meant by *meaningful* in the context of this SIOP feature. Essentially, it means the activity or activities you have chosen for a lesson are the best ones you could find that provide practice and application of the content and language concepts that are the focus of your lesson's content and language objectives. If an activity doesn't provide practice and application of your objectives, then it doesn't belong in the lesson, even if it's one of your favorites. As you read through the activities in this book, take note of the sample objectives provided for most. Be sure that whatever activity you decide to use provides students with the important practice your students need to meet *your* content and language goals for a lesson.

Ideas & Activities for Meaningful Activities

ⓐ Circle of Academic Conversations

submitted by Isabel Ramirez and Lois Hardaway, Sheltered ELA Teachers, Lewisville High School, TX

Students need help engaging in academic conversations. By working together in small groups, the students build background information about the topic and create a chart to scaffold their academic conversations. The teacher arranges students in a circle in order to structure and provide accountability for academic conversation while the large charts students create provide scaffolding for the conversation.

SIOP Feature 6: Meaningful activities that integrate lesson concepts with language practice opportunities for reading, writing, listening, and/or speaking

Additional SIOP Features: 13, 14, 15, 16, 17, 20, 21, 22

Grade Level: 6–12

Materials: Copies of the reading text; large poster paper; markers; access to dictionaries

Objectives:

- *Content:* In groups, students will reach consensus about (topic) prior to charting their ideas.
- *Language:* Students will discuss the ideas they charted by explaining and defending the ideas they generated.

Grouping Configuration: Groups of four students

Directions:

1. Students work in small groups to investigate a topic. Investigation can be done with an experiment, reading passage, Internet research, or a problem to solve.
2. Supply each group with a large piece of construction paper or poster paper for the students to use to record their findings.
3. Tell students to chart their results—their conclusion to the experiment, main idea of the reading passage, results of the Internet research, or solution to a problem. This activity can be further scaffolded by providing students with graphic organizers or sentence frames. For example, students might be asked to compare and contrast using a Venn diagram.
4. Tell students to use large print on the chart paper, as the charts should be legible for the rest of the class. It may be helpful to provide an example of what the print on the chart should—and should not—look like.
5. Each group should practice summarizing their poster before forming the whole class circle.
6. Once all of the posters are completed, the students form a large circle around the room and hold up their posters.
7. Each group takes turns summarizing its poster.

8. After each group summarizes its poster, the teacher asks guiding questions to encourage elaborated responses.

   - How did you come to that conclusion?
   - Did anyone else record a similar idea?
   - Who else came to the same conclusion?
   - Did anyone come to a different conclusion?
   - Which answer is correct? And why?

9. The students should continue discussing, defending, and questioning their posters.

a Jigsaw Story Boarding

submitted by Isabel Ramirez and Lois Hardaway, Sheltered ELA Teachers, Lewisville High School, TX

This activity engages students in illustrating and summarizing a section of a short story. A chapter or article could also be used as text. After reading an assigned passage, students individually draw a cartoon-like picture of a scene, main event, or main concept. Each student then writes a brief summary to go along with the illustrations. Then group members put the illustrations (cartoons) in sequence to make a "comic strip" of the text to share with the rest of the class.

SIOP Feature 6: Meaningful activities that integrate lesson concepts with language practice opportunities for reading, writing, listening, and speaking

Additional SIOP Features: 5, 13, 14, 16, 17, 20, 21, 22

Grade Level: 3–12

Materials: Copy of the text for each student with their assigned portions identified; large poster paper (large enough to cover four student desks) for each group; colored markers

Objectives:

- *Content:*
    1. Students will read and summarize a passage from a story.
    2. Students will correctly sequence the events in a story.
- *Language:* Students will orally present their descriptions of the summary drawing they created for the passage.

Grouping Configuration: Small groups

Directions:

1. Jigsaw a reading passage by assigning parts of each story or chapter to each group.
2. Within the groups, the students Jigsaw the reading further by each reading an assigned part.
3. On the group's poster paper, each student draws a summary of his or her assigned passage; underneath it, the student writes a summary sentence, comic strip style, to describe the drawing. Encourage students to add as much detail as possible to their pictures and summaries.

4. Remind group members to coordinate the poster so that the drawings and written summaries are in chronological order.

5. Group members work together to edit the sentences on their poster for errors. The students should also practice reading their sentences in chronological order while still in their groups.

6. When all of the posters are completed, have the class form a large circle; the groups present their posters, in chronological order, with each group member presenting his or her drawing and summary.

7. The posters can also be placed around the room and shared in a carousel activity.

Teresa Wells

Thinking about Lesson Preparation

1. Reflect again about the college teacher mentioned earlier in the chapter who was so ineffective for you. What would have made his or her lessons more engaging? What could the teacher have done to provide you with what you needed to better learn the content?

2. We've often said that the best way to learn how to write content and language objectives is to WRITE THEM. Think about how you learn something new. What thinking processes do you go through? What are the implications of your own learning process for your students' learning and how you plan lessons for them?

3 Building Background

Monkey Business/Fotolia

A Teacher's Reflection

One of the most profound things that I have learned in my SIOP training is that we need to tap into what our children already know before we start a lesson (and they know so much!). They come with a wide variety of experiences, and it is our job to help them make connections from their prior knowledge or their prior learning to new learning. If necessary, we need to give them experiences in the classroom so that they have the background they need to grasp and connect to new ideas.

—Jennifer Toledo, Teacher, Grade 4, Gauldin Elementary School, Downey Unified School District, California

Afrequent comment we hear from teachers when describing some of their students is, "My English learners don't have any background knowledge." We think what they mean is that their students often have gaps in their background knowledge and experiences related to the topic that is being taught. Everyone has "background knowledge," but English learners who are recent immigrants with limited or interrupted schooling may need substantial background building in order to be able to access grade-level content and language concepts. Other English learners who have been well schooled in their first language may need background building and academic vocabulary instruction to help them learn the new English terms and labels for familiar content concepts. In a nutshell, the focus of the Building Background component is on activating prior knowledge about a lesson topic for students who have some familiarity with it, and developing background knowledge and vocabulary where gaps exist for students who are unfamiliar with the topic.

During effective SIOP lessons with the Building Background component, you will discover:

- Your students are able to make meaningful connections between what they know and have experienced and the topic they are currently learning (Feature 7);

- Your students use new information to connect with past learning (Feature 8);

- Your students know the meanings of academic vocabulary and use the words, terms, and phrases orally and in writing (Feature 9).

Feature 7 Concepts Explicitly Linked to Students' Background Experiences

You may have heard that there have been some concerns expressed by those in the reading field about the Common Core State Standards (CCSS) (2010) and the expectation that students should be able to do close readings of complex texts without first building their background. As you know, it's a frequent classroom practice to activate students' prior knowledge before reading a story or other text. Some of the concerns associated with CCSS and current practices are due, in part, to what literacy expert P. David Pearson suggests may be teachers who are focusing too much time on the "Know" part of KWL, and not enough on the "Want to Learn" and "Learned" parts of a lesson (Ogle, 1986; Pearson, 2013). While cautioning that there also may be too much time spent with students "swapping experiences about roadrunners before reading . . . ," Dr. Pearson (2013) suggests that it's impossible for readers to withhold connections to what they know and have experienced:

Asking students to hold their prior knowledge at bay is like . . .

- *Asking dogs not to bark or*
- *Leaves not to fall.*
- *It's in the nature of things.*
- *Dogs bark.*
- *Leaves fall.*
- *Readers use their prior knowledge to render text sensible and figure out what to retain for later.*

So, what does this have to do with the Building Background component in the SIOP® Model? The implication is that we need to carefully think about both the difference between activating prior knowledge and building background (see Echevarria, Vogt, & Short, 2013, p. 67, for more information), and the difference between the instructional activities that are used to elicit students' prior knowledge and those that are used to develop students' background knowledge.

1. **Activating Prior Knowledge:** Activating prior knowledge is beneficial when students have stored information and/or experiences about the topic at hand. If most of your students are knowledgeable about the topic you're teaching, then have them do a brief activity (2–3 minutes), such as a quick write or "Tell your partner three things you know about . . . ." Take another 1–2 minutes for students to share out what they know, and move on to the rest of your lesson.

2. **Developing Background Knowledge:** If students lack information about or experiences with the topic or there is a mismatch between what they know and what is being taught, then it is critically important to fill in the gaps by developing students' background knowledge. Previously, we alluded to the popular activity, KWL (Know, Want to Learn, Learn) (Ogle, 1986), and the importance of having a *brief* brainstorming, followed by more time (and mental energy) exploring the topic and learning about it. The same philosophy extends to other activities as well. If you time the activity carefully, use your content and language objectives as your guide, and provide a focused learning task, there's less chance that students' conversations will wander off (to talking about roadrunners, for example) and a greater chance that they will use the new information to help them better understand the topic at hand.

Ideas & Activities for Linking to Students' Background Knowledge and Experiences

ⓐ Abracadabra: Magically Transformed Words!

New vocabulary can be confusing for all learners, and especially English learners, because once you have learned the meaning of a new word, how to spell and pronounce it, and how to use it in a sentence, you begin to encounter different forms or derivations of that word, which when not explained, can become confusing. For example, consider a student who has just learned the word *swim* and uses it in a sentence: *Yesterday, I swim with my family at the pool*. He might find it confusing when the teacher explains that the correct past tense of the word is *swam*. Additionally, a word like *complicate* might appear in the text as *complicated* or *complication*. This activity illuminates various forms of English words by providing younger students with *magical* opportunities to explore their derivations (forming new words using affixes; also the etymology or source of words).

Provide students with a word of the day (or week), focusing on the third category of words students need to learn (as described in Echevarria, Vogt, & Short, 2013, p. 71, Word Parts: Roots and Affixes). Students work with partners to think of a "magic transformation" of the word they already know about and write the new word on an index card. When partners introduce their new derivation or form of the word, they do so with a magic wand, a top hat, and the phrase: "Abracadabra! The transformation is . . . !" For dramatic effect, students can pull a card from a hat before reading the word to the class. The word forms and derivations are then posted for all to see, and everyone (teacher and students alike) attempt to use the words in their conversations as frequently as possible throughout the day.

SIOP Feature 7: Concepts explicitly linked to students' background experiences

Additional SIOP Features: 8, 9, 13, 15, 21, 27

Grade Level: K–5

Materials: Something that can be used as a "magic wand" (such as a rod or pencil with a star attached); a top hat or other type of hat; index cards; chart paper and/or board space for posting the Magical Word Transformations of the Day

Objectives: Most likely, you won't need to include objectives for this daily routine. However, the first time you introduce the routine, you might include these objectives:

- *Content:* I can think of, find, or create a different form of a word.
- *Language:*
  - I can explain what my transformed word means, and I can use it in a sentence.
  - I can define the word *transformation*.

Grouping Configuration: Partners and whole group

Directions:

1. Using one of the three types of academic vocabulary (content, general academic, and word parts: roots and affixes), choose a word for students to magically transform. Discuss with the class how words have different forms or derivations that change how they are used in a sentence. Provide examples using the magical props. For example,

show students the word *swim,* and then "magically" transform the word into *swam, swum* (past participle), and *swimming.* You can use technology like animation in PowerPoint® to make the original word transform before everyone's eyes. Provide an example of how each word is used in a sentence and talk about the similarities and differences in the meanings of each word. Then have students practice thinking of different forms of a word. Encourage students to talk about "magical transformations" of words with their parents or caregivers.

2. As needed, review how roots, base words, and affixes work together in the English language. For example, a verb *(swim)* can become a noun *(swimmer)* by adding the suffix *–er.* Other examples: *teach/teacher; walk/walker; run/runner,* and so forth.

3. Explain how "Abracadabra: Magical Word Transformation!" will work each day as a classroom routine.

   a. Each student has a Magical Word Transformation partner. Rather than letting students select their partners, assign them so that they are somewhat close to each other in terms of language proficiency and vocabulary knowledge.

   b. After introducing a word that most students are familiar with, have students work with their partners to think of a magical transformation. Tell students that the magically transformed word should be related to the original word and that they should be able to use the magically transformed word in a sentence. Each pair writes both their magically transformed word and their new sentence on an index card.

   c. After each pair has chosen their magically transformed word and used it in a sentence, select a pair of students to share their Abracadabra: Magically Transformed Word with the entire class. The chosen pair will take the magic wand and the hat and privately put their word in the hat. With a wave of the magic wand, they will take their word from the hat.

   d. The pair says the word, reads their definition, reads the sentence that includes the word, and explains why they chose the particular word. Repeat as needed until all students can say the word and tell one another its meaning.

   e. The index card with the transformed word and sentence is then posted on a bulletin board that has the heading, "Abracadabra: Magically Transformed Words!" For younger children, also write the word on a piece of chart paper in big type for easy reference.

4. Depending on the age of your students, you may wish to model the process for several days in a row, with a different word each day, so students understand what to do. Choose interesting, fun, and age-appropriate words for your demonstration.

5. Use the Magically Transformed Words whenever you can during the day and encourage students to do the same. One middle school teacher we know prints the Magically Transformed Word on a piece of sentence strip (in large type), adds a ribbon or string to slip it over her neck, and wears the word card throughout the period. What a great reminder that is for her students! Magical partners could also wear their magically transformed words to remind everyone that words have different forms, inflections, and derivations.

6. At the end of the week, say and review all of the Magically Transformed Words. Draw attention to students who have consistently tried to use the words during the week.

ⓐ Discuss What You Know

submitted by Stephen Lanford, Math Teacher, Mabelvale Magnet Middle School, Little Rock School District, AR

Feature 7 is about helping students make a connection between what they already know, believe, or have experienced, and the concepts and language of the lesson. The adult educators we work with are good at making connections to their personal schema. They have already earned at least one degree and are holding down a job as an educator, so they tend to be excellent learners and make connections quickly. Often teachers will come up with an anecdote or even an analogy for the SIOP concepts they are learning. They are quick to say things like, "Oh, language objectives are like (fill in the blank here with some technique they are familiar with)."

Our favorite connection was made by Stephen Lanford, the author of this activity. We were talking about the importance of allowing each child to make his or her own personal connections to the content, not just one or two children. Stephen suggests that, statistically, it is easy to predict how a *group* of people will respond, but it is very difficult to predict how an *individual* will respond. Stephen was making a connection between Feature 7, links to students' schema, and something he was more familiar with, statistics. This activity is intended to help students make similar connections between what they are learning and what they already know by providing scaffolding in the form of questions and heterogeneous pairings.

SIOP Feature 7: Concepts explicitly linked to students' background experiences

Additional Features: 16, 17, 19

Grade Level: 3–8

Materials: Prepared questions related to the language and content objectives of the lesson.

Objectives: Note that it's not really necessary to have separate objectives for activating students' prior knowledge unless you're introducing to your students the importance of making connections between what they've learned and what you're teaching. If you're introducing this concept for the first time, you might have objectives such as:

- *Content:* Students will synthesize (content concepts) by making personal connections.
- *Language:* Students will use sentence frames to discuss personal connections with a partner.

Grouping Configuration: Heterogeneously mixed pairs

Directions:

1. Pair students heterogeneously when determining partners for this activity. Think about language proficiency, reading or math ability, and the ability to work with others. Even though the students are functioning at different ability levels, make sure the groups are compatible by pairing students that are only a little above, or a little below the level of the other students.

2. Provide a list of questions about the content and language objectives designed to help students make personal connections. Below are some possible questions:
   - I think _____ is like _____
   - One thing I know for sure about _____ is _____
   - One thing I might know about _____ is _____
   - Something that I see every day that is like _____ is _____

- I think the difference between _____ and _____ is _____
- Another word for _____ could be _____
- I have seen this before when _____

3. You can provide a visual for questions to support the discussions.
4. The partners will work together to answer the questions.
5. Allow students to clarify the questions in the L1 if they are able and as needed.
6. After an appropriate amount of time, ask the students who spoke the most to stand.
7. Ask the students who are still sitting to summarize what the their partners said using the following sentence frame: "I heard you say . . . . Is that correct?"
8. Continue this activity until the groups have been able to make connections between their personal schema and the lesson's content and language objectives.

ⓐ Pair-Share-Chart

Uncovering what students already know about a topic provides valuable information, even if their perceptions are not quite correct. Think about the first time someone explained to you that our universe is heliocentric with the Earth revolving around the sun, not the other way around. In order to understand that concept, you must first recognize that the sun seems to be rising and setting every day. We use our experiences to make sense of new learning. Asking students to verbalize what they already know about a concept allows teachers to relate the concept to the students' experiences, thus making the learning more meaningful. This activity takes the familiar Think-Pair-Share and adds a charting component.

SIOP Feature 7: Concepts explicitly linked to students' background experiences

Additional SIOP Features: 6, 8, 14, 21, 22

Grade Level: K–12

Materials: Chart paper or interactive white board to record and save student responses; photos or videos of the topic or concept; markers

Objectives:

- *Content:* Students will generate ideas that they know about (topic).
- *Language:* Students will orally share how the ideas they know about (topic) relate to (topic).
- *Student Friendly:*
  - *Content:* I can think of something I know about (topic).
  - *Language:* I can tell my partner how my ideas are like (topic) that we're learning about today.

Grouping Configuration: Partners and whole group

Directions:

1. Ask students to talk to their partners about what they already know about a topic or concept. You can scaffold the students' conversations by providing a picture or short video clip, or by modeling a process, like solving an equation or writing a summary.

2. After two or three minutes of talking in pairs about the concept, have students share their conversations with the whole class.

3. As students share what they know, or think they know about a topic or concept, record their thoughts on chart paper.

4. Use the chart of student responses to introduce a new concept and help students make connections between what they know, or what they think they know.

5. Save and add to this chart throughout the lesson or unit to help students make connections between what they already know and what they are learning.

Feature 8 Links Explicitly Made Between Past Learning and New Concepts

How many times have you had a student come into your classroom at the beginning of the day or period saying, "What are we doing today?" Don't you wish you had a dollar for every time you heard this question? And, don't you wish this common question could change to "What are we *learning* today?"

Posted content and language objectives will certainly answer this question as you begin each lesson. However, we suspect another reason students ask the "What are we doing?" question so often is because:

1. They don't remember what they did yesterday in your class.

2. They don't understand that what they learned yesterday in class will be closely linked to what they'll be learning today.

3. They don't remember what they *learned* yesterday, but instead remember the fun activity they engaged in.

Of course, it could be that none of these reasons pertains to the ubiquitous question—the kids may just be using it to tell you "Hi!"

Regardless of the motivation behind the question, Feature 8 is included in the SIOP® Model because many students, including those who are English learners, need help in connecting past learning to what is being taught today. Notice the use of the word *explicit* in this feature. Review of past learning, even if it's what was taught the day before, needs to be direct and to the point.

For example, let's say that you ended the previous day's lesson with Outcome Sentences (Echevarria, Vogt, & Short, 2013, p. 217). Your end-of-lesson prompts included:

- I discovered _____

- I learned _____

- I still have a question about _____

Students completed one of the sentences during "tickets-out" and they gave their sentences to you as they left the classroom for break or the end of the period. The next day, at the beginning of class, you used the students' responses to review explicitly what was taught yesterday, and you used their questions to inform you about what you need to answer and clarify today. Your review, including referring to some pictures used in yesterday's lesson, took no more than about five minutes, but it explicitly connected yesterday's learning to today's lesson in an important, meaningful, and explicit way.

Ideas & Activities for Linking to Past Learning

ⓐ Linking Journals

Linking Journals can be used to help students practice and apply the concepts and language they're learning during a lesson. They also allow teachers to assess what students have learned. Further, Linking Journals can be used to help students remember concepts studied in previous lessons so they can connect them to new content, especially when the connections are suggested explicitly by the teacher.

SIOP Feature 8: Links explicitly made between past learning and new concepts

Additional SIOP Features: 6, 22, 23, 24, 27, 28, 29, 30

Grade Level: K–12 (Young children can draw pictures in their journals of something they remember from the lesson.)

Materials: Student notebooks or journals; detailed lesson plans with dates of specific concepts taught

Objectives:

- *Content:* Students will articulate connections they make to a recent lesson by describing them in their journals. (An example of a topic-specific content objective is: *Students will compare and contrast the characteristics of igneous and sedimentary rocks to metamorphic rock samples.*)

- *Language:* Students will orally share their journal entries using the following sentence frame: "One thing I wrote in my journal about . . . is . . . ."

- *Student Friendly:*

  - *Content:* One thing I remember about _____ is _____.
  - *Language:* One thing I wrote in my journal about _____ is _____.

Grouping Configuration: Individuals, partners, whole group

Directions:

1. Include in your lesson plans the dates when concepts were taught and student journal entries were written.

2. Ask students to write a journal entry (or draw a picture) that summarizes the content and academic language learned and practiced during the lesson. Remind students to date each journal entry.

3. Scaffold the journal entry with sentence frames and ask students to use newly learned (and posted) key vocabulary in their entries.

4. If relevant, have students draw or copy classroom artifacts like maps or timelines in their journals.

5. Have students organize their journal entries consecutively by date so they can return to them easily.

6. As lessons build on prior knowledge, you can ask your students to return to an earlier journal entry and read what they recorded about a previous lesson.

7. Students can share their journal entries with a partner, in a small group, or with the whole class.

ⓐ Structured Quick Writes

Quick Writes is an informal writing activity that takes little time (3–5 minutes) and provides students an opportunity to think about and then express what they know about a particular topic. For those students who write proficiently and think quickly, the activity can be an effective way to activate students' prior knowledge. However, for some English learners and other students who struggle academically, a "quick" write can be anything but quick, and by the time the other students have finished writing, these students have barely begun. Frustrated and embarrassed, especially if the Quick Writes are shared with partners, these students may be lost for the rest of the lesson because the opening activity was inappropriate for their language development needs.

Structured Quick Writes provide these English learners and struggling students with a template that scaffolds their writing, enabling them to recall and articulate previous lessons' content concepts. Note that this activity differentiates for your students' needs—some students do a typical Quick Write, while those who need the scaffolding complete the Structured Quick Write. If you simply distribute a handout to each student, with the Quick Write question(s) on one handout and the template on another, each student can accomplish the goal of connecting his or her past learning to today's lesson concepts.

SIOP Feature 8: Links explicitly made between past learning and new concepts

Additional SIOP Features: 6, 14, 22, 25, 28

Grade Level: 3–12

Materials: Two handouts: one with a prompt or guiding question; the second with a template.

Objectives: Note that it's not really necessary to have separate objectives for activating students' prior knowledge unless you're introducing to your students the importance of making connections between what they've learned and what you're teaching. If you're introducing this concept for the first time, you might have objectives such as:

- *Content:* Students will explain three main points about (the content topic).
- *Language:* Students will write what they remember about (the topic) from yesterday's lesson.

Directions:

1. Remind students that it's important for them to remember that what they learned in a previous lesson is usually connected to what will be taught in the following lesson.

2. If you have never had students complete a Quick Write, explain that this is a technique for helping them remember and use what they have learned previously.

3. Introduce a writing prompt or question that activates students' prior knowledge.

4. Introduce the structured template for the students who need additional scaffolding. The template includes sentence frames that provide the language students need to express their recollections of what they've learned before. It will be helpful if you include key vocabulary to trigger students' memories. These can be withdrawn as students become more proficient with English and more capable of completing Quick Writes on their own. You might want to have several versions of a template so they can be re-used depending on your content and language objectives for a lesson. Figure 3.1 provides an example of a Structured Quick Write Template.

5. The first time you have students do a Structured Quick Write, explain and model how to complete the sentence frames, and do several of them together with your students. The ultimate goal is to remove the scaffolds when students can do a Quick Write independently.

Figure 3.1 Structured Quick Write Template

Topic: Character Analysis

Directions: Think about and remember what you learned yesterday in class about the characters in the short story we began reading. Then fill in the blanks and complete at least three sentences.

1. Something I remember about a *descriptive adjective* is _____.

2. Something I remember about a *character trait* is _____.

3. While I read, I need to *infer*. I think that means I need to _____.

4. Something I remember about the *dialogue* in the story is _____.

5. A *trait* I saw in a *character* in our story, "Everyday Use: For Your Grandmama,"[1] is _____.

6. This *trait* is familiar, because _____ also has it. (write a friend or family member's name)

7. I also remember _____ about the story.

[1] *"Everyday Use: For Your Grandmama"* is a short story written by Alice Walker.

Feature 9 Key Vocabulary Emphasized (e.g., Introduced, Written, Repeated, and Highlighted for Students to See)

Academic vocabulary is but one aspect of the academic language that English learners and other students must learn in order to be successful in content classes. This vocabulary is found in challenging grade-levels texts, on state standardized tests, in academic discussions and instructional conversations, on the Internet, and in articles, poetry, novels, and most any genre. Within the SIOP® Model, we classify the range of academic words, terms, and phrases into three categories (see Chapter 3 in Echevarria, Vogt, & Short, 2013, for a comprehensive explanation of each category).

1. **Content Vocabulary—Subject Specific and Technical Terms:** Key words and terms associated with a particular topic being taught

2. **General Academic Vocabulary—Cross-Curricular Terms/Process and Functions:** Academic words used in all academic disciplines; terms frequently found in standardized tests

3. **Word Parts: Roots and Affixes:** Primarily based on English morphology, these word parts enable students to learn new vocabulary

For English learners and other students who lack academic language proficiency, it is imperative that you expand your teaching of vocabulary to include all three categories of words and terms. If you rely only on the highlighted words and terms found in your teachers' guides, your students are likely to miss out on learning the other types of academic vocabulary (such as process/function words) they'll need to meet state requirements or the Common Core State Standards.

Figure 3.2 provides examples of words in each of the three categories of academic vocabulary.

Figure 3.2 Examples of Academic Vocabulary

Content Vocabulary: Subject Specific and Technical Terms	General Academic: Cross-Curricular Terms—Process and Function	Word Parts: Prefixes and Affixes
main idea	estimate	*photo* = light
supporting ideas	discuss	photograph
setting	summarize	photography
plot (literature)	categorize	photo finish
plot (math)	list	photodynamic
triangle (music)	define	photoelectric
triangle (math)	demonstrate	photocopy
fractions	illustrate	photosynthesis

Ideas & Activities for Teaching Key Vocabulary

ⓐ Attendance Vocabulary Review

submitted by Shawana Boyd, Math Interventionist, Cloverdale Middle School, Little Rock School District, AR

This technique for reviewing key vocabulary can be implemented into the daily classroom routine of taking attendance. It offers students multiple exposures to key vocabulary on a Word Wall and it's fun! Be sure to model how to do the process beforehand and decide how students will know what words to practice. Both self-selection and teacher choice (you point to the words to be reviewed) work well, and you may wish to mix it up to make it interesting. Whatever you decide to do, be sure to have students go over the words in a choral reading (together, everyone reads the words aloud) before individuals are expected to read the words independently. The choral reading may need to be done for several days for challenging, new vocabulary words that have replaced former words on the Word Wall.

SIOP Feature 9: Key vocabulary emphasized

Additional SIOP Feature: 27

Grade Level: 1–5 (Older students can also participate in this activity, but names are usually not called aloud for attendance in secondary classrooms because of time constraints. If you have a block schedule in middle or high school, this is a good technique for reviewing content vocabulary.)

Materials: Word Wall (or space to create a Word Wall); list of student names for attendance

Objectives: Ordinarily, you wouldn't have content and language objectives for a classroom routine. However, the first time you introduce this activity, you may wish to have objectives, such as these)

- *Content:* Students will define and give examples of key content vocabulary as posted on the Word Wall.
- *Language:* Students will read and pronounce correctly key content vocabulary as posted on the Word Wall.
- *Student Friendly:*
  - *Content:* I can tell what words on our Word Wall mean.
  - *Language:* I can say correctly (or pronounce) the words on our Word Wall.

Group Configuration: Whole class

Directions:

1. Beginning in the first week of school, show students how to practice vocabulary while attendance is being taken. Teach your students to read aloud a word on the Word Wall when you call their names for attendance. When a name is called, that student either selects a word to read or reads the word that you point to.

2. In the following days, as students become more familiar with the routine and the words, and depending on their ages, explain that they can choose to either read the word or give a definition of the word. If the word is a simile, the students can either say, "simile" or "a comparison using like or as."

3. As students become even more familiar with this routine, you can add the option of providing an example of the word. So if the word is *fraction,* a student can choose to say "fraction" or "one-fourth" when his or her name is called.

4. Other adaptations of this vocabulary practice technique are to allow students to give antonyms or synonyms, or have word roots as the "word part" of the day, allowing students to read words that contain a particular word root.

5. The options allow differentiation for students with various language proficiency levels. Newcomer students with little English should always have the option of reading the word with a partner, while other students with more proficient English skills can be encouraged to provide a definition, example, or even derivation!

ⓐ Four-Corners Carousel

submitted by Takessa Hood, Chicot Primary School, Little Rock, AR

Many teachers adapt activities to meet the needs of their students and the lesson concepts they are teaching. These two well-known teaching techniques—Four Corners Vocabulary (Vogt & Echevarria, 2008, p. 40) and Carousel—actively engage students in learning key vocabulary. By combining these two activities, teachers can emphasize key vocabulary and provide a grouping configuration that promotes student engagement.

SIOP Feature 9: Emphasizing key vocabulary

Additional SIOP Features: 17, 25

Grade Level: 2–12

Materials: Large chart paper; markers; dictionaries; sticky notes

Objectives:

- *Content:* Students will draw a picture and define a key vocabulary word.
- *Language:* Students will write a sentence using the key vocabulary word.

Students will provide feedback to their peers using the following sentence frames:

- We agree with your (picture, definition, sentence) because . . .
- Another idea for a (picture, definition, sentence) would be . . .

- *Student Friendly:*

- *Content:* I can tell the meaning of a new word.
- *Language:* I can use the new word in a sentence.

  I can tell my friend that I agree or disagree with a word's meaning.

Grouping Configurations: Small groups (4–5 students)

Directions:

1. Students work in groups to complete a large, poster-sized, Four Corners Vocabulary Chart using their assigned vocabulary word.

2. Assign each group a different vocabulary word, so if there are 8 groups, there will be 8 different words for the Four Corners charts.

3. Students divide the chart into fourths and complete the corners with an illustration (top left), definition (bottom left), and contextualized sentence (top right) that includes the word. The fourth square (bottom right) is for the vocabulary word.

4. Post the completed Four Corners posters on the walls around the room, and have the students in their groups do a Carousel, or move as a group, to view each of the charts made by other groups.

5. As time permits, students can add comments on each of the posters they visit using sticky notes. Each group should be allowed to provide one sticky note comment per poster.

6. Further scaffold those students who need help, providing sentence frames to encourage them to elaborate on their responses:

   a. We agree with your (picture, definition, sentence) because . . .

   b. Another idea for a (picture, definition, sentence) would be . . .

7. You can use these charts as a word wall for the lesson. Note how much context this word wall has: a picture, a definition, and a sentence are included, in addition to the key vocabulary word.

ⓐ Link Up

submitted by Leticia M. Trower, SIOP Coach, Gaston County Schools, NC

Keeping students engaged in learning content and language can be challenging. Encouraging students to tackle higher-order questions and tasks can be equally challenging. Leticia Trower uses an interactive activity she calls Link Up to get her students moving and thinking about her lessons' content concepts and key vocabulary.

SIOP Feature 9: Emphasizing key vocabulary

Additional SIOP Features: 15, 16, 17, 21

Grade Level: K–12

Materials: Index cards with vocabulary words written on each card

Objectives:

- *Content:* Students will identify common attributes shared by multiple vocabulary words.
- *Language:* Students will justify their word groupings using the following sentence frames:
  - We are _____ and _____ and _____.
  - We go together because we are all _____.
- *Student Friendly:*
  - *Content:* I can put words into groups because they are alike.
  - *Language:* I can tell why I put a word into a group.

Grouping Configuration: Students form groups of three; the activity also incorporates whole group discussion.

Directions:

1. Give each student an index card with a vocabulary word on it—all words must be from the same theme or topic.

2. Tell students to look for other students holding word cards that go with or are in the same group as their word. Students should try and form groups of three with all the words connected in some way. Once three students decide to form a group, they should link their arms to indicate they are done.

3. Students must justify their decision to the rest of the class. Have each group justify their grouping using the following sentence frames:

   a. We are _____ and _____ and _____.

   b. We go together because we are all _____.

4. You can repeat the justification and then ask the rest of the class, "Do you buy it?"

5. The best part comes next. After the groups have formed, shared, and justified their ideas, then they have to break the link and form NEW groups of three. This is where their understanding of the vocabulary gets stretched.

6. For example, it can be easy to put together *circle, square,* and *triangle,* but creating a less obvious group of three and justifying it pushes your students' understanding of the words! A student might say, "We are *circle, angle,* and *triangle,* and we go together because a triangle has three angles, and angles are measured in degrees, and a circle is 360 degrees." This shows a much deeper understanding of the words than something like "We go together because we are all shapes."

7. Usually what happens in the first round is that the first few groups form up very quickly, and then the people with words that don't easily fall into groups of three end up working a little harder. Sometimes students will try to persuade others to leave the groups they formed and join with them. Frequently, in the second round, we see everyone in the room working to organize all the words into groups of three. This is where the higher-order thinking skills really come into play, and where we see a lot of collaborative work.

8. Here's a hint for success for this activity: Before you ask students to do this kind of word analysis, be sure to choose your vocabulary carefully and anticipate how students might connect them. Think through various permutations so you can help students as they are searching for connections.

ⓐ Pick Ten Words

submitted by Isabel Ramirez and Lois Hardaway, Lewisville High School, Lewisville, TX

This activity is an extension of Marty Ruddell's Vocabulary Self-Collection Strategy (VSS) (Echevarria, Vogt, & Short, 2013, p. 80; Ruddell, 2007). Research on VSS has shown that comprehension is improved when teachers show students how to select meaningful and important vocabulary words in texts they read. This adaptation of VSS focuses on students selecting and defining previously unknown vocabulary words following the reading of a text, and then creating a poster with the words. The final list of ten key vocabulary words is helpful to students when writing a summary of what they have read.

SIOP Feature 9: Key vocabulary emphasized

Additional SIOP Features: 13, 14, 15, 16, 17, 20, 21, 22, 27, 28

Grade Level: 4–12

Materials: Copies of the reading text; large poster paper; markers; access to dictionaries or a glossary

Objectives:

- *Content:* Students will determine the main idea of a passage using textual evidence to support their answers.
- *Language:* Students will determine the meaning of key vocabulary from a passage. Students will engage in a structured conversation and will contribute appropriately.

Grouping Configuration: Small groups (4–5 students)

Directions:

1. Hand out a reading passage, one copy for each student.

2. Invite students to read the passage with a partner or as a small group.

3. Model how to choose words that are important to the meaning of the text. For example, you might say, "The word *paraphernalia* is central to the meaning of *The Lottery* (by Shirley Jackson) because it is connected to the black box and shows the community's feeling of loss."

4. Ask each small group to select up to ten words that they think they need to learn because these words are important for understanding the meaning of the passage. These can be words the students do not know or that they have heard of, but may not know the precise meaning.

5. Once the group members have chosen their words, they next define them in writing, using their own words. The students can use resources (glossary, dictionary) to create their definitions.

6. Encourage groups to return to the text to find support or a rationale for the words they have chosen.

7. On a large piece of construction paper or poster paper, ask students to record the vocabulary words and definitions.

8. Once all of the posters have been completed, have students form a large circle around the room and hold up their posters.

9. Members of each group read their words and definitions.

10. As each group presents, students put stars by words on their poster that appear on another poster.

11. Each group is given time to present the words chosen, the definitions, and the support or rationale they found from the text.

12. After each group shares their definitions of the words, the class votes on the best definition. If there is more than one definition provided, the teacher can ask the groups to read the text for evidence about the best definition to use.

13. In the end, the class will have ten words, important to the meaning of the text, and their definitions. These words become the key vocabulary that students will learn for this lesson.

ⓐ Team TPR

submitted by Lindsay Young, Pearson SIOP Consultant

Total Physical Response (TPR) is a technique developed by Dr. James Asher that focuses on the coordination of language and movement. As an example, a teacher presents a new word and definition, and students respond with whole-body actions, a role-play, or another type of physical gesture or response. Originally, TPR's primary use was with young children and beginning speakers of the target language, but in reality, it can be used with students of all ages and at all levels of language proficiency.

In Team TPR, students work together to develop new gestures for key vocabulary or content concepts, thereby making the learning more personal to each student on the team.

SIOP Feature 9: Key vocabulary emphasized

Additional SIOP Feature: 12, 27

Grade Level: K–12

Materials: Vocabulary list

Objectives:

- *Content:* Students will determine a gesture or movement that matches a word's meaning.
- *Language:* After performing the word's meaning, students will pronounce the word correctly and will orally give its meaning.
- *Student Friendly:*
    - *Content:* I can plan a movement that matches a word's meaning.
    - *Language:* I can say the word correctly and tell a friend its meaning.

Grouping Configuration: Small groups (2–3 students)

Directions:

1. Place students into small groups and assign each group a different word or concept. *Example:* Each group gets a different science word or concept, such as *control, variable, observe, hypothesize, conclude, justify*

2. The groups work together for about 3–4 minutes to develop gestures that demonstrate the meaning of the word or concept.

3. If needed, provide scaffolding with a sentence starter, such as "In a scientific experiment, we _____" The sentence starter can be used while students do their gestures.

4. Each group takes a turn presenting their team's TPR to the class. As an example of the process, you can provide the prompt "Action!" and the group models the TPR for the class. Students might say, "In a scientific experiment, we *observe* (students point to eyes and ears)." Then you can prompt again with "Take 2!" and the whole class does the TPR together with the group, while saying the vocabulary word.

5. Assess students' memory of the words at the end of the period by doing the gestures of the meanings and having the students respond chorally by saying the appropriate words.

ⓐ Team Word Wall

submitted by Lindsay Young, Pearson SIOP Consultant, former middle school teacher, instructional coach, and certified SEI trainer in Creighton School District, Phoenix, AZ

Because visuals are such a great resource for learning new academic vocabulary, students benefit from creating some that have a personal meaning to them. Rather than the teacher always finding pictures for vocabulary word walls, students can collaborate on what their class word wall should look like.

SIOP Feature 9: Emphasizing key vocabulary

Additional SIOP Features: 27, 30

Grade Level: 1–12

Materials: Chart paper; markers

Objectives:

- *Content:* Students will draw pictures or symbols to represent key vocabulary words.
- *Language:* Students will write similes about vocabulary words using the following sentence frame: "_____ is like _____, because _____."
- *Student Friendly:*
  - *Content:* I can draw a picture of one of our words.
  - *Language:* I can say, " _____ is like _____, because _____."

Grouping Configuration: Partners, small groups

Directions:

1. Have students preview or review vocabulary words and definitions for a unit or lesson.

2. Working in pairs, ask students to sketch or draw pictures or symbols to represent key vocabulary words. The students may be less intimidated by this if you model a sketch first. Also support the students by having them think of a simile to go with their word, such as "[Key vocabulary word] is like _____, because _____."

3. Have the pairs share out in their table group or with another pair of students nearby. When they share in small groups, they have to pick a symbol that they feel best represents one of the key vocabulary words. For one minute, one "artist" in each small group draws the symbol or picture on a large index card or regular piece of paper.

4. Have the artist hand off the picture to one other person in their group. This student presents the picture to the class "_____ is like _____, because _____" and posts it on the class word wall.

5. Because the students get to choose their "best" picture, you can assess the students' confidence in their definitions. Sometimes students from different tables will choose the same word to depict. When this occurs the groups then have a way to compare their understanding of key vocabulary with others. The word wall can grow and change over time, too. What started as a word wall with only a few words depicted on

Monday can be added to throughout the week as students' understandings of the other terms develop.

6. Remember that Word Walls can become "English noise" to English learners and struggling readers if there are too many words on the wall and if they're not used instructionally. Remember that lots of words are not necessarily better. Be selective about the words that are posted and if you're not using the words during lessons, remove them. Also, beware of multiple word walls in your classroom . . . one organized and consistently used Word Wall is much better than a mass of words that are posted in various places throughout your room.

ⓐ Updating Your Status

submitted by Catherine Hopkins, Reading Instructional Specialist, Beltsville Academy, MD.

As an alternative to asking students to use a word in a sentence, have them use vocabulary words to update their status in social media, such as on Facebook. "My kids are very receptive when a vocabulary task is posed as something to do with updating their Facebook status," says Catherine Hopkins. "Students like to see what other groups say about their post. Sometimes, the comments are quite funny."

For students who do not have a Facebook account or who are unfamiliar with social media, note that this vocabulary activity takes place on sentence strips, rather than on the computer. Ask all students to create a personal "profile" using some of the descriptors on Facebook (such as favorite song, movie, book, sports, musical instruments played, family members, special events or vacations, and so forth). Classmates can then respond to posts that are written on the sentence strips that can be hung on the wall or on pocket charts. Use your judgment about the appropriateness of this activity for younger students who may not know what Facebook is all about.

SIOP Feature 9: Emphasizing key vocabulary

Additional SIOP Features: 7, 12, 15, 20, 27

Grade Level: 5–12

Materials: Sentence strips that can be hung on the wall and markers

Objectives: Once students know the routine, you probably will not need objectives for this activity. To introduce it, you may wish to use the following objectives.

- *Content:* Students are able to use new vocabulary words correctly in writing.
- *Language:* Students will update their Facebook status using newly learned words.

Grouping Configuration: Individual, small groups

Directions:

1. Give students a sentence strip and a marker.
2. Choose a vocabulary word from a previous lesson.
3. Students must use the vocabulary word to update their status. Catherine explains, "For example, my 5th graders had trouble with the word *frequently*. They wrote things such

as: *Jason frequently falls down,* and *Nelson does not like taking tests so frequently. That one came after a two-week testing period . . ."*

4. Students demonstrate an understanding of the word, or they may need more clarification, which you and the other students can provide.

5. Hang the sentence strips on the wall and change them each day.

6. Allow students some time each day to read the updates and make comments.

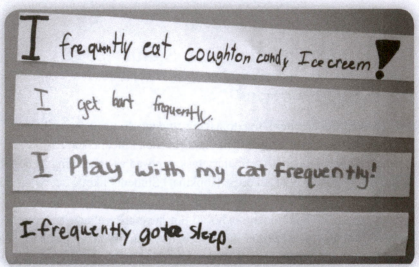

Marilyn Amy Washam

Thinking about Building Background

1. Reflect on each of the features of the Building Background component. Which is the easiest for you to implement? Why do you think this feature is easier than the others? Which is the most challenging and why? What resources and/or information about your students would you need to implement this component more fully?

2. If possible, observe the first day of a lesson of a colleague who teaches the same grade level or subject area as you do. If this is impossible, ask a fellow teacher to videotape a lesson on the first day so you can watch and discuss it with him or her. How did the teacher activate students' background knowledge? What kind of background building did the teacher do? How was key vocabulary introduced, practiced, and applied during the lesson? What did you learn from the lesson that you can apply in your own classroom?

4 Comprehensible Input

A Teacher's Reflection

If the Comprehensible Input component is done correctly, it allows students to better understand the material because it is presented in a way that doesn't just simplify the materials, but is put into terms which give the students the best chance for success.

—Todd Koenig, English Teacher and SIOP Coach, West Middle School, Downey Unified School District, California

Have you ever had this happen? You've worked hard on planning a lesson and feel that you're entirely prepared to teach it. In fact, you're looking forward to teaching this particular lesson because it's about one of your favorite topics and you just know your students will really enjoy learning about it, too. However, once you begin teaching, things start falling apart. The students are restless and appear particularly uninterested in what you're saying. You try to speed things up in an attempt to get everyone ready to begin the fun activity you've planned. You go through the directions for the activity quickly, and then tell the students to begin.

This is when things really go downhill. While a few students begin working, most look around at students in other table groups to see if they know what to do. Frustration mounts for both you and your students, especially when it's discovered that no one really understands the task that everyone is to accomplish. The topic that you're fond of has become one that your students dislike, largely because they're frustrated. The activity that you planned has turned out to be anything but fun or productive.

So, what happened? It's easy to blame the inattentiveness of your students on the fire drill that preceded the lesson, or the change in the weather, or the ineffective substitute you had yesterday, or the kids having had too much Halloween candy (but it's February), or whatever else you can think of. But, in reality, if you really think about it, your lesson went south because your goals for the lesson and the instructions for the activity weren't clear to your students. In a nutshell, your students didn't understand, and they didn't know what to do.

The Comprehensible Input component is intended to make sure this doesn't happen again in your classroom for any of your students, but especially for English learners. The component's features, when implemented consistently, provide students with access to effective, understandable instruction, and directions for tasks that are written and modeled for comprehensibility.

During effective SIOP lessons with the Comprehensible Input component, you will discover:

- Your students are able to understand what you are saying, and they are able to engage and respond appropriately to your instruction because it is comprehensible (Feature 10).

- Your students can follow your written and oral directions for academic tasks and activities (Feature 11).

- Your students react to the various ways you make your instruction comprehensible by engaging meaningfully with you and their peers (Feature 12).

Feature 10 Speech Appropriate for Students' Proficiency Levels (e.g., Slower Rate, Enunciation, and Simple Sentence Structure for Beginners)

This feature requires that you know your students' language proficiency levels in English, and if possible in their home languages as well, so that you can provide instruction and materials that are understandable. If you're not familiar with the WIDA (World-class Instructional Design and Assessment) levels of second language acquisition (WIDA Consortium, 2007), review them in the section that follows, and read the examples of what you might expect for possible responses from an English learner at each of the levels.

Over the years, there have been several variations of what constitutes a "level" or "phase" of language acquisition, and in your district and state, you may be using names and descriptors that are somewhat different from the WIDA levels. Whatever you use, the reality is that language development is more fluid than a series of steps, and it often depends on the context of the speaker's discourse, such as a chat room, family reunion, or science classroom. It is important to remember that when appropriate comprehensible input is provided consistently to English learners during content instruction at whatever their level of English proficiency, both their content knowledge and their language proficiency improve.

It is unrealistic to expect a beginning English speaker to fully engage in a small group discussion without considerable scaffolding that includes language support, sentence frames, modeling (more than once, if needed), pre-teaching or jumpstarting key vocabulary and signal words, and a comfortable, no-risk classroom environment. Obviously, these kinds of supports need to be considered during lesson planning. Think about this question: Should any student who is learning English be excluded from any activity, such as group work, until he or she is a fluent English speaker? We believe the answer is no. Therefore, all aspects of your instruction must be comprehensible, not only for this student who is a beginning speaker, but for your other students as well.

Ideas & Activities for Making Your Speech Comprehensible

a Formula 5-2-1

submitted by Lindsay Young, Pearson SIOP Consultant, former middle school teacher, instructional coach, and certified SEI trainer in Creighton School District, Phoenix, AZ

This idea, similar to Chunk & Chew (Vogt & Echevarria, 2008, p. 164), promotes frequent opportunities for student-to-student interaction even in lessons that require a lot of explicit instruction. It has a flexible time frame that helps to balance linguistic turn taking among students and teacher. It also helps to make your speech more appropriate for students with less English proficiency by speaking for shorter periods of time. Because there is frontloading of information, followed by processing time for students to think about and/or rehearse their answers, this idea can also be used to make sure you're providing sufficient wait time for students to process new information.

SIOP Feature 10: Speech appropriate for students' proficiency levels (e.g., slower rate, enunciation, and simple sentence structure for beginners)

Additional SIOP Features: 16, 18

Grade Level: K–12

Materials: Pictures, copies of text, examples of concepts being taught

Objectives: Not applicable

Grouping Configurations: Partners, small groups, whole class

Directions:

1. To promote frequent opportunities for interaction, use the formula of 5-2-1:

   5 = Limit your explicit instruction to *5* minutes of teacher talk, providing comprehensible input, such as modeling, showing pictures, or using gestures.

   2 = Give students *2* minutes to process the information by thinking quietly, talking to a partner, or engaging with a small group.

   1 = Call on a non-volunteer to share for *1* minute what was processed; or assess students' understanding by using an active response technique (e.g., white boards, response pads), before delivering the next 5-minute chunk of explicit instruction.

2. Note that for the secondary grades, 10 minutes of explicit teaching, followed by 2–3 minutes of student processing may be more appropriate.

3. What's important to remember is to refrain from turning 10-minute chunks of teacher talk into 45-minute blocks of time with little to no opportunity for student processing.

i Levels of Language Proficiency

At present, many states have adopted the following WIDA English language proficiency standards. If you have an ESL specialist in your school, he or she has probably evaluated your students who are English learners with whatever language assessment is used in your state. Use this assessment information to guide your lesson planning for English learners. If you don't have access to more formal language assessment data, use the following WIDA levels to informally assess your students' English proficiency, based on their oral language, writing, and reading skills in English.

When you have school personnel who speak the same language as a student, you may be able to obtain information about his or her language and literacy development in the first language (L1). If a student speaks a language that school personnel do not speak, you may be able to informally assess the home language and literacy proficiency by enlisting the help of a community member who speaks that language and English as well. This person may have books and/or newspapers written in the L1, and these may be used for an informal reading and writing assessment. Any information you can gather about L1 proficiencies and students' educational experiences in the first language is helpful as you plan lessons.

There's one more very important point to remember. Students who are speaking English at lower levels of proficiency are not necessarily functioning at lower levels of cognitive ability. These students frequently use the higher-order thinking skills and strategies learned in their first language and transfer them to English. However, as beginning English speakers, they still may have difficulty understanding academic content and expressing knowledge in English.

 WIDA Levels of Language Proficiency (Echevarria, Vogt, & Short, 2013, p.313; WIDA Consortium 2007)

- **Entering (Level 1)**   Students do not understand or speak English with the exception of a few isolated words or expressions; they are often newcomers and need extensive pictorial and nonlinguistic support. They need to learn basic oral language and literacy skills in English.

  • Possible student response: (pointing to picture) *"dog"*

- **Beginning (Level 2)**   Students understand and speak conversational and academic English with hesitancy and difficulty; understand parts of lessons and simple directions; are at a pre-emergent or emergent level of reading and writing English, significantly below grade level.

  • Possible student response: *"big dog run"* or *"I see the big dog."*

- **Developing (Level 3)**   Students understand and speak conversational and academic English with decreasing hesitancy and difficulty; are post-emergent, developing English reading comprehension and writing skills; are able to demonstrate academic knowledge in content areas with assistance; students can speak and write sentences and paragraphs, although with some errors.

  • Possible student response: *"The big brown dog runs down the street."*

- **Expanding (Level 4)**   Students understand and speak conversational English without apparent difficulty, but understand and speak academic English with some hesitancy; they continue to acquire reading and writing skills in content areas with assistance.

  • Possible student response: *"The enormous brown dog chased the tennis ball down the street."*

- **Bridging (Level 5)**   Students understand and speak conversational and academic English well; they are near proficient in the reading, writing, and content area skills needed to meet grade level expectations; students use general academic and technical vocabulary. Students at this level have often exited the ESL or ELD program, but their language and academic performance is still monitored.

- Possible student response: *"Before responding to his owner, the large Labrador Retriever chased a tennis ball down the street."*

● **Reaching (Level 6)** Students are now fully English proficient; they read, write, speak, and comprehend English within academic classroom settings; their oral and written communication skills are comparable to native English speakers at their grade level; they have exited the ESL or ELD program, but their language and academic performance is still monitored.

- Possible student response: *"After his owner whistled, the enormous Labrador Retriever spotted a rolling tennis ball, ignored the irritating whistle, and raced down the street, chasing his favorite toy."*

 **ⓐ M&M's® Word Quest**

This activity provides practice with a group of words that frequently trip up English learners and struggling readers: words with multiple meanings. The English language is full of these words, and many are found in academic content disciplines. It is important that you are aware of them, both in your oral speech and in your written assignments, so that you can point them out to English learners and struggling readers. This activity provides motivation for students to be on the lookout for the "M&M's® Words," because the reward for finding one is a yummy M&M's® candy!

Here's a quick review:

● There are two types of multiple meaning words:

- *homonyms* (or homographic homophones): words that sound alike *(The owner chooses to <u>store</u> the empty shoe boxes at the rear of his <u>store</u>.)*

- *heteronyms* (or homographic heterophones): words that sound different *(The lady drove down the <u>windy</u> road on a very <u>windy</u> day.)*

To make things even more challenging for English learners (and other students), within these two groups there can be other differences in multiple meaning words:

● **Tense:** *The class will <u>read</u> the third chapter after they've <u>read</u> the second.*

● **Punctuation:** *After the <u>fall</u>, the elderly woman was unable to walk until it was <u>fall.</u>*

● **Parts of speech:** *<u>Point</u> to the spot where the pencil <u>point</u> made a mark.*

● **Capitalization** (and in this case pronunciation): *The august, old gentleman died on August 5, 2013.*

You can search on the Web and find many lists of examples of words with multiple meanings.

SIOP Feature 10: Speech appropriate for students' proficiency levels

Additional SIOP Features: 5, 9, 13, 14, 22, 27

Grade Level: 3–6

Materials: Chart paper or white board; markers; M&M's® candies

Objectives:

- *Content:* Students will identify words that have multiple meanings.
- *Language:* Students will write and read sentences using multiple meaning words.

Directions:

1. Teach (or remind) students about words with multiple meanings and explain why they're sometimes confusing when we read. Explain what a "quest" is.

2. Provide examples of multiple meaning words, especially those found in the content you teach, such as:

   a. math: *product* (answer to multiplication) and *product* (item at the store)

   b. literature: *plot* (events in a story) and *plot* (section of land in a cemetery)

   c. science: *cycle* (life cycle) and *cycle* (something to ride on)

   d. history: *right* (guaranteed by the Constitution) and *right* (euphemism for being conservative politically) and *right* (opposite of left)

3. As you do a mini-lecture, read aloud a story, or read an article with multiple meanings, ask students to "turn up their antennae" for multiple meaning words. The antennae are their two index fingers, held straight up next to their ears. Any time they hear or read (if they also have a copy of the text and are reading along) a word with more than one meaning, have them signal by wiggling their "antennae," and then writing the word on the M&M's® Word Quest handout (a sheet with the name of the activity at top of page with pictures of round candies, and lines for students to write multiple meaning words). It's fine to scaffold by having students work in pairs or work from a list of possible multiple meaning words—whatever helps all students participate.

4. At the end of the reading, students tally the words they found in their quest. For each identified multiple meaning word, reward with an M&M's®. If students have made a valiant try, but missed a word or misspelled it, it's okay to reward them, too!

5. When students find a word with multiple meanings while engaging in independent reading, they can note (highlight or write) the word and receive an M&M's® for each at the end of the lesson. It's important that all words that are found and shared with partners and the whole class.

6. To collect the multiple meaning words, use chart paper, create a word wall, have students create their own multiple meaning word books, and/or create mobiles (with hangers or string) that can hang from the ceiling, with the multiple meaning words that students have found during the M&M's® Word Quests attached.

7. Most likely, in the initial stages of working with multiple meaning words, students will be working primarily to get an M&M's®. Gradually withdraw the candy rewards and substitute other validation for finding examples of these important words during a Word Quest.

Feature 11 Clear Explanation of Academic Tasks

This SIOP feature just makes sense, doesn't it? What teachers would give an unclear explanation of what they want their students to do or how they want them to accomplish a task? But if you're like us, you'll remember some times when you carefully planned a lesson and thought you had explained everything well. You turned the kids loose to do their work, and a bunch of hands shot up with a chorus of voices asking, "*What* exactly are we supposed to do?" Then you scurried around the room answering questions, repeating the instructions, and generally doing all the work that the students were supposed to be doing. Sound familiar?

While this scenario may not adversely affect high-achieving students (too much), for English learners and students who struggle, this is a recipe for academic disaster. Within the SIOP® Model, we maximize instructional time and accelerate achievement—we do not bog it down in needless repetition of directions. This feature focuses on providing clear instructions (with cartoon-like illustrations, if needed), delivering the directions orally and in writing, modeling any task that might be confusing or complicated, and checking understanding of the instructions before students begin working. It doesn't mean that you'll slow down your instruction; instead, you save time in the long run by making things clear the first time around, and your students will be more likely to be successful in accomplishing the tasks and activities you assign.

Ideas & Activities for Providing Clear Academic Tasks

ⓘ No More Than Three!

This is a simple reminder that students need instructions that are presented both orally and in writing. Some of the steps may also need to be be modeled, especially if they're complicated. Think of a time when someone gave you oral driving directions to a business or home. If there were more than 2–3 turns, you probably needed to write them down, especially if they were in an unfamiliar part of town. It's almost impossible for humans to remember more than three directions when presented orally. So, save yourself and your students some time, and never give more than three oral directions at once. Write them down for your students and they'll be grateful that you took this important step in your lesson.

SIOP Feature 11: Clear explanation of academic tasks

Additional SIOP Features: 14, 19

Grade Level: K–12

Materials: Chart paper, PowerPoint® slides, or white board

Objectives: Not applicable

Directions: Not applicable

Hints for Success:

- Remember that your directions for a task, experiment, or anything else that students are to complete or produce, need to be: a) written for students to read and reference; b) orally read and explained; c) modeled, step-by-step, if needed; and d) reviewed with students at the end of each lesson.

- To ensure students understand procedures, processes, and instructions, check for understanding regularly, throughout each lesson:
  - Can somebody tell us all what it is you're to do?
  - What's your next step? Are you allowing time to do it?
  - Turn to your partner and explain step by step what you'll be doing. Refer to the directions on the board if you need help remembering.
  - What are you to do first? Second? Third? Last?
  - What do you have left to do?

- As a rule of thumb, if more than three people need your help to understand what they are to do, stop and clarify (re-model, if necessary) for the entire class. It's worth the few minutes it will take and it will save time in the long run, because you won't have to run around the classroom telling each group again what they're to do.

ⓐ Tell Your Partner!

A common classroom practice is to ask a student to repeat directions for a task that you've just presented. Most often, the student who volunteers to go through the directions is one who always seems to know what to do. Your English learners and struggling students are not likely to be the ones who are asked to repeat the instructions or who volunteer to do so. One way to ensure that your students know what to do and are able to explain the steps of a process, task, or activity after you've presented them (orally and in writing), is to have them Tell a Partner. This is an excellent routine to establish in the beginning of the year. It will let you know immediately if anything is unclear or if anyone is confused. If students want to read the directions from chart paper you've prepared and explained, that's just fine. They're using the resources that are available to help them be successful during the lesson.

SIOP Feature 11: Clear explanation of academic tasks

Additional SIOP Features: 14, 19

Grade Level: K–12

Materials: The list of directions you have prepared and explained

Objectives: Not applicable

Directions: You may not need to follow these directions when introducing this activity. However, for English learners with low proficiency in English and for young children, following these steps will teach your students what they're to do during Tell Your Partner.

1. Write the directions for a task in sequence on chart paper, the board, or wherever students can see them and refer to them throughout a lesson.

2. Read the directions aloud, one at a time, and ask students to share each direction with their partner, alternating back and forth with each new direction.

3. Eventually, as this becomes a routine, you won't need to pause after each direction. Once you've gone through all of the written directions and have modeled steps as needed, have students engage in Tell a Partner, alternating with each direction on the list.

4. If students still have questions about what to do during a task, something hasn't been explained well, either when you've done the explaining or when a student has. Back up and try again, until everyone understands. Be patient and trust the process. Students will eventually learn to listen more carefully while you give directions, and that's a good thing!

Feature 12 A Variety of Techniques Used to Make Content Concepts Clear (e.g., Modeling, Visuals, Hands-On Activities, Demonstrations, Gestures, Body Language)

For one of the classroom videos we filmed of SIOP lessons, we interviewed English learners in high school about what teachers do that makes their learning more challenging in content classes. Without a hesitation, these teens responded that some of their teachers talked too fast, talked too much, and didn't explain things well. They all agreed that some of these teachers "aren't patient."

When asked what teachers do that makes it easier for them to learn in content classes, these English learners all started chattering about their American Literature teacher. They said, "She draws pictures, acts things out, explains things slowly, repeats directions sometimes, shows a video, finds things on the Internet, puts us in groups to work . . . she'll do whatever it takes so that we can understand what she's teaching. And, she's patient. She never forgets we're here." In a nutshell, these insightful students described what this particular SIOP feature is all about. You consistently do whatever works to enable all of your students to comprehend the lessons you teach.

Ideas & Activities for Making Content Concepts Clear

ⓐ Apps for Pronunciation Practice

In addition to learning the meaning of new vocabulary words, English learners need help pronouncing them. You can write new words down for students to see while modeling slowly how to pronounce them. Many students benefit when you explain how to shape your lips or where to place your tongue on teeth. There are many computer applications that record your voice and play it back in a whimsical fashion. Students can see a bear pronouncing their word or sentence or hear their own voice pronouncing words in really high, squeaky tones or really deep tones. These apps encourage students to engage in repeated pronunciation practice, which can benefit English learners (and other students) as they develop their English muscles to improve verbal acuity and learn new English words.

SIOP Feature 12: A variety of techniques used to make content concepts clear

Additional SIOP Features: 4, 25, 27, 29, 30

Grade Level: Best suited for elementary, but all students might enjoy the whimsy while learning to pronounce new words

Materials: Smart phone; tablet; iPad; an application that records and plays back your voice (some options are *Voice Changer Plus, Voice Recorder, Squeak My Voice, Talking News*); a list of words or phrases for students to practice

Objectives:

- *Content:* Students will incorporate new terms or phrases into their speech.
- *Language:* Students will practice pronouncing new words or phrases.
- *Student Friendly:*
  - *Content:* Our job today is to use our new words when we talk.
  - *Language:* Our other job today is to practice pronouncing (saying correctly) our new words.

Grouping Configuration: Individual, pairs, small group, whole group share out

Directions:

1. Provide students with smart phones, tablets, or iPads, at least one per group, but each student could have his or her own device.
2. Make sure the app you want to use is installed on each device.
3. Provide a vocabulary or phrase bank, like a word wall.
4. Model acceptable behavior and discuss unacceptable behavior
   - *Acceptable behavior*—asking for help when you are not sure how to pronounce a word, providing productive feedback to your table partners on their pronunciation, and "controlled" giggling!
   - *Unacceptable behavior*—pronouncing words not on the word wall, not taking turns with your table partners
5. Set the timer for 5 minutes and tell students to record the first word on the chosen app and play it back for the group. If the app allows students to change their voices, you

can indicate the setting. You might say, "Everyone pronounce the word *qualitative* using the Echo feature (on *Voice Changer Plus*)." Each student records his or her pronunciation and plays it back to the group. The second time around the teacher might ask students to pronounce the word *quantitative* using the Haunting feature.

6. At the end of the 5 minutes, have students save their last pronunciation practice to share with the class.

7. Allow students at each table to share their last pronunciation practice with the whole class.

ⓘ Befuddling Words Bulletin Board

Just as multiple meaning words and phrases can be frustrating and perplexing (another great word) for English learners and other students, the same goes for idioms, figurative language (similes and metaphors), unusual words, and of course, content vocabulary that is especially challenging. This is a simple word wall that can be very helpful to English learners and other students. The purpose is for students to identify words that they come across that are especially confusing—such as *befuddling*!

Create a bulletin board or special space on your classroom wall where students can post befuddling (or challenging) words. As students encounter these words in their reading, during discussion, while watching television, or from another source, they write them on sticky notes and post them on the Befuddling Words Bulletin Board. Other students respond if they know the word's meaning, and they write a definition (in their own words) on the sticky note that was posted by the other student. Once the words are defined (and you agree with the definition), print the words in large type (or have students help with this) on tag board or sentence strips and post on the bulletin board under "Former Culprits."

Any type of word can become part of this word wall: content words related to particular topics that are being studied; cross-curricular words; words found in literature or textbooks; words heard on TV or in conversations, and so forth. As students place their befuddling words on the board, talk about them and use them in your lessons, as well as in your directions, if relevant. This idea helps demystify frustrating words and allows English learners and other students know that everyone has problems once in a while with certain words.

SIOP Feature 12: Variety of techniques used to make content concepts clear

Additional SIOP Features: 9, 14, 20, 22, 27

Grade Level: 1–12 For younger children, you can use easier words for *befuddling* and *culprit,* or just teach the meanings of these interesting words. Young children (and older) will enjoy knowing these words!

Materials: Sticky notes; bulletin board; dictionary (have one close to the bulletin board); headings for the bulletin board: Befuddling Words, Former Culprits

Objectives: Not applicable

Directions:

1. Teach students the meaning of *befuddling.* You could use *confusing* or *perplexing,* but *befuddling* is so much more interesting and fun to say. Also, it reminds students that we can figure out words we don't know.

2. Introduce the Befuddling Words Bulletin Board and present its purpose: to identify words that we don't know and can't figure out, and to have our classmates suggest meanings for the words we post.

3. Be sure to take the sticky note down when students no longer find a word *befuddling*, and move it to the "Former Culprits" list. The number of new befuddling words on the board may vary throughout the year, depending on the topics being studied.

ⓐ Scavenger Hunt

submitted by Ashanti Ravenell, Teacher, Prince George's County Public Schools, MD

Scavenger Hunts can occur at the beginning of a lesson as students are trying to understand a concept for the first time or they can take place at the end of a lesson while students are reviewing a concept and the teacher is assessing what has been learned. During this activity, students practice and apply new concepts and/or academic vocabulary by searching for specific examples of the concepts or vocabulary around the room, in their journals, or in their textbooks.

For example, in a geometry unit, students do a Scavenger Hunt, looking for examples of geometric figures such as *triangles, rectangles,* and *circles.* During an elementary reading block, children are asked to look for names of things that include the digraphs *sh* and *ch,* such as *shoes, children, shapes,* and *Chapstick.* In Literature, students are directed to find examples of descriptive adjectives in a story or article they're reading. In Science, students could search for examples of *solids* (books, doors, tables); *liquids* (bottled water, juice, water fountain); and *gases* (spoiled banana that's giving off ethylene—yes, that's a stretch, but aren't you impressed we know that?). Once students have completed the Scavenger Hunt, everyone shares the names of the items that they discovered.

SIOP Feature 12: A variety of techniques used to make content concepts clear

Additional SIOP Features: 4, 6, 7, 25

Grade Level: 2–8

Materials: Objects around the room, including textbooks, student journals, pictures, magazines, picture books; checklist of items to be found

Objectives:

- *Content:* Students will find examples of (key concept or key vocabulary).
- *Language:* Students will orally share how the items they found are examples of (the assigned topic).

Grouping Configuration: Individual, small groups, whole class

Directions:

1. Have students look around the classroom or school for objects.
2. Ask students to use a checklist to check off objects they found.
3. Debrief the class by having students share their checklists.
4. Make connections between the objectives and the lesson's concepts.

ⓐ Time Lines on the Ceiling

submitted by Todd Ferguson, SIOP teacher, Mabelvale Middle School, AR

Content information is more accessible when teachers establish a context for what is to be learned. For example, an historical event becomes more meaningful when interesting and relevant images or photographs of it are displayed. Similarly, a timeline of events before, during, and after the key event helps students place it in relationship to all the other events surrounding it.

Todd Ferguson, a World History teacher, has his students create timelines for each continent, which include all of the major events studied during the year. These are posted on the classroom ceiling! At the beginning of the first semester, students scan their World History textbook for dates and events to put on their assigned timelines. This activity also allows the students to preview what they will be learning and learn how to use their textbooks. Mr. Ferguson's classes look up on the ceiling to refer to their timelines daily as they cover new topics.

SIOP Feature 12: A variety of techniques used to make content concepts clear

Additional SIOP Features: 6, 13, 14, 15

Grade Level: 2–12

Materials: Long narrow strips of chart paper, markers, rulers to make a straight line, textbooks, staples or tape to attach the timelines to the ceiling.

Objectives:

- *Content:* Students will preview the text to determine key events and dates on (topic).
- *Language:* Students will use adverbs of time to discuss how to order the events on the timeline (such as, *first, second, third, next, subsequently, finally,* etc.).

Grouping Configuration: Small groups (4–5)

Directions:

1. Discuss and show examples of timelines.
2. Assign portions of each timeline to students who are working in small groups.
3. Remind students how to scan a chapter for specific information.
4. Have students scan the assigned chapter to find important events and dates to add to their section of the timeline.
5. Attach the timelines to the ceiling to refer to throughout the year.
6. Encourage students to check the timeline for missing information. If a student discovers missing information from the timelines, the student or the class is rewarded for the discovery. The timeline is then revised, as needed.

Todd Ferguson

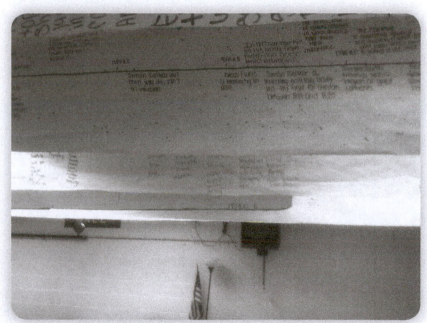

Todd Ferguson

Thinking About Comprehensible Input

1. How do your students respond when they obviously understand what you're teaching? How do they respond when they obviously don't understand? How do you feel when you're the one teaching the students in both situations?

2. Reflect on your current instructional practices for English learners. What do you do to make your instruction and materials comprehensible to all of your students? What might you be doing that sometimes makes it difficult for some of your students to understand what you're teaching?

3. If you teach older students, who may or may not be English learners, ask them the following question: "What do I do during class that helps you understand better?" Then ask, "What do I sometimes that makes it difficult for you to understand?" Most students are able to answer these questions, and you may find their responses to be very helpful."

5 Strategies

A Teacher's Reflection

The biggest impact I see in my classroom occurs when strategies are part of the students' bodies. When I see a student taking a test on measures of central tendency and he's using the five-finger check to make his box and whisker plot, I know the student can demonstrate his learning!

Molly Richardson, 6–8 Resource Room Math,
Olympic Middle School, Auburn, WA

Reflect for a moment about two students you've taught recently in your classroom. Does either of them share aspects of one of the following learner profiles?

1. Student #1 is a problem solver and a strategic thinker. Even though he sometimes has difficulty with a challenging piece of text or an abstract problem, he is usually able to think it through and figure it out. He enjoys academic challenges, and even though he sometimes gets frustrated, he appears confident that in the end, he'll succeed with whatever he sets out to do.

2. When Student #2 gets stuck on a problem or with challenging text, she frequently appears anxious and she doesn't seem to know what to do. Often, her hand is the first one raised after you've given directions and the other students have begun working. She looks around to other students for clues about how to proceed, and if she can't figure out what to do, she sits and waits for help, or she engages in what Cris Tovani (2000) calls "fake reading," described as going through the motions of being a good reader (decoding well, fluent oral reader), but comprehending very little.

You may have noticed that we didn't provide an age or grade level for either of these students. How old do you think they are? If you're an elementary teacher, you probably pictured a student in the grade you teach. If you're a secondary teacher, you probably did the same. Is the age of the student really relevant here? We think not because very young children can be strategic thinkers and problem solvers—some are and some aren't. The same goes with adolescents. And, you may be surprised to realize that for the most part, the way we approach problems and abstract concepts doesn't entirely have to do with intellect, but it certainly has to do with how we *think*. It's probably no surprise to you that while the first student in the example is academically achieving at grade level as measured by state assessments, the second student is stuggling academically and is underperforming.

The purpose of the Strategies component in the SIOP® Model is to help all students become strategic thinkers—those who have a repertoire of learning strategies that enable them to solve problems, think critically, and feel confident that in the end, they can figure out what to do to be successful. The big difference in the two profiled students is that Student #1 has learned strategies to be successful in figuring things out, while Student #2 appears to struggle when faced with challenges, in part because the strategies she uses (e.g., watching for clues from classmates, waiting for help, and fake reading) aren't effective. She completes her class work, mostly satisfactorily, but she lacks confidence, is often anxious, and has developed few helpful strategies. Her teacher can assist by teaching and modeling a variety of learning strategies, incorporating in lessons questions and tasks that require higher levels of thinking, and then providing appropriate scaffolding as needed, so that this student can be successful and make academic progress.

During effective SIOP lessons with the Strategies component, you will discover:

- Your students develop, practice, and use a variety of learning strategies while they're practicing and applying the key content and language concepts you're teaching (Feature 13).

- Your students respond to your efforts to effectively scaffold instruction for them, by being able to meet your lesson's content and language objectives (Feature 14).

- Your students improve their critical thinking skills, as demonstrated by their reading, writing, listening, and speaking during content lessons (Feature 15).

Feature 13 Ample Opportunities Provided for Students to Use Learning Strategies

Essentially, the goal of this feature is to help individuals like Student #2. While she's able to do her school work and she's reading and writing nearly on grade level, her lack of learning strategies is making her feel anxious and frustrated when she's confronted with challenging situations and problems to solve.

Learning strategies enable students to self-monitor and self-regulate, so that they create personal, conscious plans for figuring things out. For example, think of a time when you were stuck reading something challenging. As a capable, strategic reader, you probably employed a variety of strategies, such as rereading; highlighting key points; taking some notes; identifying vocabulary that might be tripping you up; making connections to what you already knew about the topic; stopping to summarize what you've read; asking questions and seeking answers while reading; among others.

Within the SIOP® Model, we focus on three types of learning strategies to teach English learners and others students (for more information, see Echevarria, Vogt, & Short, 2013, 2014a; 2014b):

1. **Cognitive strategies:** Learners organize the information they are expected to acquire through the process of self-regulated learning. Examples include: previewing text before reading; establishing a purpose for reading; consciously making connections while reading, highlighting or underlining text; taking notes; reading aloud for clarification.

2. **Metacognitive strategies:** Learners engage in the process of consciously their own thinking, using metacognitive strategies that imply awareness, reflection, and interaction. Examples include: predicting, inferring, generating questions, monitoring, clarifying, evaluating, summarizing, synthesizing, visualizing.

3. **Language learning strategies:** Learners purposefully use a variety of strategies to increase progress in speaking and comprehending a new language. Examples include: skimming, scanning, reviewing when reading; analyzing and using forms and patterns in English; making logical guesses about words; breaking words into component parts; using gestures to communicate; substituting known words for unknown; self-correcting when speaking; guessing and deducing.

To be successful academically and to develop academic language proficiency, all students must learn how to become strategic learners, readers, writers, and speakers, and that's what this Strategies component is all about.

Ideas & Activities for Providing Practice with Learning Strategies

Ask a Clarifying Question

Personal Connection with Marilyn Amy Washam

When I was 16 years old in 1983, I went to Argentina as a foreign-exchange student. I spoke no Spanish and met very few people who spoke English. When communication broke down, especially when I found myself alone with one other person, I used a phrase to help me learn more Spanish and keep the conversation going. "¿Como se dice en español?" ("How is it said in Spanish?") The phrase worked because:

1. The answer was usually one or two words.
2. I could repeat the words.
3. The other person would either correct me or nod in agreement.

This was my language learning strategy, and it worked well for me.

English learners can benefit from language learning strategies to help them learn more English on their own. This idea focuses on one phrase that English learners can be taught to help them clarify what they hear, but this phrase is also helpful for many students. We often ask teachers how their students communicate when they do not understand a concept or directions, and all across the country teachers seem to provide the same response—"I didn't get it." For us, and I think most teachers, this statement is frustrating. "What did you not get? What did you get? Can you elaborate?" Teach students to paraphrase or summarize in order to clarify uncertain concepts or directions can be helpful for all students, not just English learners. Imagine if your students raised their hands when they did not understand and said, *"I heard you say _____. Is that correct?"*

SIOP Feature 13: Ample opportunities provided for students to use learning strategies

Additional SIOP Features: 14, 15, 16, 19

Grade Level: 3–12

Materials: Chart paper, markers

Objectives:

- *Content:* Students will ask clarifying questions.
- *Language:* Students will use the following sentence frame to ask a clarifying question:
  - I heard you say _____. Is that correct?

Grouping Configuration: Whole group, small group, pairs

Directions:

1. Ask students to discuss with their table partners what they do in class when they are uncertain about a concept or even directions for an assignment.

2. Allow the class members to discuss their ideas and then share them while you post a few on a chart, making sure to add the students' names.

3. Tell students that another effective way to ask for help is to paraphrase or summarize what you think someone said or meant to say.

4. Provide the sentence frame "I think I heard you say _____. Is that correct?"

5. Explain that this technique allows you, the teacher, to understand exactly what part of the concept or directions a student is struggling with.

6. Model the technique by summarizing the ideas students shared earlier, while pointing to the sentence frame. For example, *"Charlie, I heard you say that one way to clarify uncertainty is to raise your hand and ask the teacher for help. Is that correct?"*

7. Have students practice the sentence frame using the answers that you charted previously.

8. Explain that students will be required to use the technique at least once during the lesson.

9. The first day, you can stop the lesson and ask one student (partner A) to use the technique with another student (partner B). Eventually, you can suggest that students use the technique during group work or once during the lesson. Students should feel comfortable with the phrase, hear it used, and have opportunities to use it.

ⓐ Learn to Define the Word

submitted by Leslie M. Middleton, Instructional Coach, Rochester City School District, NY

This activity introduces students to vocabulary words in text and helps them infer the words' meanings using context clues. Students practice listening to, pronouncing, and writing vocabulary words.

After reading a text once or twice, students are directed to look for the words that have been introduced and to use context clues to infer the words' meanings. Explain and model the learner strategy of using context clues to infer meaning. For example, write the following on the board:

> My friend's family is _____ and when I go out to breakfast with them they all order a tofu scramble with lots of vegetables. Once I ordered it, too, and I thought it tasted good, even though I missed cheese, eggs, and sausage.

Notice that the key vocabulary word, vegans, is missing, and students must try to figure out the meaning of the missing word using context clues, rather than their knowledge of a *vegan diet*. Provide several similar examples before you begin this activity; it's almost like a game and students enjoy trying to figure out the missing word or words. Of course, for younger students, use age-appropriate, relevant words and concepts for your examples. Remind students that learning new words by using context clues is an effective strategy to use while reading.

SIOP Feature 5: Ample opportunities provided for students to use learning strategies

Additional SIOP Features: 2, 9, 14, 15

Grade Level: 2–12

Materials: A place to display words (white board or bulletin board); a text that includes the vocabulary students will be learning; student journals; a graphic organizer with pictures of the words students will be defining

Objectives:

- *Content:* Students will collaborate with others to come to consensus on the meaning of a word.
- *Language:* Students will determine the meaning of vocabulary words in text by using context clues.
- *Student Friendly:*
  - I can work with others to figure out what words mean.
  - I can use context clues to figure out what words mean when I'm reading.

Grouping Configuration: Individual, partners, whole group

Directions:

1. Display each vocabulary word, one at a time, for students to see. This can be done on an interactive white board or a dry-erase board. Select the number of words judiciously, depending on the age of your students and their levels of English proficiency. Of these words, some should be new to almost everyone, some should be a bit familiar, and a few should be familiar words that almost everyone knows. Remember that the goal is to teach and provide students with practice using *context clues,* not *decoding,* so it's better not to have all unfamiliar, new words.

2. Ask students to define any of the words they know, and talk together about the definitions of those that are new.

3. Have students record the words in their journals, Cornell note-taking style. Have them leave the right half of the page blank for recording the definitions later. (At this point, the students have NOT recorded any definitions, only the words.)

4. Review what context clues are and how to use them when reading. This is very important for English learners who may know a term in their L1 but not in English. If you have English learners who haven't learned to read well in either their L1 or English, you may want to partner them with students who speak the same L1 and can clarify how to use context clues (if this possible), or you may want to work with these students in a small group while the other pairs are working together.

5. After the class has read through the text, have the students go back into it to search for the vocabulary words you introduced. Ask them to infer definitions of each word using context clues and textual evidence. Provide each student with a graphic organizer handout with pictures of each word.

6. Working with a partner, students are to write the word and definition next to its picture on the graphic organizer.

7. Once students finish the graphic organizer, have them join another group to compare their answers.

8. The four (or five) group members must come to consensus on the correct definitions.

9. The class meets as a whole group to share their definitions and come to consensus on one definition for each word, using the context clues and other textual information as evidence.

10. The students write these definitions in their journals in the blank space beside the vocabulary words they previously listed.

ⓐ Read-Aloud, Think, & Summarize
adapted from Sarah Russell, High School English Teacher, Washoe County School District, NV

The purpose of this activity is help English learners and other students practice and improve their reading, listening, and speaking skills. In pairs, students alternate reading aloud, listening, and summarizing an assigned text. The focus for each partner, depending on the role, is to read clearly, listen carefully, and summarize the text's key ideas. Students who have participated in this activity have reported that they have learned to read better as a result of working through text with a partner.

SIOP Feature 13: Ample opportunities provided for students to use learning strategies

Additional SIOP Features: 14, 15, 16, 22, 25

Grade Level: 4–12

Materials: Text appropriate to students' reading levels; sticky notes; list of key vocabulary with brief definitions

Objectives:

- *Content:* Students will summarize key content concepts after listening to text read aloud.
- *Language:*
  - Students will read and listen to text passages.
  - Students will use key vocabulary when summarizing key content concepts.

Grouping Configurations: Partners

Directions:

1. Determine the pairs of students who will work together for this activity. Consider the following when partnering students:

   a. *Reading levels:* Pair students who are at similar reading levels, if possible. Ideally, partner a grade-level reader with someone who is slightly less skilled in reading; partner an above-grade level reader with someone who is a bit less skilled, but not a poor reader. When you partner students with one who excels in reading and the other who struggles a lot with reading, it's unfair to both people and not very productive. If you have students who have significant problems with reading, work with them on this activity in a small group. If all of your students have serious reading problems, this may not be an appropriate activity for them.

   b. *Compatibility:* Select partners who will work well together and will stay on task. It is fine to partner a more rambunctious student with one who stays on task, but two of your rambunctious students reading together probably won't be successful. For this particular activity, it's better not to let students choose their own partners.

2. Select the texts that students will be reading. This is an equally important step if the activity is to be successful, and it's critical that no partners be expected to read and summarize frustration-level passages. If you have at- and above-grade level readers working as partners, grade level text (or even a bit above grade level) will work well. If you have below-grade level readers working together, adapted text should be used.

3. Model with a student how everyone should read, listen, and summarize with their partners:

   a. If everyone is reading from a passage that is about one particular topic, distribute a list of key vocabulary, including brief definitions. Limit the number of key vocabulary words to 4–5 terms. If more words need defining, the passage may be too difficult for this activity. Check to see if any of the vocabulary words are totally new, and if so, define them with a sentence or two to provide context.

   b. The student reads aloud from a passage.

   c. You listen, without looking at the text, and jot key points on a sticky note.

   d. After the student has finished reading aloud, you orally summarize the most important points, using your sticky note, and including key vocabulary in your summary.

   e. It's important to summarize the most important points and not read from a list. The key points may or may not be in order, depending on the text read.

   f. After you summarize, the reader may add any missed points or correct any misunderstandings or misconceptions; he or she should also try to include key vocabulary in these comments.

   g. Switch roles, and continue to model, if needed.

4. Debrief with students each time you have them do this activity. How did it go? How many of the key vocabulary words were included? How have their summaries changed with more experience in orally summarizing what they heard? What have they learned about reading aloud to another person? What will they try next time to make the process work even better?

5. The first few times students engage in this activity, monitor closely and assist as needed. Eventually, partners should be able to go through the steps independently, while you work with a small group. Once everyone is comfortable with the process, mix up the partners, but continue to attend to the difficulty level of the texts.

6. Assess students' participation, oral reading, use of key vocabulary, and oral summaries. Have the partners complete a brief self-assessment of how well each did with the Read-Aloud, Think, & Summarize activity.

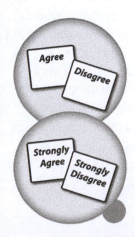

ⓐ Take Your Position

Part of teaching students how to engage in strategic, higher-level thinking involves providing opportunities for them to take a position and support it with evidence. All students can learn to explain clearly why they think a particular position is worth supporting, beyond an emotional response. For older students, this is a critical skill to develop so they will be prepared for college or career choices. With this activity, you can teach your students:

1. What it means to "take a position."

2. How to explain the position taken.

3. How to justify the position with evidence.

SIOP Feature 13: Ample opportunities for provided for students to use learning strategies

Additional SIOP Features: 6, 15, 21, 22, 25

Grade Level: 2–12

Materials: Signs for *Strongly Agree, Agree, Strongly Disagree, Disagree*; a variety of resources, such as newspapers, magazines, websites, books

Objectives:

- *Content:* Students will take a position on an issue after reading and/or talking about it.
  - Students will use texts and electronic resources to find evidence to support their positions about (an issue).
- *Language:* Students will use persuasive language to explain their rationale for the position they have taken on (the issue).
- *Student Friendly:*
  - *Content:* I can decide whether I agree or disagree with (topic or position).
  - *Language:* I can talk about why I agree or disagree with (topic or position).

Grouping Configuration: Individual, partners, small group, whole class

Directions:

1. During reading and/or discussion, help students identify possible issues related to a topic. For example, for children, the issue could be something related to the school, such as instituting healthier lunches, decreasing school bus services to save money, or requiring uniforms. For older students, select an issue related to a topic being studied, such as the use of DNA to convict criminals years after a crime was committed (science); the positions of the colonists and British soldiers prior to the "shot heard around the world" (history); whether parent permission should be required for the "day-after pill" (health); or whether something equivalent to a "Scarlet A" should be used today to identify those who break community-imposed rules (literature).

2. During class, have students examine several positions that could be taken regarding the issue of the day. Students can work with partners or a small group to investigate the position they may wish to take, using a variety of resources for research. Even though they're working with other class members, they don't have to take the position of those in their group.

3. On the day of Take Your Position, post the signs (Strongly Agree, Agree, Strongly Disagree, Disagree), in each of the four corners of the classroom. Post the day's issue on the board or chart paper.

4. On cue, students stand (with their notes), and go to the corner that best represents their individual (not group) positions. You may find that only two positions are selected by the groups, such as Strongly Agree and Disagree. That's okay—the sizes of the groups by position don't need to be even. If everyone goes to one group, you have a problem: the issue may not be controversial enough and you may need to select another. Resist letting students be "neutral"; they must take a position by one of the signs. If only one person picks a particular position, he or she can either stay and defend it alone or move one way or the other to take a different position. Sometimes, there's safety in numbers.

5. Once in their new groups, students compare the notes from their research and create their group's argument. Ask students to make sure that each person in their group knows the evidence well enough to support the group's position.

6. There are several options for the next step in the process:

   a. Hold a debate. Be sure to explain clearly the steps of the debate, go over the "rules of the game," and provide sentence frames for those students who need them.

   b. Number students off within the same-position groups, and randomly call two numbers at a time. The students with those numbers in each group will each argue the position and provide the supporting evidence gathered by group members. Language objectives could include the language of persuasion and how to disagree appropriately with another speaker ("On the other hand. . . ." "While I respect your opinion, I suggest. . . .").

   c. Have students in each group create a poster or PowerPoint® presentation that illuminates their position and provides evidence from resources.

   d. Have students in groups write a position paper, patterned after a newspaper editorial or other opinion pieces.

   e. Engage students in a Value Line activity (Vogt & Echevarria, 2008, p. 94). "Draw" an imaginary line across the classroom floor. Place a sign with *Strongly Agree* at one end of the line; place another with *Strongly Disagree* at the other end. Ask students to consider the position they've taken and go to a spot on the line (between the two extremes) that best represents their perspective. Students can't form a clump at the middle, but must distribute themselves along the line, talking with other students and moving their bodies toward one end or the other. You could do a Value Line after students have moved to the corners and developed their reasons for the positions they've taken.

7. Individual student participation can be assessed in a variety of ways, including:

   a. Read and assess a summary written by each student of the position taken with relevant supporting evidence.

   b. Create a rubric with a 0–4 rating system. Include descriptors for each number. The rubric can be used for assessing oral presentations, debates, poster sessions (where students explain their posters), and so forth.

Feature 14 Scaffolding Techniques Consistently Used Assisting and Supporting Student Understanding (e.g., Think-Alouds)

Often teachers express enthusiasm and gratitude when they learn about a new game or activity that will help their students engage in a lesson, but sometimes they also express concern that playing games and providing too much scaffolding is diminishing the rigor and watering down the content. We have heard teachers ask something like, "How is all of this scaffolding preparing our students to be ready for college and careers? Shouldn't they be able to work on their own?"

First of all, scaffolding should not make lessons "easier" for students. Instead, scaffolding provides students with greater access to content and language concepts. Activities, techniques, teaching methods, and games are tools we provide our students to help them explore the content, practice academic language, and gain access to knowledge and skills they have not already developed.

Further, we devise games in order to extend the duration during which students engage with the content and language concepts (see Row Races Review, p. 177). We provide structures and rules in order to help students acquire and refine interpersonal skills or learner strategies (see The Pattern of Accountability, see p. 106). Teachers incorporate various teaching methods to make the content more comprehensible and to help students practice becoming better learners (see Verbally Scaffolding for Higher-Order Questions, p. 99).

Before choosing a technique or activity, assess your students' knowledge of the lesson's content and language key concepts. How much scaffolding will your students need in order to meet the objectives? Also assess their interpersonal skills and the learner strategies they know and use. Are they able to collaborate with peers? How do they react when facing a challenge? If students are unable to work as a team to solve a problem, create a structure that will give them practice working with others effectively. Once students have mastered a game or activity, make the activity more complex by adding a new requirement and/or by taking away some of the scaffolding.

Activities, techniques, teaching methods, and games should always provide learning challenges for students. If your students are not developing their learning strategies, content knowledge, and English language proficiency, make adjustments to the scaffolding you are providing them. Scaffolding should always help your students become capable, independent learners who are prepared for college and career.

Ideas & Activities for Providing Scaffolding

a Academic Conversation Sentence Frames

It is important to allow students time to talk about content concepts and academic language, but all too often, asking students to discuss a topic in small groups results in off-topic, social conversations. There are probably many reasons why small group conversations wander off topic, including: students not knowing what to say or how to say it, not having the social skills to keep an academic conversation going, and/or not feeling motivated to have the conversation in the first place. In this activity, sentence frames are used to keep student conversations moving, to scaffold academic language, and to place students in charge of making sure the conversations stay on topic. Since one student is in charge and there are specific rules for using the conversation cards, students can begin to hold themselves accountable for their own discussions.

SIOP Feature 14: Scaffolding techniques consistently used assisting and supporting student understanding

Additional Features: 13, 16, 25, 26

Grade Level: 1–12

Materials: A deck of index cards, 10 or more with sentence starters written on each one.

Objectives:

- *Content:* Students will participate effectively in a range of conversations with diverse partners, building on others' ideas and expressing their own clearly.
- *Language:* Students will include the following vocabulary words when completing the sentence frames (include words from the lesson).
- *Student Friendly:*
  - *Content:* I can tell my ideas about (topic) to my classmates.
  - *Language:* I can use these vocabulary words when we talk about (topic). (List 2–3 vocabulary words.)

Grouping Configuration: Small groups (3–4 students)

Directions:

1. Arrange students in small groups.
2. Designate one student in each group to be in charge of the conversation cards (the "deck master"). Provide each group's deck master with a deck of ten conversation cards prior to the beginning of the lesson. Each conversation card includes a sentence starter to help students engage in meaningful talk about a concept, problem, or text.
3. Explain that the deck master will hold on to the cards until the teacher asks students to ponder a question, problem, or text.
4. The deck master selects a card and hands it to one of the other group members, who uses the sentence starter to ponder the question, problem, or text. Or, the deck master

can "fan" the cards and each student can pick one of the sentence starters. Examples of sentence starters are:

- What do you think _____ means?
- Does anyone disagree with _____? Why?
- One example of _____ that I can think of is _____.
- One question I have about _____ is _____?
- One idea I have about _____ is _____.
- I think the key ideas are _____, _____, and _____.
- Another way of stating this is _____.
- I agree that _____.
- What I find most interesting is _____.
- Something that puzzles me is _____.

5. After the student completes the sentence frame, he or she hands the conversation card back to the deck master.

6. The deck master continues to hand out cards to the others in the group, one card at a time, until the teacher ends the small group conversations.

7. The deck master holds on to the cards until the next time the teacher prompts him/her to assign a card.

8. Since this activity assigns responsibility to one student in each group, it might be helpful to explain to the students that being *in charge* means having responsibilities. The deck master holds the cards; selects one at a time for a classmate (or fans them for each student to select); makes sure each student has an opportunity to read a card and complete its sentence frame; keeps the conversation moving; and returns the cards to you at the end of the activity.

9. For subsequent academic conversations when sentence frame cards are used, remind students that each group member will eventually have a turn to serve as the deck master.

ⓘ Differentiating Student Products

Have you ever seen a class of students complete an assignment or task in the same amount of time? There are always students who finish earlier than anticipated, students who finish in about the same time frame that you planned, and students who will not complete the assignment no matter how much extra time you allow. This becomes very frustrating if your goal is for students to complete the assignment or "product" so that you can talk about it together or move on to something else. What do you do with students who are finished too early? Do you give them more work? What about students who need more time? Do you ask them to complete the assignment for homework? And . . . is it *really* necessary for all students to work on the same tasks at the same time, so that they all finish together? If the answer to this last question is "No," doesn't lesson planning for such diverse students become a nightmare?

We don't think so because with differentiated student products, your focus is on the extent to which each student is making progress in meeting the lesson's content and language objectives. The best way to explain this shift in focus is that you are more aware of your students' *learning,* not just the products they produce. As an example of why this is so important, Amy shares a personal story about her son when he was in kindergarten.

I know that I have watched my own son struggle with cutting and pasting letters to pictures in order to learn to read. He hates to cut and paste, and that was ALL they did in kindergarten. I found a private teacher who had these wooden puzzle letters and Pete loved working with them. He also loved working with computer programs and actually writing words. He still hates to cut and paste. I kept telling his kindergarten teacher that we could work on cutting and pasting, perhaps with other concepts he was better at, but we needed to work on phonics in a modality that he was more comfortable with. She really did not understand what I was saying.

We hope you can see from this example that this particular idea isn't about activities as much as it is about how students go about meeting a lesson's objectives. For example, students with more advanced English proficiency might be able to work with a concept in writing for the entire class period. However, other students may not be able to do this because of gaps in their literacy skills. Struggling to write continuously for a long time prevents these students from grappling with the lesson's content concepts and academic language. They may generate a few sentences, but they'll probably miss the key concepts.

Many teachers want all of their students to accomplish the same amount of learning during a class period, but this is impossible. A more achievable goal is for students to learn more about a topic than they knew when they began the lesson, and this may require differentiated tasks and products. It is better for a student to write one complex sentence on his own about a concept than to copy an entire essay that he does not understand.

Our goal should be that every student gets to that point in the learning process where some grappling occurs, even if it only happens for a short amount of time. If you occasionally or often differentiate student products, you may find that your students will be able to meet their objectives, albeit in different ways.

SIOP Feature 14: Scaffolding techniques consistently used, assisting and supporting student understanding

Additional SIOP Features: 6, 12, 14, 23, 26

Grade Level: K–12

Materials: Not applicable

Objectives: Not applicable

Directions:

1. Take a look at the following objectives and think about the ways students may demonstrate their learning of them.
2. As you do so, list some ideas for possible products that would provide practice and application of the key concepts and vocabulary and that would promote student engagement in academic conversations. For example:

Students will make personal connections while reading a story.

Note that this could be an objective after teaching and modeling the reading strategy of making connections. Possible differentiated options for students to meet this content objective include:

- Students individually create journal entries and share and compare them with other students.
- Students verbalize text-to-self connections using teacher-prepared sentence frames.
- Students use teacher-prepared sentence frames to verbalize text-to-self connections while reading a passage, such as "I understand why the main character feels sad because _____."

Another example is:

> Students will use the words *dividend, divisor, quotient,* and *remainder* to explain how to solve long division problems.

Possible products are:

- Students work individually to play Internet or computer games. Sites like http://www .aaamath.com/div-terms.htm#section3 allow students to race against the clock to identify the parts of division problems, using the following terms: *divisor, dividend, quotient,* and *remainder.* The "product" in this example is actually a score for correct answers.
- Students work in pairs to solve a division problem. After they find their solution, they write an explanation of how they solved the problem using the following terms: *divisor, dividend, quotient,* and *remainder*.
- Students make posters with division problems. They visit each poster during a Gallery Walk (Vogt & Echevarria, 2008, p. 115), and use the words *divisor, dividend, quotient,* and *remainder* to explain each poster's problem.

ⓐ Sentence Analysis

English learners, along with struggling readers and writers, need instruction in vocabulary as well as sentence structure. Many English learners and some native English speakers have not had enough exposure to conventional English to begin noticing the more complex patterns of the English language. Consequently, they often write in simple sentences. Teaching students how to write complex sentences provides them with the tools they need to think critically and respond to higher-order questions or tasks.

SIOP Feature 14: Scaffolding techniques consistently used assisting and supporting student understanding

Additional SIOP Features: 13, 15

Grade Level: 4–12

Materials: Markers; chart paper with each of the following sentence categories written on one piece:

- *Cause and Effect*: Because it is raining, the children can't go outside to play.
- *Dependent*: If it stops raining, the children will be able to go outside to play.
- *Conflicting*: Although it is raining, Juan is outside playing.

- *Concurrent*: While it is raining, the class is listening to the teacher tell a story.
- *Sequential*: After it rains, the children can go outside to play. Before it rained, the children were looking forward to playing outside.

Objectives:

- *Content:* Students will analyze complex sentences to determine their sentence structures.
- *Language:* Students will read and write complex sentences with varied sentence structures.

Grouping Configuration: Individual, partners, small groups

Directions:

1. Provide students with three examples of any type of sentence, such as Cause and Effect:

   a. *Because the boy is hungry, he eats.*

   b. *Because the gate was left open, the dog got out.*

   c. *Because the children were cooperating, they were given extra time to play the game.*

2. Ask students to think-pair-share with a partner and then in their group about what the three sentences have in common.

3. Ask groups to share their conclusions as you chart their answers on a poster titled *Cause and Effect Rules*. For example:

   a. Cause and Effect Sentence Rules

      - Sentences can start with *Because*.
      - A comma separates two ideas.
      - The first idea makes the second idea happen.

4. When the class agrees that the rules are correct after double-checking them with each sentence, students write their own sentences, using the Rules. Scaffold this step according to the age and language proficiency of your students. For example, some students are asked to analyze a simple sentence, such as *Because the boy is hungry, he eats*. Other students are able to analyze more complex sentences, such as *Because the basketball team was behind by three points, with the clock at 48 seconds, and one timeout remaining, the coach substituted his best defensive player.* Differentiate with varied levels of sentence complexity.

5. Students work in pairs or as a whole class to edit their sentences, using the rules they created as their guidelines.

6. After students have learned the basic rules of writing a sentence with a particular structure, ask them to apply the rules in writing. Again, you can scaffold the level of complexity of the sentences students will be expected to write. Examples of sentences you could assign include:

   a. Write a *dependent sentence* about what happened in an experiment.

   b. Write a *cause and effect sentence* about the main idea of a paragraph.

   c. Write a *conflicting* or a *concurrent sentence* comparing how you and another student solved a problem.

7. Have students find examples of the different types of sentences in their textbook chapters or other reading materials (magazines, newspapers, and so forth).

8. Once students have mastered a particular type of sentence, explain that there are other words and phrases that can be used to create the same meaning, and add them to the Rules poster, such as:

Cause and Effect Sentence Rules

- Sentences can start with *Because*.
- A comma separates two ideas.
- The first idea makes the second idea happen.
- Sentences can also start with *Since* or *As a result*.

You may be thinking that this type of analysis is too sophisticated for your students. That may be the case now. However, with explicit instruction and ample practice, students (including English learners and other students) can learn to recognize and write various type of sentences, with increasing sophistication. This skill is one that will facilitate students' progress in meeting the Common Core literacy standards for both reading and writing.

Feature 15 A Variety of Questions or Tasks that Promote Higher-Order Thinking Skills (e.g., Literal, Analytical, and Interpretive Questions)

It's interesting to ponder how we have "taught" English learners in our schools over the past few decades. Here's a partial list of ways we've tried to meet their needs.

1. We've placed many students whose home language is not English in special education, regardless of whether they really qualified or needed services.

2. We routinely placed English learners in low-track classes in the secondary grades, regardless of whether that was appropriate for their needs.

3. We placed English learners in mainstream classes with little to no language support.

We have "immersed" English learners, held them back, provided social promotions . . . and watched many drop out of school as soon as they could legally do so. What we have *not* done, for far too many English learners, is develop their critical thinking skills and strategies through scaffolded, appropriate, and accelerated academic and language instruction. That's what this SIOP feature is all about.

Many of you "grew up" as a teacher learning how to write different levels of questions using Bloom's Taxonomy of Educational Objectives (Bloom, 1956), or perhaps it was the more recent revised Taxonomy (Anderson & Krathwohl, 2001). In your lessons, you've probably tried to keep higher levels of questioning in mind as you teach. However, research has shown that 80% of teacher questioning is at the Literal/Knowledge/Remember level (Watson & Young, 1986). We believe this is primarily because it's hard to be standing in front of your class teaching, while at the same time figuring out how to phrase a question at the Synthesis or Create level.

Therefore, we suggest that during lesson planning, you think not only about including higher-level tasks for students to complete, but also plan in advance the higher-order questions that you will ask. This is the only way to ensure that English learners and your other students are challenged to critically and strategically think about key content concepts. We've said this before (Echevarria, Vogt, & Short, 2013, p. 141), and we'll say it again: *Just because English learners don't speak English proficiently, doesn't mean they can't THINK!*

Ideas & Activities for Planning Higher-Order Questions and Tasks

ⓐ Bingo with a Twist!

submitted by Andrea Rients, Social Studies Teacher, Shakopee High School, Shakopee, MN

This is Bingo with a new twist! Students will engage in varied levels of questions about key content and language concepts while they try and win at Bingo.

SIOP Feature 15: A variety of questions or tasks that promote higher-order thinking

Additional SIOP Features: 13, 14, 20, 21, 25, 27, 29, 30

Grade Level: 1–12

Materials: Student Bingo "boards" (sheets of paper are fine); prepared questions

Objectives:

- *Content:* Students will identify (properties, elements, or characteristics of content concepts studied).

- *Language:*

  1. Students will work with a partner to determine the best answer to Questions about (topic) on a Bingo card.

  2. Students will use evidence to support their answers to the Bingo card questions (from past learning or with evidence from the text).

- *Student Friendly:*

  - *Content:* I can work with my partner to answer Bingo questions.

  - *Language:* I can tell why I think my answer to a question is correct.

Grouping Configuration: Partners

Directions:

1. Write questions for the 20 (4 down) or 25 (5 down) Bingo boxes or for older students, tell each set of partners to write three questions about the topic. Then, you select the 25 questions for the Bingo card, adding some of your own if the topic isn't covered well enough by the students' questions.

2. Provide each set of partners with a Bingo card with questions printed on it.

3. With their partner, students write answers to the Bingo questions, trying to answer all questions in a row: vertically, horizontally, or diagonally.

4. Prior to a test (such as at the end of a unit), students are to answer the questions without any resources, especially if you want to assess what might need to be reviewed or re-taught. Or, you may permit students to use class notes as a reference. Those who have kept good notes will be at an advantage over those whose notes are incomplete or disorganized.

5. Discuss and model how to participate in effective, academic discussions during Bingo, especially how to talk about why partners decided on a particular answer to a question.

6. Sentence frames may be helpful for some students:
   - This is the answer to our first (second, third, etc.) question: _____.
   - We think this is the correct answer because _____.
   - It says _____ in the book, so our answer to this question is _____.

7. All sets of partners must be able to explain why they answered each question as they did. They can use information from former lessons or experiences, or by providing textual support.

8. For each game, there can be *one* vertical, *one* horizontal, and *two* diagonal winners (either leg of the X).

9. Partners who think they are winners should call out "Bingo!" and present their answers, as well as their sources for their answers, including textual support if applicable.

10. Ask the rest of the class for verification of the pair's answers.

11. Once one group gets a vertical Bingo, the rest of the pairs must change their strategy and try for a different row to get a Bingo.

12. Use the "black out" option (all questions on the Bingo card are answered correctly), so those who complete a Bingo are still engaged throughout the game.

13. Be prepared: Bingo with a Twist! can easily take a full classroom period.

ⓐ Concept Ladder

submitted by Kimberly Howland, SIOP Trainer, Washoe County Schools, NV

A concept ladder is an organizer that synthesizes student understandings of a topic or event and scaffolds student articulation of higher-order questions. Students search for answers to their own questions, as well as questions generated by their peers, so that learning is guided but also self-directed. Over time, students begin to see how their thinking builds from understanding the basic facts of a concept, event, or situation to critically thinking about its impact. If you are familiar with Question-Answer Relationships (Raphael, Highfield, & Au, 2006; Vogt & Echevarria, 2008, pp. 79–81), we suggest that you teach the QAR levels and provide students with practice in identifying them before you teach them how to write questions at different levels of a taxonomy. The QAR levels are:

- **Right There:** The answer to the question can be found easily in one or two sentences in the text.

- **Think and Search:** The answer is in the text but several sentences, paragraphs, or pages have to be put together to find the answer.

- **Author and Me:** The answer involves what I know, what I believe, or what I have experienced *and* what happened in the text.

- **On My Own:** The answer is not found in the text. The answer is only about my thoughts or experiences and a theme or idea from the book.

- For children in grades K–2, use a simplified QAR:
  - *On the Page*: I'll find the answer to the question right on the page.
  - *In My Head*: The answer to the question isn't on the page. I have to think and figure out the answer myself.

SIOP Feature 15: A variety of questions or tasks that promote higher-order thinking skills

Additional SIOP Features: 6, 13, 14, 16,17, 20

Grade Level: 1–12

Materials: Concept Ladder graphic organizer; copy of the Process Verbs (Appendix B); a text to read

Objectives:

- *Content:* Students will read closely to determine what the text says and make logical inferences from it.
- *Language:* Students will write questions about the text they are to read using verbs from varied levels of (QAR or Bloom's Taxonomy or the Revised Bloom's Taxonomy).
- *Student Friendly:*
  - *Content:* I can read a story and understand what it means.*
  - *Language:* I can ask good questions about what I am reading.

Grouping Configuration: Begin working whole group, shift to pairs, then individual students once students are ready to work independently

Directions:

1. Provide students with a copy of the Concept Ladder graphic organizer (see Figure 5.1).
2. Tell students that they are creating their own guide for reading a text using various levels of questions.

Figure 5.1
Concept Ladder

Source: Created by Kimberly Howland.

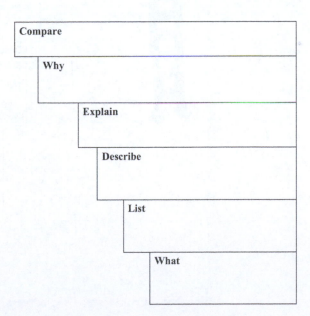

3. Explain to students the concept of different levels of questions, and review the QAR levels as an example.

---

* Note: We don't usually use *understand* in an objective because it's not really measurable. However, *infer* is a tough verb to use with small children. *Understand* is more understandable for them and it fits this objective, so we're using it!

4. For English learners and other students with more advanced levels of English proficiency, provide a copy of the Process Verbs (Appendix B). Briefly discuss each of the levels of the Revised Bloom's Taxonomy (see an overview on pp. 124–125, Echevarria, Vogt, & Short, 2013).

5. Model how to use the Process Verbs (Appendix B), by writing a question at each level of the taxonomy (or QAR).

6. Explain that a question is written on each "rung" of the Concept Ladder using a key term from the taxonomy to begin the question.

7. Work together as a class to create the first rung question, then allow students to work with partners to create the second and subsequent rung questions.

8. After students have completed their ladders, they can begin reading the assigned text, using the questions on their Concept Ladders as a guide for reading. Your purpose is to teach students how to identify and ask questions at varied levels of cognition, so keep in mind that you can differentiate this activity by providing texts with varied levels of complexity. If some students are asked to do this with exceedingly difficult text, they won't be successful at writing the questions or reading. For students with lower language and reading proficiency, have them complete the Concept Ladder with an adapted text as they may need the scaffolded support.

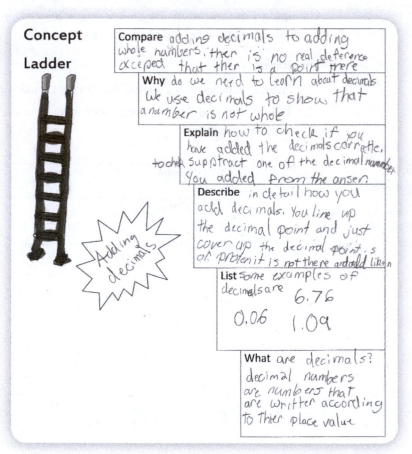

Marilyn Amy Washam

9. Another option is to allow students to exchange Ladders with peers and practice answering other students' questions.

10. You can also choose to use students' Ladder questions in the Row Races Activity for assessment (see Review & Assessment, p. 100).

ⓘ Verbally Scaffolding for Higher-Order Questions

In order to get all students to engage in answering academic questions, we can use verbal scaffolding, which includes preparing and asking a limited number of questions; repeating and rephrasing the questions; pointing out key words and ideas for students to focus on; providing wait time for students to think and process; and discussing ideas with a partner or small group.

SIOP Feature 15: A variety of questions or tasks that promote higher-order thinking skills

Additional SIOP Features: 10, 11, 12, 14, 16

Grade Level: K–12

Materials: Dry erase board to write on; visuals; copy of text

Objectives: Not applicable

Grouping Configuration: Mostly whole group, but at times during the discussion, students might pair up in order to grapple with a question

Directions:

1. You can prepare your students for a whole class academic discussion by having them read a text or work on a problem before discussion begins.

2. Prepare a limited number of questions to ask students. Think of ways to rephrase them.

3. Ask your first question and allow students time to think and process (at least 10–15 seconds).

4. Use the following techniques to clarify, as needed:

   a. Repeat the question.

   b. Rephrase the question.

   c. Ask what certain words in the question mean.

5. Resist answering the question yourself (something we teachers *love* to do!).

6. When a student responds, use follow-up questions to continue the discussion:

   a. Who can tell me more about that?

   b. What else did you think about?

   c. Who had a similar idea? What is it?

   d. Who had a different idea? What is it?

   e. What made you think of that?

   f. Where did that idea come from?

7. If students are struggling to engage in the conversation, use the following techniques:

   a. Provide visuals such as timelines or pictures.

   b. Allow time for students to go back to the text or problem and study it again.

   c. Allow time for students to talk to their table partners about the question.

   d. Provide sentence frames and allow students time to complete them before calling on anyone to answer.

   e. Have students use white boards to write their responses. Use the group response cues (*Think! Write! Show Me!*), and have students share their answers with each other.

8. Keep a record of the conversation outcomes on chart paper for students to reference later in the lesson.

Thinking about Strategies

1. Analyze the learning strategies that you routinely use when you:

   a. Read a complex text.

   b. Write an essay or other type of extended text.

   c. Try something new for the first time.

   Which strategies work best for you? How do you know they're effective? How did you learn these strategies? Do you recall ever being taught them? If not, how did you learn them? Answers to these questions will help you become more effective in teaching learning strategies to your students, especially when you use think-alouds.

2. Keep a record of the questions you ask your students (in one subject area or during one period) over the three-day period. Analyze them as to the levels of cognition (Bloom's Taxonomy, the Revised Bloom's Taxonomy, or Depth of Knowledge). What percentage of the questions are at the literal/Knowledge/Remember level? What percentage is at a higher level? What do you need to do to increase the percentage of higher-order questions for your students?*

---

*   Note: Audio or videotaping lessons over a three-day period is the best way to do this analysis.

6 Interaction

Hasloo Group Production Studio/Shutterstock

A Teacher's Reflection

I have found that providing opportunities for more small-group, student-to-student interaction provides a non-threatening environment for students who are English learners, thus increasing their participation.

—Charlotte Rippel, Ward Elementary School, Downey Unified School District, California

Think for a minute about these questions: What language are your English learners likely to speak before they come to school? If they have friends who speak the same L1, what language do they speak during breaks (recess or passing times) and lunch? What language do they speak after school until they go to bed? You're probably thinking: My students who are English learners most likely speak their home language outside of school. And you're probably right.

Now consider how much time these same students spend speaking English during the school day. If you look at research on the balance of teacher talk to student talk, you'll find that during school, the teacher is talking most of the time while students are listening. If this is the case in your classroom, then when are your students practicing academic English?

The focus of the Interaction component is on creating a better balance of student talk and teacher talk in SIOP classrooms, where students are using academic language with partners, in flexible small groups, and in conversation with the teacher. In order for English learners to converse in English, they need to be provided sufficient wait time to process, perhaps in their first language, and then in English. Clarification in their home language, if possible, may be necessary for beginning English speakers to understand and to be understood.

Jana Echevarría shared the following anecdote to remind us all that even though students are learning English, they will have difficulty becoming fully fluent if they are not able to use it regularly with other English speakers.

Personal Connection with Jana Echevarría

When I was an English teacher at a university in Taiwan, the benefit of practicing speaking and listening in a second language became apparent. Most of my students had studied English for many years, but their experience was limited to a "book knowledge" of the language. They could read and write but had great difficulty speaking and understanding spoken English. I decided to give an oral test to convey to them the importance of being able to actually use the language. I met with each student individually and asked a series of questions. I recall a couple of students responded with, "Thank you very much" regardless of what I asked! I still chuckle at the memory.

During effective SIOP lessons with the Interaction component, you will discover:

- Students who formerly didn't speak much in class are now more verbal because you are planning lessons that include multiple opportunities for them to engage meaningfully in English with you and other students (Feature 16).

- English learners and other students have more opportunities to use academic language when talking about key content concepts when you plan lessons that include a variety of flexible grouping configurations (partners, small groups, whole class) (Feature 17).

- English learners and other students use academic language more in class when they are provided with enough wait time to process information and plan what they are going to say (Feature 18).

- Students participate more fully during class when clarification is provided in a student's home language (L1) (Feature 19).

Feature 16 Frequent Opportunities for Interaction and Discussion between Teacher/Student and Among Students, Which Encourage Elaborated Responses about Lesson Concepts

When teachers begin planning lessons with the Interaction component, some worry that if they provide "frequent opportunities for interaction and discussion," they won't be able to cover their content standards because students will spend too much of each period talking to each other. This may happen when teachers and students alike forget the second half of this feature: ". . . elaborated responses about lesson concepts." The second part of the feature is as important as the first, and it is about providing time within lessons for students to practice and apply key content and language concepts through interactions with others.

Here is an example of an American History task that includes student-to-student interaction and elaboration of responses. Note that the teacher has provided each student with a copy of this assignment:

For this activity, use the newspaper accounts we just read from the *Helena Harold* (July 4, 1876) and the *San Diego Union* (July 9, 1876). With your partner, come up with an explanation of why the twice-court martialed General George Armstrong Custer thought he could successfully attack the camp of Chief Sitting Bull. Instead of waiting for forces under Generals Crook and Terry, Custer had little more than 200 men when he approached the Sioux camp on Montana's Little Big Horn River.

1. What prompted Custer to attack without waiting for the others?

2. What might General Custer have said to his troops to inspire them?

3. How do you think his men responded to him as their leader?

4. What do you think the Sioux Indians were saying as they saw Custer and his men advance?

Remember to use the key vocabulary words that are listed on the board as you're discussing these questions. Jot your ideas so that you can share them when you join another pair (or triad) of students.

Notice how focused this assignment is on key content concepts, key vocabulary, and the use of language to ponder what Custer and the Sioux thought and said. Note also that this task won't necessarily take a long time if the teacher has explained clearly what to do and has provided the necessary background information and resources that students will need. As you read through the next three activities that promote student-to-student interaction, think about the following questions:

1. What academic language will your students be practicing during this activity?

2. What academic content might students be practicing and applying?

3. What background knowledge and vocabulary do students need to have command of to be able to participate fully?

Ideas & Activities for Providing Opportunities for Classroom Interaction

ⓐ Buzzing
submitted by Lee Wilson, Dodd Elementary School, Little Rock School District, AR

Lee Wilson learned about this activity during Reading First training and adapted it for his students. Buzzing helps young children learn to engage in academic conversations by listening to their partners and speaking with appropriate "inside" voices as they respond to their teacher's prompts.

SIOP Feature 16: Frequent opportunities for interaction and discussion between teacher/student and among students, which encourage elaborated responses about lesson concepts.

Additional SIOP Features: 13, 17, 18, 19, 25

Grade Level: K–2

Materials: Visuals that stimulate and generate student conversations; picture books photographs or illustrations, sentence frames for children who need additional support

Objectives:

- *Content:* Students will make predictions about events in a story.
- *Language:*
  - Students will orally share predictions.
  - Students will listen to their partner's predictions.
- *Student Friendly:*
  - I can predict what will happen in our story.
  - I can tell my partner my predictions and listen to his (or her) predictions.

Grouping Configuration: Partners

Directions:

1. Model how to engage in Buzzing, emphasizing that students should whisper when they "buzz," and listen carefully to their buzzing partners.

2. Ask students a question, or direct them to talk about a topic or picture.

3. Have students sit facing one another. If students are sitting on the rug or on a mat, ask them to sit elbow-to-elbow, knee-to-knee.

4. Student #1 buzzes (whispers) to student #2 about the assigned topic for 30 seconds.

5. After 30 seconds, student #2 buzzes to student #1 for 30 seconds.

6. If an English learner doesn't understand his buzzing partner, clarification in the L1 may be offered, if available.

7. Provide sentence frames to students who may need extra support. You can add rebus pictures (draw them or use clip art) in sentence frames to further support beginning English speakers and readers.

8. After one minute of buzzing, ask a student to tell what his or her partner buzzed about. Then ask two more students to share what their partners buzzed about.

9. Examples of Buzzing tasks:
   - *Buzz One:* How does the Rhino feel? How do you know? Do you think his feelings will change?
   - *Buzz Two:* What do you think will happen in the story to make the Rhino feel grumpy?
   - *Buzz Three:* Using a sentence frame for telling your prediction, say: "I predict that _____ will happen."

10. After the Buzzing practice and before reading the story, debrief how well your students told their predictions and how well they listened to their partners.

11. After the story, return to the students' predictions, and determine, with students' help, which were confirmed, which were disconfirmed, and why they were either confirmed or disconfirmed.

ⓐ Chart and Share

submitted by Isabel Ramirez and Lois Hardaway, Sheltered ELA Teachers, Lewisville High School, Lewisville, TX

Students need assistance in learning how to engage in academic conversations. By working together in small groups to investigate a topic, they develop background knowledge. Then they create a chart together with the information and vocabulary gleaned from their investigation. During the subsequent academic conversation, students use their chart as a scaffold to emphasize their topic's key concepts and vocabulary during their presentations to the class.

SIOP Feature 16: Frequent opportunities for interaction and discussion between teacher/ student and among students, which encourage elaborated responses about lesson concepts.

Additional SIOP Features: 6, 7, 14, 21, 22

Grade Level: 6–12

Materials: Copies of text for reading; large chart paper; markers; access to dictionaries and other references

Objectives:

- *Content:* Students will organize their findings on a poster after investigating [topic] on a poster.
- *Language:* Students will summarize their findings and defend their ideas using textual support.

Grouping Configuration: Small groups of 4–5

Directions:

1. Students work in small groups to investigate a topic. Investigations can be done with an experiment, reading passage, Internet research, or a problem to solve.

2. Supply each group with a large piece of chart paper for recording the group's findings.

3. Tell students to chart their results (conclusions, main ideas, Internet research, or solutions). This activity can be scaffolded by providing students with graphic organizers or sentence frames to use while creating their posters. For example, a group of students might be asked to compare and contrast two scientists' discoveries on a Venn diagram prior to completing their poster.

4. Remind students to use large print on the chart paper as the charts should be legible to the entire class. It may be helpful to provide an example of what the print on the chart should look like.

5. Have each group member practice orally summarizing the poster so that all are prepared to participate. (Prior to this step, some students may benefit from modeling, either by you or another student, how to do an oral summary.)

6. Once all of the posters are completed, ask students to form a large circle around the room and hold up their posters for all to see.

7. Have groups take turns summarizing their posters. After each group has summarized, ask a few guiding questions to kick-start the conversation. The following questions and others can be printed on sentence strips so students have an idea of what to ask their peers.

    a. How did you come to that conclusion?

    b. Who else came to the same conclusion?

    c. Did anyone come to a different conclusion?

    d. Did anyone else record a similar result?

    e. Which answer is correct? How do you know?

    f. Where did you get your information?

    g. Are you sure the information is accurate? How do you know?

    h. Was there any time during your investigation that you questioned the accuracy of something you read? If so, what did you do next?

8. During the oral summaries and the following conversations, students should refer to their posters and their references as they discuss, defend, and question the ideas they recorded.

ⓘ The Pattern of Accountability

submitted by Lindsay Young, Pearson SIOP Consultant; former middle school teacher, instructional coach, and certified SEI trainer; Creighton School District, AZ

Some teachers avoid student-to-student interaction because they worry that students will go off-task or they have concerns that an activity with interaction will be difficult to manage. The Pattern of Accountability is a management technique employed to develop effective and productive student interaction. When students recognize patterns of interaction in the classroom, they know what will happen next and they can prepare themselves with their best responses. Students also have an opportunity to rehearse their responses in pairs or small groups before answering in a whole group setting. Through this pattern, students feel supported in their learning and accountable for participating in interactions with classmates.

SIOP Feature 16: Frequent opportunities for interaction and discussion between teacher/ student and among students, which encourage elaborated responses about lesson concepts

Additional SIOP Features: 25

Grade Level: K–12

Materials: Timer; sticks in a can with students names

Objectives: Not applicable

Grouping Configuration: Individual, partners

Directions: Follow these steps for the Pattern of Accountability to keep student engagement levels high.

1. *Time:* Give students a predetermined amount of time for their interactions. Using a timer is an effective way for students to learn how long they are expected to engage with their partners. For example: "You have 2 minutes to share an idea about how to solve this math problem."

2. *Turns:* Assign who will speak first and monitor turn-taking to encourage equal participation. For example: "Partner A is the student closer to the clock. Partner A speaks first; partner B listens first. Switch after 1 minute."

3. *Assess:* Monitor by walking around and listening to student responses during the interaction. Then call on non-volunteers or have students give a group response. For example: Pull a stick from the can and call on the student whose name is on it. "Juan, what did your partner say was the best way to solve this math problem?" Wait for Juan's response. "Knock 3 times on your desk if you solved the problem the same way as Juan."

Feature 17 Grouping Configurations Support Language and Content Objectives of the Lesson

You probably noticed that for each of the preceding interactive activities, we suggested grouping configurations of partners and/or small groups. When SIOP teachers model how students should look and sound when they're working together in partners and groups, student behavior improves because meaningful group work becomes frequent and routine.

Providing many opportunities for students to interact with each other requires that you organize your classroom in such a way that students can face each other, lean in close to communicate and hear each other, and share their ideas and work. Fortunately, student desks are no longer bolted to the floor as they once were, because with a bolted desk it's nearly impossible to work with a partner or in a small group. Today, there's little excuse for having long rows of desks that all face the front of the room (what Debbie Short, our SIOP co-author, refers to as the "cemetery model"). In fact, in SIOP classrooms, there's seldom a "front" to the classroom, students' desks or tables are grouped together, the teacher circulates frequently, and he or she teaches from nearly any spot in the room.

Ideas & Activities *for Planning Grouping Configurations*

🛈 Grouping Ideas
submitted by Andrea Rients, Social Studies Teacher, Shakopee High School, Sokopee, MN

For some activities, it works best to let students work with whomever they wish. But for other tasks, it's better to group students heterogeneously, perhaps using criteria. For example, consider the following to facilitate creating heterogeneous groups:

- Students' L1 language and literacy levels, if other than English
- Students' English language and literacy levels, including reading
- Students' personalities: for example, outgoing or shy; level of leadership skills; ability to get along with classmates (or not); and so forth
- Students' learning styles: for example, prefers working alone or prefers working with others; stays on task (or not); accomplishes and/or completes assignments (or not); works best with hands-on activities; enjoys reading and writing (or not)
- Academic needs and strengths. Jot a note about each student's academic needs and strengths, so you can quickly pull together a small group that might benefit from a mini-lesson.
- Student choices. Ask students to indicate who they like to work with; usually you can group students so that they can have at least one friend in their group.

Along with heterogeneous groups, occasionally students may need to be grouped homogenously so that they can practice collaborating and problem solving. Of course, there are many times when groupings can be spontaneous, surprising, and even whimsical. The following ideas created by Andrea Rients add whimsy to the classroom without interrupting the essential learning.

SIOP Feature 17: Grouping configurations support language and content objectives of the lesson

Additional SIOP Features: 16, 25

Grade Level: K–12

Materials: Index cards, deck of playing cards, stickers

Objectives: Not applicable

Grouping Configuration: Partners and small groups

Directions:

 Clocks and Calendars: The purpose of this grouping idea is to remind you to establish new sets of partners for a particular time frame, such as at the beginning of a semester, quarter, or new unit. For the remainder of that time period, whenever you say, "Find Your Partners," students will know who to work with for a think–pair–share activity or other partner work. The benefits include more efficiency for students who work together long enough to rely on one another and get things done.

Deck of Cards: Randomly pass out a playing card to each student as the students walk in the door or when you transition to another subject. You can have students meet with people of the same number, color, or suit of their card. Don't let them know which one you will choose so they will be less likely to trade!

Famous Pairs: For fun, give students a card with the name of a famous pair or group, and their job is to find their partner or other group members. Examples include: Fred and Wilma Flintstone; Larry, Mo, and Curly; Prince William and Princess Kate; the President and First Lady; the Beatles or a current rock group, and so forth. For young children, the cards can have pictures, such as two cats, dogs, horses, geese, etc.

Shuffle the Deck: Write the name of each student on an index card. Also include notes from the categories listed previously (L1 and L2 language and literacy, personality, learning style, etc.). Shuffle the deck and randomly select students for work groups, or shuffle and deal the cards for groups of varying sizes. You can also shuffle the cards and then pick one to call on a student (similar to sticks-in-a-can). As needed, you can organize the cards by students' academic needs and strengths, so that you can quickly pull a group of students together for a mini-lesson, pre-teaching, or re-teaching.

Silent Grouping: As students walk into class, ask them to line up silently according to their birthdays. They will not be allowed to talk so they will need to come up with a different way of communicating (signs or gestures). Once they are lined up, you can quickly place them in groups of varied sizes, depending on your purpose. Silent grouping also works well with tallest to shortest, and oldest to youngest, and so forth.

Stickers: No matter how young or old they are, students enjoy stickers, and they are easy to give out as students walk into class or as you transition to a different subject. Use pairs of stickers or have several groups of 4 to 5 that are alike. Students are to find their partners or groups by locating classmates with the matching stickers.

Pairs Squared

submitted by Lindsay Young, Pearson SIOP Consultant, former middle school teacher, instructional coach, and certified SEI trainer; Creighton School District, AZ

This idea works well following the activity "Go to Your Corners." In "Go to Your Corners," students move to a corner of the room based on a posted sign or directions from the teacher. For example, corners could be labeled as *Basketball, Baseball, Football, Soccer* (sport you enjoy the most) or *Cake, Cookies, Ice Cream, Pie* (favorite dessert). Once in the corner, students quickly find a partner or form a triad. After students are paired, the partners mix around the room to find another pair to form a group of four. This idea can be used to make mixed ability groups where students have one partner at the table with whom they have something in common and two more partners who have a fresh perspective or different learning strengths.

SIOP Feature 17: Grouping configurations support language and content objectives of the lesson

Additional SIOP Features: 6, 21, 22, 25, 27

Grade Level: K–12

Materials: None

Objectives: Not applicable

Grouping Configuration: Individual, pairs, small groups

Directions:

1. The following directions pertain to a math application of this idea. Of course, any subject area works equally well once you identify what each corner represents. Young children will need more guidance, but they can certainly learn to articulate what they understand and can tell another child, so this idea can be effective for K–2 students, too.

2. Assign students to corners of the room based on strengths exhibited on the last test or quiz, such as: "If you know your multiplication facts really well, go to corner #1. If you are very good at long division, go to corner #2. If you are good at factoring, go to corner #3. If you are good at solving word problems, go to corner #4." Some students may not feel confident that they're "good" at doing any of the four choices. If this happens, remind students that "good" isn't the same as "expert," and encourage them to select the corner that is the most comfortable.

3. Have students pair up in the appropriate corner to discuss their areas of strength.

4. Have pairs or triads from different corners "square up" to make groups of four or five; then have them sit together. The new groups work on math problems using each of their strengths to support each other.

5. Always debrief after small group work to find out how well students worked together.

ⓐ Study Buddy Teaming

submitted by Leslie M. Middleton, Instructional Coach, Rochester City School District, NY

In this activity, students work in pairs and in teams of four to share and compare answers, while learning to collaborate and come to consensus. Throughout the lesson, you are circling the room to ensure the students are on-task and meeting their learning objectives. Before the lesson, carefully explain the performance criteria for the Study Buddy pairs and teams so that the students know what is expected of them. Some performance criteria are:

1. Stay on topic.

2. Listen to others without interrupting.

3. Share your ideas.

4. Provide feedback to classmates on their ideas.

Each of these communication skills may need to be explained and/or modeled, such as providing appropriate feedback to peers.

SIOP Feature 17: Grouping configurations support language and content objectives of the lesson.

Additional SIOP Features: 13, 14, 16, 29

Grade Level: K–12

Materials: Questions, problems, or tasks for students to complete in a group; student journals

Objectives:

- *Content:* Students will work with others to come to consensus on a topic or problem.
- *Language:* Students will provide group members with effective feedback by using the following sentence frames:
  - I agree with your answer because _____.
  - I agree with your answer and also think that _____.
  - One question I have about your answer is _____.
- *Student Friendly:*
  - *Content:* I can agree with a classmate's idea.
  - *Language:* I can say why I agree with a classmate's idea.

Grouping Configuration: Pairs, small groups, whole class, individual

Directions:

1. Students work in pairs or with their Study Buddy to read text, solve a problem, or answer a question.
2. Once a Study Buddy pair has completed the work, they team up with another Study Buddy pair to form a Study Buddy Team.
3. Study Buddy Teams share their work, compare and justify answers, and come to consensus on the final product.
4. The Study Buddy Teams submit their final products, answers, or conclusions to the whole class, one Team at a time.
5. After the activity, students independently summarize the findings of their Team in their learning journals.

Feature 18 Sufficient Wait Time for Student Responses Consistently Provided

You've probably heard about the research on wait time after asking a question; we teachers seldom pause more than a second before calling on a student to respond (Echevarria, Vogt, & Short, 2013, p. 156). For many English learners and other students as well, coming up with an answer to a question in a second is impossible. Whereas in some cultures lag time between utterances is considerably longer, in schools in the United States, it is insufficient for many students, including most English learners.

In SIOP classrooms, teachers give English learners and other students ample time to think and process in their home language, if necessary, before responding in English. Balancing the need for students to process information and the need to move a lesson along can be tricky. We hope the following ideas and activities will assist you in achieving this important balance.

Ideas & Activities for Providing Wait Time

ⓐ Life Saver

submitted by Lindsay Young, Pearson SIOP Consultant, former middle school teacher, instructional coach, and certified SEI trainer; Creighton School District, AZ

Having enough processing time to think through a response is important not just for English learners, but for native English speakers as well. When teachers ask higher-order thinking questions, all students need sufficient mental processing time to come up with their best answers. We need to keep in mind that the purpose of questioning is to assess what students understand, not merely for them to answer with a correct response. With the Life Saver activity, you can provide students with the time they need to respond to a question, and encourage them to use a "life preserver" to help them with their answer, if they need it.

SIOP Feature 18: Sufficient wait time for student responses consistently provided

Additional SIOP Features: 21, 23, 24, 28

Grade Level: 3–12

Materials: Chart paper for types of Life Savers

Objectives:

- *Content:* Students will determine if they know an answer to a question about (topic), and seek assistance if they don't know it.
- *Language:* Students will answer questions about (topic) and explain why they think their answer is the best one.
- *Student Friendly:*
  - *Content:* I can decide if I can answer a question about (topic), and ask for help if I need it.
  - *Language:* I can answer a question about (topic), and say why I think it's correct.

Grouping Configuration: Partners, whole class

Directions:

1. Show students a photo of a Life Saver (life preserver) and ask if anyone knows what it's for and how it works.

2. Explain how the concept of the Life Saver will be used while the class is engaged in a game of review before a quiz or test. During the mock game show, if students don't understand a question, are unsure of the answer, or need more time, they can say, "I'd like a Life Saver!"

3. Students can also say "Life Saver" during any type of lesson whenever they need a bit more thinking time after a question has been asked.

4. Make a chart or poster as a reminder to students of how the Life Saver can be used:

   - *Text a Friend:* The student who has been asked a question can ask a classmate for help with an answer. They will have one minute to talk privately. When the minute is up, both students return to their seats and the question is answered by the student who asked to text his friend. For younger students, you may wish to have an old, out-of-commission cell phone so they can pretend to text a friend.

- *Either/Or:* Provide two answers for the student to choose from. He or she decides which answer is better and explains why.

- *Ask the Class:* Provide multiple choice options for the class. When a student asks for this option, class members read the possible answers and respond with their fingers as to which they think is the best answer. After the class "votes," the student decides which answer is the best and explains why. Students respond with:

  - Choice 1: Show index finger
  - Choice 2: Show 2 fingers
  - Choice 3: Show 3 fingers
  - Choice 4: Show 4 fingers

5. You may find it necessary to limit the number of Life Savers available so students don't overuse the support. For example, tell students they have only three Life Savers per week, or whatever time frame you deem reasonable.

6. Your students will enjoy receiving a candy shaped life preserver for correct answers to questions!

ⓐ Think Before You Answer

As mentioned previously, most of us interpret wait time as the amount of time you give a student to answer a question after the question has been asked. But remember that wait time also can be provided immediately after posing a question and *before* you call on a student to answer. By posing a question and providing sufficient time for everyone to think about it before calling on someone, all of your students are thinking about an answer, not just one.

SIOP Feature 18: Sufficient wait time for student responses consistently provided

Additional SIOP Features: 12, 14

Grade Level: Pre-K–8

Materials: Board or chart paper for questions and answers; paper, journals, or interactive white boards for writing answers to questions; sand timer for timing wait time

Objectives: Not applicable

Grouping Configuration: Individual, pairs, whole class

Directions and Options for Providing Wait Time

1. Ask a question and have students turn to a partner and discuss. After a minute or two, call on two or three students to tell you what they talked about with their partners. You can also ask the students to tell you what their partner talked about.

2. Ask a question and have students write the answer on paper or a white board. For all group responses, give the following cues: *Think*; *Get Set* (get ready to show the paper or white board but keep the answer covered); *Show Me!*

3. Have students share their answer with a partner. This can be either a table partner or someone at another table. Call on two or three students to tell both their answers and their partner's answers.

4. Do a Think-Pair-Share. This technique is very familiar but it still works well, IF students remember the "Think" step. Most begin talking right away, so remind them each time to think quietly before speaking.

5. Ask students to think about the question for 20–30 seconds before discussing or writing the answer. Use a sand timer so students can see how much time they have left to think.

6. For younger children, demonstrate the thinking process with a Think-Aloud technique, and point to your brain while thinking aloud. Teach students to point to their brains and tap their fingers while they are thinking about the answer to a question. After the students are done thinking, ask them to pretend to kiss the palms of their hands and touch the palms to their forehead ("kiss their brains"), indicating that they are finished thinking about the question and are ready to discuss their answers.

7. Find Someone Who _____. This can be used for a quick partner share. Ask students to share their answers "with someone who has shoes like you" or a similar shirt, hair color, eye color, birthday month, and so forth.

ⓘ Wait Time, More Time!

For some teachers, it's very difficult to remember to wait before calling on a student to respond. If you're one of them, considering using one of the following ideas:

- Use a one-minute sand timer. You and your students will be amazed at how long a minute really is when everyone is quiet and students are thinking. If you can't stand waiting a full minute, watch the sand or your wall clock, and wait for thirty seconds. Be sure to watch the sand timer in private, because if your students can see it, they'll all be watching the sand fall, rather than thinking about the question you posed!

- Use "sticks-in-a-can" to randomly call on students. For those of you who don't know about this idea, you simply purchase tongue depressors or craft sticks and print one student's name on each stick. Put all the sticks in a can and pull one at a time. Your students won't know whose name you've pulled until you read it aloud. If you use sticks-in-a-can, provide extra wait time before you ask a question by following these steps:

  • Put all the sticks in the can.

  • Ask the question.

  • Slowly look around the room at each student while the class is thinking.

  • Pull the stick.

  • Wait a few more seconds. Tell students to get ready with their answers.

  • Call the student's name that's on the stick.

- Count to five after you've asked a question. You're probably thinking, "Really? I paid for this book and THIS idea is included?" Yep, it's here because it works. If you've never met MaryEllen, then you don't know that she talks VERY fast . . . and she also teaches VERY fast. Her poor students can hardly keep up with her. So, counting to five works for her. If she has pants pockets, she puts her hand in her pocket and counts slowly to five, one finger at a time. It probably takes about five seconds, which is four seconds longer than she usually waits for a student to respond. The point here is . . . do whatever you need to do to let your students think and process before you expect an answer to a question. And that includes using BOTH hands in your pockets if you need to! Ten seconds are better than five . . . and aren't you glad you bought this book?

Feature 19 Ample Opportunities for Students to Clarify Key Concepts in L1 as Needed, with Aide, Peer, or L1 Text

This SIOP feature indicates that teachers may clarify key concepts in a student's home language so that English learners are clued in to the learning goals of the lesson. It is not suggesting that instruction and feedback be mostly provided in the L1, unless the instruction is in a bilingual or dual immersion program. In these programs, instruction is carefully designed in both languages with the goal of developing students' bilingualism and biliteracy.

In classes where English is the medium of instruction, some teachers of English learners may be overusing the home language or using it in a haphazard way, which neither develops literacy in the home language nor provides appropriate English language development. They might be more successful, especially with beginning English speakers, with a preview-review approach, where a brief jumpstart (pre-teaching) is provided in the L1, the lesson is taught in English, and if needed, a review is also provided in the L1. In this situation, teachers use SIOP techniques to support comprehension in English and use students' L1 strategically to enhance understanding.

The "right" amount of L1 use is not always easy to determine. Jana taught English learners who expressed resentment of their teachers for speaking to other English learners in a language they didn't understand, and not to them. She remembers, "I had high school Vietnamese students who were learning more Spanish than English! Their parents were unhappy and there was also friction between the groups. It is an equity issue as well as a pedagogical one."

So, while there is controversy surrounding the use of L1 for instruction, there is no doubt that clarification in the home language is beneficial, if used judiciously by the teacher, classmates, or an instructional assistant. Also, because research clearly shows that language skills in the L1 transfer to the L2, strategic use of L1 can be supportive. Just remember that in classrooms where English is the language of instruction, the goal is to teach content and academic language in English, with as-needed L1 support and validation of students' home languages.

Ideas & Activities for Providing Clarification in the Home Language

ⓘ Previewing Material in Children's Home Language (L1)

Echevarria, Short, and Peterson (2011) suggest that teachers use children's fascination with new toys that are introduced to the classroom as a way of teaching them new language concepts. When showing new playthings, you introduce vocabulary words and language that students can use to play with the toys. Include this before a lesson so that the students are familiar with the toys and the language to use while playing (p. 50). Whenever possible, engage English learners in a conversation about the new toys in their home language.

SIOP Feature 19: Ample opportunities for students to clarify key concepts in L1

Additional SIOP Features: 6, 16, 21

Grade Level: Pre-K, Kindergarten

Materials: New toys introduced to the classroom

Objectives: Not applicable

Grouping Configuration: Small group, whole group

Directions:

1. When you introduce new toys or activities to the classroom, try to explain the purpose and the rules for the new toys in both English and the children's L1.

2. For example, with a new Lego® set say, "These are the parts" and give the names for each, saying, "This is what they can do." Repeat this in English and in the child's L1, if possible (by another student or adult, if you don't know the language yourself).

3. Allow the students to talk about the new toys in their L1. You might find out that the students have experience with the toys already or that they have questions about the toys.

4. You can also demonstrate what should not be done, such as putting items in their mouths. Since understanding the rules is important to maintaining classroom safety, rules for using new toys should also be discussed in the child's L1 whenever possible.

5. For items that go in the dramatic play area, (e.g., drug store) say, "These are the names of the new pieces of equipment; here are the roles that can be played." You can also ask students to tell you the name of the new toys in their home language to see if they are familiar with these items.

6. Provide specific language, in both L1 and English, that can help the students while they are playing with the new toys.

7. Model the language by saying "I want a _____" or "Can I help you?" or "Welcome to _____," explaining to students what the sentence frames mean in their L1.

ⓘ Translators to Clarify Key Concepts in L1

Often teachers ask us how to incorporate Feature 19 when they do not speak the students' L1 or have a paraprofessional who speaks the children's first language. While not speaking your students' L1 is inconvenient, there are techniques to incorporate Feature 19, including using technology and other available resources.

SIOP Feature 19: Opportunities for students to clarify key concepts in their L1

Additional SIOP Features: 4, 5

Grade Level: 3–12

Materials: Bilingual dictionaries, electronic translators, Google Translate

Objectives: Not applicable

Grouping Configuration: Individual, pairs, and small groups

When using bilingual dictionaries and electronic translators, keep the following suggestions in mind:

1. Older students who are literate in their L1 can use an electronic translator, bilingual dictionary, or online translator to help them translate unfamiliar words and phrases they encounter in class.

2. These resources should be made available to English learners at all times during the lesson as they provide a much needed scaffold to help students better comprehend the concepts and language they are learning.

3. Be sure to assess their learning often because electronic translators and bilingual dictionaries do not always provide clear translations of complex terms.

When using student translators, keep these suggestions in mind:

1. Find a student translator. This is a bilingual student who speaks the L1 of the English learner.

2. Determine your student translator's proficiency in his L1, as well as his willingness to translate for other students.

3. From time to time, place the student translator in groups with English learners who have the same L1 but speak less proficient English. It helps if you have several student translators so that you can vary your grouping from lesson to lesson.

4. If the student translator is not literate in the L1, he should only be asked to translate directions and familiar terms.

5. No matter how fluent in the L1 that the student translator seems to be, make sure to scaffold the translations by helping the student translator understand exactly what to translate. Here are some items that your student translator may be able to translate:

   • Short, simple directions like "Read page 76."

   • Questions like "Do you understand how to solve this problem?"

   • Short explanations of visuals and examples like "This picture shows the stages of the water cycle, and the words on the pictures identify each stage. I want you to be able to label each stage with one of the underlined words."

- Questions or statements from other less English proficient students. For example, the student translator may translate a question from another student into English by saying, "He is asking if he will be able to use his notes on the test."

6. Always make sure that the relationship between the student translators and the English learners they are helping is positive and productive. Many students will enjoy the responsibility of helping another student, and translating may actually deepen their understanding of the concepts and language because they have to process everything differently as they work to translate. But some students may resent having to translate. If this is the case, find someone else or use another technique. Do not use unwilling students as classroom translators.

Thinking about Interaction

1. One question that's really interesting to ask teachers is whether they prefer to work alone or in a group. If you were to ask your fellow teachers at school, they probably wouldn't wait an instant to declare, "I prefer to work alone," or "I prefer working in a group." Humans must be wired for one choice or the other, because there's seldom a pause when adults are asked this question. If that's true and young people have the same proportion of those who prefer working alone or working with others, then why do we insist that students work often with their classmates if some really want to work alone? The primary reason is that learning is a social activity and we generally learn best by interacting with others. Certainly, we learn language best by using it with others. We include this topic for reflection so that you'll consider your own students. Who might prefer to work alone over working with others? For those who have this preference, how do we honor it and still have an interactive classroom? And if you, their teacher, prefer working alone, are there implications for you in creating more opportunities for interaction in your classroom?

2. Remember that within the SIOP® Model, we advocate a balance of linguistic turn-taking between teacher and students. What do you think the percentage of teacher talk is in your classroom? How can you find out what it is? Think about videotaping yourself teaching. No one but you needs to see the videotape. What do you think you could learn by watching yourself teaching a lesson or two?

7 Practice & Application

A Teacher's Reflection

I've noticed a big difference in students' understanding of math concepts when they are first allowed to construct meaning on their own or with a partner.

Lisa Mitchener, Grade 4 Teacher, Gauldin Elementary School,
Downey Unified School District, CA

The Practice & Application component reminds us that the best way to learn something deeply is by practicing it while we have someone alongside who can model how to do it correctly and who can steer us in the right direction if we veer off course. We've known for years that it's important for students to rehearse newly learned concepts and apply them to real-life situations with hands-on practice. We've learned to ride a bike by riding, play tennis or golf by playing, cook by cooking, play the piano by playing, and teach by teaching. Without practicing, lessons and instruction do not result in mastery, whatever it is that we're learning to do.

When planning SIOP lessons and selecting activities, also remember to include opportunities for your students to practice and apply academic language related to the content. For mastery, students need to be reading, writing, speaking, and listening to academic English in every lesson you teach.

During effective SIOP lessons with the Practice & Application component, you will discover:

- Your students will have deeper understandings of your lessons' key concepts and vocabulary because of the opportunities they have to practice and apply what they're learning in meaningful, hands-on ways.

- Students' proficiency with academic English (reading, writing, listening, speaking) improves because of multiple opportunities to use it during your lessons.

Feature 20 Hands-on Materials and/or Manipulatives Provided for Students to Practice Using New Content Knowledge

Hands-on materials are important for English learners and other students so they can connect abstract concepts with concrete experiences. When students organize, count, classify, stack, experiment, rearrange, create, dismantle, observe . . . and also move their bodies, they can practice multiple times in numerous ways. Also, for English learners who are beginning speakers, hands-on practice with manipulatives reduces the language load, enabling them to demonstrate what they know and can do through varied modalities.

Please understand that this SIOP feature doesn't suggest that you have to include lots of "cutesy stuff" for each lesson. Rather, when you are writing SIOP lesson plans and you come to this feature, think about what you can do to have your students actively practice rather than passively sit. The 99 ideas and activities in this book include opportunities for active participation and interaction, and nearly all of them are appropriate for implementation of this particular SIOP feature.

Ideas & Activities for Providing Hands-on Materials and/or Manipulatives

ⓐ File Folder Vocabulary Games

Personal Connection with MaryEllen Vogt

I taught middle school for many years as a reading specialist and special educator, working with students who had a wide variety of problems with reading. Even though many of them did not like to read, nearly every one of them enjoyed these games and they actually pleaded with me to play them. I started with about ten file folder games that I made over the summer. I encouraged students to select a game when they had finished their work or had some free time. They could choose to play alone or with a partner, and they received points for playing the entire game (matching correctly all the word cards to what was written in the squares on a folder).

I differentiated the games by varying the difficulty levels of the vocabulary and topics. I also used a small colored dot on each cover to indicate the difficulty level so I could match students to the appropriate game, or I could suggest from across the room that a student pull a "red" game, or whatever level I thought would be challenging enough . . . but not too much. Students were able to progress through the various levels, but I'm not sure they ever suspected that I had such a system.

Each summer, I made more file folder games until they filled a large file box. I probably ended up with more than fifty file folder games. Years later, when I saw a former student, without fail, he or she would recall the file folder games and how much fun they were to complete. I think my students liked them so well because they felt successful when they could correctly make the game's twenty matches. For students with reading problems, some serious, feelings of success with reading were infrequent. And, for some reason, students didn't seem to perceive these games as "work." They just liked to play them.

For students and teachers who are used to lively computer games, the file folder games may seem a bit tame. Don't let that discourage you from introducing them to your students, especially English learners and students who struggle with reading. The language and literacy practice they'll engage in will help improve their reading ability and build their confidence as well.

SIOP Feature 20: Hands-on materials and/or manipulatives provided for students to practice using new content knowledge

Additional SIOP Features: 4, 6, 7, 9, 13, 16, 21, 22, 27

Grade Level: 2–8

Materials: Colored file folders; tag board; markers; stickers; quart-size plastic bags (with zip closing); large paper clips; spelling and vocabulary references (e.g., *Words Their Way with English Learners: Word Study for Spelling, Phonics, and Vocabulary Instruction,* 2011, by Bear, Helman, Invernizzi, Templeton, and Johnston).

Objectives: *Note:* Ordinarily, you don't need to post objectives for a practice activity such as this. However, if you're using a file folder game for practice and application of a particular content concept, such as roots and affixes, then you might use objectives such as the following:

- *Content:* Students will match words to other related words (or phrases, definitions, explanations, synonyms, antonyms, etc.) about (topic).
- *Language:* Students will read words and phrases while matching them with other words or phrases.

Grouping Configuration: Partners, individual

Directions:

1. Purchase a packet of multi-colored file folders. Each folder will be a game, so buy as many file folders as you wish to turn into games.

2. Purchase colored sheets of cardboard or cut up old file folders into 1-1/2" × 1-1/2" squares. The small squares need to be a different color than the corresponding file folders. You'll need 20 cards for each game board (or 40 if you're really ambitious).

3. Open a file folder and on the right side, using a ruler, draw with a slim marker 20 two-inch squares (4 horizontal; 5 vertical. You'll have some space at the top of the folder that you can use for writing categories or adding stickers, or you can leave it blank. If you want to have 40 cards and spaces, repeat this step on the left side of the folder. Older students can handle making 40 matches; it's way too many for younger ones.

4. If you're using 20 cards, use the left side of the opened file folder for the game's instructions. If you're using 40, you can write the directions on the front of the folder.

5. On the outside front cover, write the name of the game in large letters horizontally, so if the folders are in a file box, they can be easily read and retrieved.

6. Examples for games include the following. Keep in mind that you can create more than one game with many of these categories.

   - *Roots, base words, affixes:* Words, such as with the root *prod* and affixes, *-ive, -ite, -y* are printed in the file folder square; *productivity* is printed on a card. This is challenging!

   - *Antonyms:* Print pairs of antonyms, with one antonym on a card and the other in a square on the file folder, e.g., hot/cold; fast/slow, etc.

   - *Synonyms:* Print synonym pairs, one on a card and the other on the file folder, e.g., sad/unhappy; excited/enthusiastic, etc.

   - *Homonyms:* Print one word of a pair such as *blue/blew, flew/flue, allowed/aloud, be/bee* on a card and the other on the file folder. You can make this more challenging by having the homonyms on the cards and the meanings of each homonym on the file folder squares.

   - *Rhyming words:* Choose pairs of rhyming words, with half written on cards and half written in the squares on the file folder.

   - *Syllables:* Print the numbers 1, 2, 3, or 4 on the cards for number of syllables; then print single-syllable and multi-syllabic words in the squares on the file folder.

- *Idioms:* Write the idioms on the cards (*He is straight as an arrow*); then write the meaning on a square on the folder (*He follows the rules*). Other examples include: *She's a small fry. = She's a small child. He sure gets my goat! = He's really annoying!* There are many websites to help you—just search for "idioms." (Idioms are fun and they're great for English learners.)

- *Definitions:* Print the words on cards and the meanings on the squares on the folder.

- *Parts of speech:* (nouns, verbs, adjectives, adverbs) Print cards that have words from these categories; then write the names of the categories (nouns, verbs, etc.) on the folder's squares.

- *First and last names:* These can be names of teachers, presidents, historical figures, pop culture icons, students in the class, or whoever you wish. Write first names on the cards and last names on the squares in the file folder.

- *Compound words:* Print the first half of the compound on a card and the second half on a square in the folder.

- *States and capitals:* Write the capitals on the cards and the matching states on the squares on the file folder.

- *International cities and countries:* Write the capitals on the cards and the matching countries on the squares on the file folder.

- *Amphibians and reptiles:* Write the names on cards and the classifications and/or descriptions on squares on the file folder.

- *Math concepts:* Write the problems on the file folder squares and the answers on the cards.

- *Food Pyramid:* Print the different foods on cards and the categories on the file folder squares.

You get the idea. Basically, you can create any kind of game you wish with two things that match. Ask your students for ideas and for help. Older students can certainly help with creating the File Folder Games by coming up with the concepts, matching words, and phrases. Doing this also provides good practice with language and content concepts!

ⓐ Read and Respond Paper Toss

Read and Respond Paper Toss integrates all four modalities of language—listening, speaking, reading, and writing—while allowing students to engage in a game-like activity with their peers. The listening component in this activity is emphasized as students are required to listen to others so they can respond appropriately.

SIOP Feature 20: Hands-on materials and/or manipulatives provided for students to practice using new content knowledge

Additional SIOP Features: 6, 16, 17, 21, 22, 25, 27, 28

Grade Level: 2–10

Materials: Paper, pencils/pens, sentence frames, word wall (optional)

Objectives:

- *Content:* Students will write at least two reasons why (something related to topic).
- *Language:* Students will listen to and summarize statements made by their peers about (topic).

Grouping Configuration: Groups of 4–6

Directions:

1. Ask each student to complete the sentence frame: "Write at least two reasons why _____." or a sentence frame of your choice (and change content objective accordingly).

2. Students then stand up and form a circle around their table group.

3. Each student crumples into a ball the paper he or she used to complete the sentence frame.

4. All students toss their paper balls into the center of the table and mix them up.

5. One student chooses a crumpled paper ball from the pile and reads the sentence to the group.

6. One of the other students in the group must respond to the sentence using the following sentence frame: "I think I heard you say _____. Is that correct?"

7. After a student has responded to the sentence, the next student chooses a crumpled paper ball and reads it to the group. Another student responds using the sentence frame.

8. Once all of the crumpled paper balls have been read and responded to, the group sits down to indicate they have completed the activity.

9. Students compile the papers with the sentences for the teacher to take up for later use or assessment.

Feature 21 Activities Provided for Students to Apply Content and Language Knowledge in the Classroom

The purpose of this feature is to remind teachers of the primary reason for including activities in lessons: they're for students to practice and apply content and language concepts. Perhaps you have attended a large teachers' conference with lots of publishers' exhibits. You also probably saw several "mom-and-pop" booths that were selling a wide variety of activity books. These smaller booths in the exhibit hall are where the most teachers gather because, as teachers, we all want lots of activities to choose from. That's probably why you're reading this book!

However, not all activities are created equal. While some are lots of fun for students and teacher alike, they may not provide practice for a lesson's content objectives, or an opportunity for students to use academic language. Therefore, this feature is included in the SIOP® Model so we remember that students learn by doing. In reality, all of the activities in this book could be housed in this feature, because they all provide students with practice and application of content and language concepts. Think carefully about the activities you currently include in your lessons, and if they don't meet the criteria of enabling students to practice and apply *both* content and language objectives, consider whether they're worth keeping in your instructional repertoire.

Ideas & Activities *for Planning Opportunities for Students to Practice and Apply Content and Language Concepts*

ⓐ Student-Generated Tests

submitted by Andrea Rients, Social Studies Teacher, Shakopee High School, Shakopee, MN

Teacher Andrea Rients believes that student-created tests provide a great review because they allow students to think through the testing process while they are brushing up on information they've been taught. By creating tests for their peers, students are practicing both the content and language knowledge of a lesson. Students must revisit the text and the objectives to select appropriate topics for their test questions, and they must hone their writing skills in order to create effective question-and-answer choices.

SIOP Feature 21: Activities provided for students to practice content and language knowledge in the classroom

Additional SIOP Features: 27, 28, 29, 30

Grade Level: 3–12

Materials: Paper for students to create their tests; resources for test questions, such as textbooks, Internet websites, and student notes

Objectives:

- *Content:* Students will determine central ideas or themes from a unit of study.
- *Language:* Students will write test questions that include convincing false statements.

Grouping Configuration: Individual, pairs, whole class

Directions:

1. Allow students to work in pairs to create a test for their peers. Depending on your students, you may wish to assign partners or let students self-select.

2. Give students a set of parameters for creating the test, such as true or false, multiple choice, or short answer. Model how to write test questions by creating some examples with the whole class.

3. Tell students that the test questions should fall under the umbrella of the lesson's content and language objectives.

4. Ask students to use words from previous lessons' vocabulary lists in their questions.

5. Students may need instruction on how to create effective "false" statements. You can provide instruction on this technique through modeling and stating some specific guidelines. For example, ask students what makes a test question tricky; then discuss the characteristics of a tricky test question. Together, generate some false questions or statements about the content and language concepts.

6. Students should also create an answer key for their test.

7. Have each student switch his or her test with another student.

8. Students take and correct the tests made by their peers, either individually or with a partner.

9. If handled respectfully, you can allow students to discuss the quality of the questions on the tests they took. If you wish, post the test questions and have a whole class discussion about specific questions, possible answers, and why answers were either correct or incorrect. Why were some questions more challenging than others?

10. Students really will enjoy seeing (and being able to answer!) their own questions if you select some for a unit or other follow-up test.

ⓐ Who Am I?

submitted by Andrea Rients, Social Studies Teachers, Shakopee High School, Shakopee, MN

Whether students are doing research on new topics or reviewing content and language from previous lessons, this activity will encourage them to actively engage in practicing the content and language concepts of the lesson. To build background for the activity, you may wish to have students interview each other and play "Who Am I?" based on their classmates' biographical information. Once you have used this activity successfully, you might look at Riddle Brainteasers (p. 137), so you can incorporate more direct language instruction your lesson.

SIOP Feature 21: Activities for students to apply content and language knowledge in the classroom

Additional SIOP Features: 16, 20, 22, 27, 28

Grade Level: 2–12

Materials: Resources for researching lesson topics, large index cards

Objectives:

- *Content:* Students will list characteristics of (names, topics, or themes).
- *Language:* Students will determine the identity of (names, topics, or themes) by listening for specific characteristics.

Grouping Configuration: Individuals and partners

Directions:

Version 1

1. As a model, provide students with a list of characteristics and have them guess who the famous or influential person is who possesses the traits. For example:
   - Some say that I am a robber-baron, but I believe that I am a captain of industry.
   - I made my millions in the steel industry.
   - I have a famous music hall named after me.
   - I have donated millions of dollars to the arts and education.
   - Who Am I?
   - Andrew Carnegie!

2. Assign students the names of individuals associated with a particular period or content concept you've been teaching and have them create a "Who Am I?" card by researching and listing three or four facts about the person.

3. Ask students to find a partner, share their "Who Am I?" card, and try to guess each other's name.

4. Have students trade cards, find another partner, and share again. Students can share and trade three times before returning to their seats.

Version 2

1. Give students a blank body outline in the middle of a page.

2. Give them a time period, theme, culture, climate, or geographical region, and ask them to "recreate a person" from this time period, culture, or region.

3. Have students create a poster with visuals and images that illustrate the main ideas of the time period, theme, culture, climate, or geographical region of their person. When they're finished with their posters, they can attach them to the wall and stand by them to wait for further instructions.

4. All students then participate in a Gallery Walk, moving with a small group to each poster, reading the information, and trying to guess who the person is that is described.

Feature 22 Activities Integrate All Language Skills (Reading, Writing, Listening, and Speaking)

The most challenging aspect of this component may be making certain that students are using reading, writing, listening, and speaking when they're practicing and applying content concepts. In some subject areas, such as mathematics, physical education, art, or choral and instrumental music, it may seem that having students practice academic language isn't as important as it is with more language-based disciplines (English, language arts, literature, and foreign language, for example). However, as mentioned previously, the more you can include academic language practice in your lessons, whatever your discipline, the more likely it is that students can talk, read, and write knowledgeably about your lessons' content concepts. Also, English learners in particular must be reading, writing, speaking, and listening throughout a lesson if they are to become fluent and competent users of academic English. Depending on what you teach, another way to think about this is that you probably want your students to speak and write like an "expert" in your discipline, such as a mathematician, historian, scientist, author, artist, athlete, musician, economist, or chef!

Ideas & Activities for Integrating All Language Skills

Nearly all of the ideas in this book enable you to integrate the language skills in your lessons, whatever subject you teach. And we've included one more in this chapter that is especially effective for getting your students to read, write, speak, and listen to English.

ⓐ Build a Pyramid

You may be familiar with this idea because it's somewhat similar to an old game show. The purpose is for students to use reading, writing, listening, and speaking while practicing and applying key content and language concepts.

SIOP Feature 22: Activities integrate all language skills (e.g., reading, writing, listening, and speaking)

Additional SIOP Features: 4, 6, 9, 15, 21, 27, 28

Grade Level: 6–12

Materials: Paper for Concept Clues sheet; Pyramid drawn on chart paper or Pyramid projected on technology such as interactive white boards, televisions screens, large pieces of chart paper (depending on the number of topics you are studying) index cards, tape if you are not using technology

Objectives:

- *Content:* Students will determine important content and language concepts about (topic).
- *Language:* Students will write and read clues and answers about (topic).

Grouping Configurations: Partners, whole class

Directions:

1. Start by having students work in small groups to brainstorm all they learned about a topic they have been studying. Provide categories for the unit of study. A category for Language Arts might be *figurative language* while a catergory for math might be *polygons*. Ask students to use their resources such as anchor charts, notes they have taken, personal dictionaries, or their textbook to brainstorm concepts they have learned about each category. For example, concepts studied for figurative language might be *simile, metaphor, hyperbole,* and *personification.* Examples of concepts studied for polygons might be *regular, irregular, rectangle, square, equal, side,* and *angle.* Each student in the group should record these concepts studied on his or her own sheet of paper and title it Concept Clues.

2. After they finish writing, ask students to use their resources to write clues on the Concept Clues sheet for each concept they brainstormed. Students can jigsaw the concepts or work together as a group on each concept. A clue for *simile* might be using the words *like* or *as.* A clue for *square* might be *regular polygon with four equal sides.* As you can see, the clues are really just definitions or ways to remember the meanings of terms or other key vocabulary.

3. Ask students to write each concept they brainstormed on an index card, and then sort their examples into three levels of difficulty—easy, medium, and challenging. Asking this question might help guide students in this step: *Which examples of concepts studied were easiest to define, and which were the most difficult?*

4. Create a chart for each topic the students brainstormed. If you have four topics, you need four charts. Write the topic at the top of each chart, and have students place the index cards with the concepts they remembered about the topic on the charts, placing the most challenging concepts at the top and the easiest concepts at the bottom. The purpose of the chart is so students can organize their concepts from easiest to hardest and the class can discuss each concept that was brainstormed. Your role is to ask why students think that some concepts are more difficult than others, and to help them with organizing the hierarchy for each topic.

5. After the charts are complete, have a class discussion about the order of the examples, asking if the examples of concepts studied are placed under the correct topic, and if they are placed in the correct level of difficulty. This most likely will be the end of the lesson for Day 1.

6. On Day 2, on your your interactive white board, television screen, PowerPoint® slides, or chart paper, create graphic organizer pyramids prepared with three levels, one pyramid for each category. Add the concepts the students generated to the pyramids, placing the easiest examples to define on the lowest levels and the most challenging examples on the highest levels of the pyramids. If you are using technology, animate the examples so that they are hidden and will appear one at a time. If you are using chart paper, tape the index card examples onto the pyramid face down, with three at the bottom, two in the middle, and one at the top. Now, the pyramids (and hopefully, the students) are ready for the game! (See Figure 7.1)

7. Each round of the game is played with pairs versus pairs. Arrange students in groups of four with one pair, who will be providing the clues, looking at the pyramid, and the

Figure 7.1   Example of a Build a Pyramid Activity

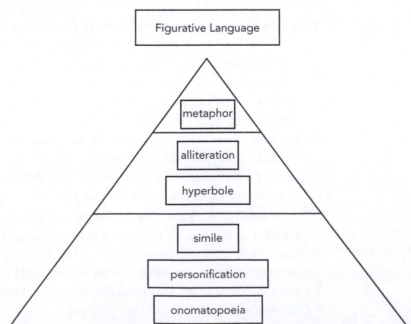

other pair, who will be listening to the clues and guessing the category, facing away from the pyramid but able to see the other pair. The pair facing the pyramid (the Clue Providers) is shown the category and provides clues to the other students (the Clue Responders), who try to guess the category. The Clues Providers may read the clues off the Concept Clues sheet, or the partners may use their own examples and definitions, but they may not say the name of the category.

8. The opposing pair, working together in the role of Clue Responder, has one minute (or more, if you wish) to see how many of the concepts or vocabulary terms they can identify accurately.

9. The Clue Providers are also the score keepers. While one of the Clue Providers is reading the clues during the one-minute round, the other is recording the number of correct answers given by the Clue Responders.

10. Play continues with the two pairs changing roles. Note that you can have numerous pairs of Clue Providers and Clue Responders that ask and answer questions at the same time, so that all students are engaged.

11. After several rounds (you decide how many), the two sets of partners with the highest scores move to the final round. One of the sets of partners faces the wall with the pyramid. If there's a tie, you can have a playoff with two sets of pyramid categories and examples. Have some extra examples of topics studied that are especially challenging in the event of a playoff.

12. You can use the students' answers to the questions for assessment to determine if re-teaching is necessary, and you can use the questions for a subsequent test or unit exam. The students can use the Concept Clues sheet to review for a test.

ⓐ Riddle Brainteasers

This activity allows students to practice and apply content concepts while developing academic language. Writing a riddle gives your students practice with academic language. Solving the riddles that peers have written provides students with the opportunity to grapple with a lesson's content and language concepts. If you don't have time to explicitly teach the language necessary for Riddle Brainteasers, use the Who Am I? activity (p. 132) as an alternative.

SIOP Feature 22: Activities integrate all language skills (i.e., reading, writing, listening, and speaking)

Additional SIOP Features: 6, 22, 25

Grade Level: 2–10

Materials: Large chart paper; markers; dictionary; thesaurus; handouts explaining and providing examples of figurative language such as metaphors and similes (comparisons using *like* or *as*)

Objectives:
- *Content:* Students will infer the meaning of riddles about (the topic).
- *Language:*

1. Students will use the following sentence frames to write a riddle about (the topic):
   - I see _____.
   - I hear _____.
   - I look like _____.
   - I sound like _____.
   - I like _____.
   - I do not like _____.
   - I feel like _____.
   - I am _____.

2. Students will use synonyms and figurative language to construct a riddle about their assigned concept.

Grouping Configuration: Individual, partners, triads, or groups of four

Directions:

1. Assign a concept or have students choose from several concepts that your class is studying.
2. Either in small groups or individually, have students brainstorm everything they know about their assigned concept.
3. Have students focus on three words from the brainstorming session.
4. More advanced students can look up the three words in a dictionary and/or thesaurus to find synonyms or interesting phrases that they can use when writing riddles.
5. Provide several examples of riddles written on the interactive board or chart paper so that students can see and hear the format as you read each riddle. As a student figures out the answer, ask him or her to write it in a different color on the interactive white board (or chart paper). Also, ask the person who solved each riddle how he or she came up with an answer.
6. Remind English learners that when reading a riddle, the word *who* refers to a person. The word *what* in a riddle refers to a thing. The word *where* in a riddle refers to a place.
7. Show examples of riddles from former students or from other sources. Here are some examples of riddles for older students. There are many examples for younger students on the Web.
   a. I get wetter and wetter the more I dry. What am I? (A towel)
   b. I have a tail and I have a head, but I have no body. I am NOT a snake. What am I? (A coin)
   c. I fall, but I do not break. What am I? I break but I do not fall. What am I? (Night falls and day breaks)
   d. I am something to eat. You throw away my outside and cook my inside. Then you eat my outside and throw away my inside. What am I? (An ear of corn)
8. Ask students to write from the point of view of the person, place, event, or thing they have chosen, using the first person. Provide sentence frames, such as:
   a. I see _____.
   b. I hear _____.

c. I look like _____.

d. I sound like _____.

e. I like _____.

f. I do not like _____.

g. I feel like _____ .

h. I am _____.

9. More advanced students who do not need the sentence frames can be encouraged to use figurative language to describe their concepts.

10. Once students have completed their riddles, they can write them on large chart paper without the answer, and entitle their posters "My Riddle Brainteaser: _Who_ Am I?" or "My Riddle Brainteaser: _What_ Am I?" or "My Riddle Brainteaser: _Where_ Am I?"

11. Post the riddles on the walls around the room.

12. As students visit each poster, they write their guess to the riddle on a sticky note and attach the sticky note to the poster.

13. After all students have posted a sticky note guess on each of the posters, read the riddles to the class or have students read their own aloud.

14. After you or the students have read the riddle, you can read some of the sticky note guesses and have students explain what, in the riddle, led them to their guess.

a. How many of you guessed _____?

b. What words in the riddle led you to make that guess?

15. Allow several students to explain why they think their guesses are correct before asking the author or authors of the riddle to tell and then explain the answer.

Marilyn Amy Washam

Marilyn Amy Washam

Thinking about Practice & Application

1. The Common Core State Standards (2010) include grade-by-grade listening and speaking standards. Regardless of whether you teach at the elementary level or in a subject area at the secondary level that the Common Core Standards target, increasingly teachers are being asked to improve their students' literacy skills, including listening and speaking. How can you do that in the subject(s) you teach? How will the ideas and activities in this chapter, as well as in the rest of the book, foster improved literacy skills in your students? How will you use the ideas and activities to assess your students' literacy skills?

2. One of the challenges with this component is that students need different amounts of practice and application to achieve content and language objectives. They also need differing amounts of time to practice something new. This is one of the great challenges of differentiation: how do you manage groups that are doing different things at the same time? Many teachers think this requires totally different assignments for students with different needs. We have learned that it is more effective to provide different levels of scaffolding, rather than create different assignments.

   For example, some of the reasons that students take longer with an assignment are because it's too hard, too difficult to read, or there's no frame of reference for the student to make a connection. For these students, we might adapt the assigned text by highlighting key concepts and vocabulary; offer a partially completed graphic organizer that helps the student manage the amount of information; or provide an adapted study guide that leads students through the assigned text, defining challenging words, explaining difficult concepts, and so forth (see Chapter 2, Echevarria, Vogt, & Short, 2013; p. 41–43 for more ideas).

   It's important to remember that having students practice and apply content and language concepts with assignments that are way too difficult is a waste of valuable instructional time—and it's very frustrating for students. As you plan lessons and choose activities for students to practice and apply the content and language concepts, how will you be certain that all of your students are able to successfully complete the assignment? What, specifically, might you need to do to scaffold English learners and other students who may have difficulty and need more time for practice?

8 Lesson Delivery

Contrastwerkstatt/Fotolia

Teachers' Reflections

By beginning my lessons with brief but engaging/interactive activities, the students have immediately bought into the lesson. They clearly understand what the concept is and are ready to begin the task.

—Molly Richardson, 6–8 Resource Room Math, Olympic Middle School, Auburn, Washington ⟩⟩⟩

Greater student engagement (90–100%) provides students with more practice time, and less time to misbehave. This benefits all students as well as the teacher.

—Charlotte Rippel, Grade 3, Ward Elementary School,
Downey Unified School District, California

This SIOP component is where the rubber meets the road. If the most carefully written lesson plan falls flat during delivery, was it a good lesson? We've all experienced a time (or two) when a lesson that we felt confident about:

1. Didn't resonate with students.

2. Was too challenging.

3. Was too easy.

4. Was interrupted by the intercom, a fire drill, or something else.

5. Was cut short because time simply ran out and our goals weren't reached.

It's not a good feeling, is it?

The purpose of the Lesson Delivery component is to make sure that when we teach a lesson, the content and language lesson objectives that were the focus during our planning are also the focus during our teaching. High student interest and engagement result when your lessons are targeted, well paced, and well planned.

During effective SIOP lessons with Lesson Delivery, you will discover:

- Your students strive to meet the content and language objectives throughout a lesson.

- High levels of student engagement are evident throughout the lesson.

- All students are able to keep up with the lesson because it's paced appropriately—not too fast and not too slow.

Feature 23 Content Objectives Clearly Supported by Lesson Delivery

The power in posting and reviewing content objectives with students is realized fully during lesson delivery. If students aren't meeting, or making progress toward meeting, a lesson's content objectives, you can immediately change course and clarify, reiterate, or reteach, as needed. In contrast, without specifically focused content objectives, it's easier to delay assessing students' knowledge and retention of key concepts until a quiz or exam. In SIOP lessons, however, that's just too late. We need to be able to know throughout each instructional period, whether a 15-minute phonics lesson or a 52-minute biology lesson, the extent to which students are learning the key content concepts you're teaching.

In addition, another important reason to have content objectives is that they can prevent what's referred to as "bird-walking" (Hunter, 1982). This is what happens when you introduce a topic such as "mountain ranges" and several of your students run away with the lesson, regaling the class with their Colorado (or anywhere else) camping adventures. The beauty of content objectives is that you can regain attention by bringing the focus back to the lesson's key content concepts.

Because content and language objectives are so closely linked, the ideas and activities for this feature follow Feature 24: Language objectives clearly supported by lesson delivery.

Feature 24 Language Objectives Clearly Supported by Lesson Delivery

As with content objectives, language objectives keep a lesson's focus on the language concepts that are being taught, reviewed, and practiced throughout the instructional period. Students sometimes need to be reminded that a particular activity has been selected because it affords them a chance to use key academic vocabulary and language concepts in a meaningful way. Also share with your students that it is through the use of academic language that they can practice and apply the concepts that are the focus of the lesson's content objectives.

Ideas & Activities for Supporting Content and Language Objectives

ⓘ All Eyes on the Objectives

SIOP Features 23 and 24: Content and language objectives supported by lesson delivery

Additional SIOP Feature: 1

We have previously discussed in Chapter 2 the need to write clear and targeted objectives. But writing such objectives is only effective if the lesson you deliver helps students meet them. Activities, while necessary and effective, can sometimes pull students away from learning the content concepts and language concepts for which they will be held accountable. Think about a lesson that you taught that was supposed to help students learn important concepts but ended up being more about how to cut out figures or fold paper. How does this happen? The lesson begins with the best of intentions, but somehow gets derailed by complicated instructions, time-consuming building background activities, or off-topic comments that turn into long discussions.

To prevent this from happening, use the following ideas to stay focused on your objectives:

1. Always keep your objectives posted for both you and your students to see.

   - Be careful not to post objectives behind screens that will be pulled down during a lesson or on an interactive white board that will be used for other activities during the lesson.

   - Post the objectives in the same location in the room every day so that students will know where to look for them.

   - Make sure the objectives are written large enough so everyone can read them from any location in the room.

2. Refer to the objectives throughout the lesson.

   - In addition to presenting the objectives at the beginning of the lesson, return to them throughout the lesson as needed to maintain students' focus.

   - Use the objectives to explain why lesson activities are meaningful.

   - Refer to the objectives when students have begun to understand the key concept, or they produce something that shows they are learning the key concept. For example, when students have a conversation about what they observed in an experiment, you can refer to the objectives to remind them to incorporate the key vocabulary, as is stated in the objectives.

   - Also refer to an objective at the end of the period to remind students that they will continue to work on it the next day. You can have students jot on a Tickets Out card whether they met each objective. The responses on the cards can be used to assess how far students have come or need to go in learning the objectives; they also can be used to remind students of the objectives at the beginning of class the next day.

3. Incorporate the language of the objectives into the lesson.

   - Make sure that activities include the language suggested in the objectives. For example, if the language objectives state that students will be able to "describe the phases of the moon," make sure that the activities require students to say the names of the moon's phases, read about them, listen to information about them, and/or write something about them during the lesson. With this language practice, students should be able to meet the language objective.

- Plan the product so that it will clearly show the degree to which students have met the objectives.

- When reviewing the objectives at the end of the lesson, refer to the lesson's activities and ask students to tell how each activity helped them meet the objectives.

ⓐ Talking Tokens

submitted by Stephen Lanford, Geometry Teacher, Mabelvale Magnet Middle School, Little Rock School District, Little Rock, AR

Often we write objectives and plan lessons that do not turn out quite the way we had hoped. Our best plans for student interaction often fall apart when one student in the group takes over while others sit back and say nothing. Talking Tokens is designed to hold all group members accountable for participating in both listening and speaking during academic conversations, which in turn can lead to a more successful delivery of the lesson's objectives.

SIOP Feature 24: Language objectives clearly supported by lesson delivery

Additional SIOP Features: 16, 17, 18, 27, 28, 29, 30

Grade Level: 2–12

Materials: Prepared questions for groups to answer; some sort of tokens or cards to indicate which students should stand

Objectives:

- *Content:* I can discuss (topic) with my peers.
- *Language:* I can use the following vocabulary words to discuss (content concept): (key vocabulary words).
- *Student Friendly:* Same objectives as above; "I can" statements are appropriate for both older and younger students.

Grouping Configuration: Partners

Directions:

1. Arrange students in pairs; for this activity it's better that students do not select their own partners.

2. Prepare a set of questions about the content; you will post the questions one at a time on the interactive white board or elsewhere.

3. Ask students to discuss the first posted question with their partners.

4. As you are monitoring each group's discussion, determine which student in each pair has contributed the most to the conversation and then hand that student a token.

5. When all groups have been monitored and one person in each group has received a token, tell the students who earned tokens to stand up.

6. The students who are still sitting and without a token are asked to summarize the conversation in which the partners were engaged. Performance criteria can be added to the summaries by asking these students to use words on the word wall or to complete a sentence frame.

7. When you walk around the room to listen to each sitting student summarizing the conversation to his or her standing partner, retrieve the tokens; they will be distributed toward the end of the next conversation.

8. After all of the sitting students have summarized their conversations, pose the next question and ask the partners to begin discussing it.

9. Continue to monitor the conversations and pass out the stand-up tokens to students who make the most contributions in their pairs.

10. In case of a tie (the goal *is* for all students to participate equally), hand a token to each student in the pair. While standing, the partners take turns summarizing in the conversation.

11. If some students are not participating fully with their partners after a few questions, you may need to go back and review how to meaningfully engage in a conversation with another person. And, depending on your class, this review also may need to precede the opening round of questions.

12. The number of tokens each student earns during this activity can be tallied and charted by the individual students. The totals can be used for earning points or rewards if you wish.

ⓘ Weaving Content Objectives into Activities for Young Children

Since preschool and kindergarten students are often engaged in self-directed learning, centers, or playtime, it is necessary to rethink how we support content objectives throughout the day for our young English learners. Instead of introducing the content objectives to the whole class at the beginning of a lesson, a preschool teacher might weave them into the learning activities that are occurring throughout the day. Sometimes, the content objectives might be shared as students are learning a new concept during a science experiment, but other times you might reinforce them while children are engaged in self-directed play or are reading a book (Echevarria, Short, & Peterson, 2012).

SIOP Feature 23: Content objectives clearly supported by lesson delivery

Additional SIOP Features: 1, 4, 28, 30

Grade Level: Pre-K, Kindergarten

Materials: Provide a variety of activities that include books, art projects, building materials, and play stations located around the classroom; interactive white board or chart paper to post objectives; large photos to provide context for the objectives

Objectives: Not applicable

Grouping Configuration: Individual, small group

Directions:

1. Post the content objectives, including a picture for clarification, in the learning area where children will participate in an activity.

2. Engage children in exploration of a topic using hands-on activities.

3. After students are engaged in an activity, begin to ask them questions about what they are experiencing and learning. The questions should be related to the lesson's content objectives.

4. Read and talk about the content objectives and relate them to the activity the children are engaged in.

5. Throughout the lesson, refer back to the content objectives to remind children of their learning goal(s).

ℹ️ Weaving Language Objectives into Activities for Young Children

Language objectives, similar to content objectives, also can be woven into learning activities for young English learners. Echevarria, Short, and Peterson (2012) emphasize that children will *learn* language when they are given opportunities to use language. In addition to explicit teaching of English, younger English learners benefit from practicing English during play time, hearing books read aloud, chanting and singing rhymes and songs, and experiencing repetition and imitation of lively texts.

SIOP Feature 24: Language objectives clearly supported by lesson delivery

Additional SIOP Features: 2

Grade Level: Pre-K, Kindergarten

Materials: Activities that use books, art projects, building materials, and play stations around the classroom; interactive white board or chart paper for posting language objectives; large photos or illustrations that provide context for language objectives

Objectives: Not applicable

Grouping Configuration: Individuals, small groups

Directions:

1. Post the language objectives, including a picture for clarification, in the learning area where children will participate in an activity.

2. While children are engaged in exploration of a topic, introduce the language objective by modeling the language that they will be learning and using. Have them say words and phrases with you, chorally or as an echo, clarifying pronunciation and intonation as needed.

3. As children are engaged in the hands-on activity, begin to ask them questions about what they are doing and why they are doing it. The questions should be leading the children toward the language objectives.

4. Help children become aware of the language they are learning by naming concepts and/or terms, repeating these names and terms, and having children imitate the language you're using.

5. To further reinforce the language objectives, point occasionally to the posted objectives in the learning area.

6. Continue to weave the language objectives into the lesson throughout the day by reminding children of the new language they were introduced to previously. Recap the new language often and encourage children to imitate and repeat what you say.

Feature 25 Students Engaged Approximately 90% to 100% of the Period

Occasionally, teachers question us about why the SIOP® Model requires such a high percentage of student engagement. Our response is that English learners (and other students, for that matter) cannot afford to spend less than 90% to 100% of a lesson period involved in learning. Of course, this doesn't mean that students must be hanging on to every word you say, while busily making something. What it does mean is that while students are participating in activities, they are absorbed with doing meaningful tasks that enable each of them to practice and apply the content and language concepts. Note the phrase *each of them*. You know what often happens when students are supposed to work in groups: one or two students do all the work while the others watch or worse—just sit. And, as all teachers know, "if students don't know what to do, they will find something to do, and misbehavior or inattention ensues" (Echevarria, Vogt, & Short, 2013, p. 195). This SIOP component suggests that *all* students, during each and every lesson, must be engaged *meaningfully* for nearly all of the class time.

Ideas & Activities for Keeping Students Highly Engaged

ⓐ Boxing Questions

submitted by Olga Jimenez, Science Teacher, Solis Middle School, Donna, TX

Keeping students involved with each other is easy; keeping students engaged in tackling complex content concepts requires a teacher's skill, as well as a few tricks. Olga Jimenez has developed quite a few "tricks" in the activities she uses to keep her students engaged while learning science. Boxing Questions incorporates movement and competition to keep students engrossed in practicing a lesson's content and language concepts.

SIOP Feature 25: Students engaged approximately 90% to 100% of the period

Additional SIOP Features: 4, 15, 16, 27, 28, 29, 30

Grade Level: K–12

Materials: Medium-sized boxes, such as copy paper boxes; medium-sized baggies labeled with team names; prepared questions on index cards; large baggie for teacher's questions; space for students to line up and walk a few feet to the boxes; a place to keep score (such as an interactive white board, white board, or chart paper)

Objectives:

- *Content:* Students will determine which statements or observations are (true/false; correct, incorrect, qualitative/quantitative, etc.)

- *Language:* Students will justify their answers using the word *because* … (a sentence frame could be used, as well as more challenging academic vocabulary, such as *therefore, in addition to, as a result, furthermore, moreover*).

- *Student Friendly:*

  - *Content:* I can decide whether something is … (true or false, right or wrong, big or small, hot or cold, and so forth).

  - *Language:* I can say why I think something is … (true or false, right or wrong, big or small, hot or cold, and so forth).

Grouping Configuration: Small groups for teams, whole class

Directions:

1. Prepare answer boxes by labeling the outside of the box with the answers to the questions you will ask. If you are asking True/False questions, one of the boxes can be labeled True and the other False. Other ideas are: Agree/Disagree (teams must justify their answers); A, B, C, D (for multiple choice questions; show questions on an interactive white board and/or with PowerPoint® slides); Correct or Incorrect; and so forth. Each box should include a baggie that is clearly labeled for each team. The baggies remain in the box during the game. Note: An alternative to using the small baggies in each box (for each team), is to color-code the question strips. If there are four teams, then make four sets of questions, each in a different color. Instead of putting the questions in their team's baggie, students simply drop their team's question in the appropriate box. At the end of each question, the colored strips are tallied for

each team. The colored tags speed up play but may take more of your time to print out the questions on the different colored papers. It's your call.

2. Divide the class into teams. Larger classes might divide into three or four teams; smaller classes might divide into two teams.

3. Have each team line up behind an established line that will represent where students will start and finish the race for each round.

4. Place the labeled answer boxes in a horizontal row several yards in front of the established start and finish line.

5. Stand on the line, holding your baggie of questions. Remember that the answers to each question are labeled on the boxes.

6. The first student in each team takes a question from your large baggie, reads it, runs to the boxes, and places the card in his or her team's baggie in the box that indicates what the team thinks is the correct answer (or if you're using colored question cards, the card is placed directly in the box). The student then runs back to the finish line so that the next student on the team can take a card.

7. The object of the game is to collect the most correct answers.

8. At the end of the game, students return to their seats, and you (or a student) read the questions put into the teams' baggies that were inside the answer boxes (or separate the cards by team color). After you read each question, the class determines if the question was put into the correct Answer Box. Ask students to explain their answers. If a question was put into the baggie incorrectly, ask the students to explain why the question does not belong there.

9. Either you or a class member can keep score as you read the questions and the class determines if the questions were put in the correct answer box.

10. The team with the most points, or correct answers, wins!

ⓘ Proximity and Participation

SIOP Feature 25: Students engaged approximately 90% to 100% of the period

Additional SIOP Features: 12, 14, 16, 17

Grade Level: K–12

Have you ever noticed what happens when you have a group of students who are fooling around when you're teaching and you're across the room shooting daggers at them with your eyes? Do they immediately straighten up and pay attention, do they basically ignore you, or do they straighten up for a few minutes, and when you turn away, they're right back to fooling around? What happens if you wander over to stand by their table for a while? Do they settle down and look up to you as though you're the most important person in the room? What happens to this group when you walk away? How about a group of students who aren't necessarily fooling around, but they're not participating until you move toward the group, look each one in the eyes, smiling and expectant? If you stand there long enough, have you noticed that most of the students in the group will look interested and engaged . . . until you move to another group? What do these examples tell you about your proximity?

For years, teaching experts have suggested that when we are close in proximity to students when we're teaching, they are more highly engaged in lessons. Your experiences may not mirror exactly the examples given above, but we suspect they're close. There are several things you can do to increase your proximity to students, and at the same time increase their engagement during lessons, including the following:

1. Be mindful of your eye contact with students during lessons. Mentally, divide your classroom into quarters and then into eighths. As you are teaching, if you can't be moving to each of the eight "squares," try to have eye contact with someone in each. Alternate your attention from back to front and side to side, focusing on the perimeters and the center of the room. This doesn't mean that you are dizzyingly flipping your head from one spot to the next throughout a lesson. What it does mean is that you're aware of what's going on in all parts of the classroom and that you are consciously attempting to make eye contact with as many of your students as possible. The more eye contact you have with them, the more they'll participate and the higher their engagement will be.

2. If you have several table groups that aren't working well together and you've tried to mix students up and move the trouble-makers to different groups and it's still not working, do an interaction analysis of who you're talking to (and with) during a lesson. Create a chart of the table groups and attach it to a clipboard. While you are teaching and as you are "working the room" for greater proximity, put a check by a table group each time you communicate with someone in the group; also attempt to give positive and specific feedback to students, rather than corrective "get-to-work" comments. You may find that you are talking more with some students and talking very little with others.

   In a study that MaryEllen did some years ago with a struggling ninth grade math teacher, she analyzed the interactions of the teacher and her students and found that the teacher had interactions only with students in the first two rows (from side-to-side) of the classroom. If students sat in the last two rows, they had few if any interactions with the teacher, while those students in the middle had occasional interactions with her. Not surprisingly, although the teacher wasn't aware of this, the students were, and those who didn't want to interact with her and were uninterested in participating in algebra lessons simply chose seats in the back of the room. When the teacher rearranged the classroom, providing aisles through which she could walk, and implemented a seating chart that she regularly changed, she was able to have more proximity to and interaction with all students. The classroom climate changed markedly with these simple modifications.

3. Videotape yourself teaching. Put a video camera on a tripod, turn it on, and teach. While the resulting video can be uncomfortable for you to watch later ("I swear I'm losing 20 pounds and I'm NEVER wearing that shirt again!"), get over it. No one has to watch the video except for you . . . and you may be surprised to discover patterns of interaction that are preventing students from being engaged in your lessons. Who are you talking to? What happens when you move closer to or farther away from a group? Are you missing anything when your back is turned on a group? How can you achieve greater proximity and student engagement?

4. Keep in mind this important adage when you plan lessons: *Proximity Increases Participation.* As you select activities for your out lessons, consider where you will be standing and how you'll be moving during the lesson. Think about when you'll check in with groups (part of Review & Assessment), and how you'll keep track of interactions between you and your students. Focusing on your proximity to students and their reaction to it may result in students' greater participation and overall engagement.

ⓐ Research and Share

When teachers introduce new material or complex concepts, or there is simply too much material to cover in the time allotted, there is a tendency to lecture through the material in order to cover everything. Research and Share allows students to begin practicing and applying the content through a discovery method so that you can interact with them in small groups, assess their understanding, and present the information within the context of what students have discovered on their own.

SIOP Feature 25: Students engaged approximately 90% to 100% of the period

Additional SIOP Features: 6, 13, 14, 15, 16, 17, 20, 21, 22

Grade Level: 4–12

Materials: Textbooks or other research resources (Internet); markers; large sheets of chart paper with a topic printed at the top. Post these posters around the room.

Objectives:

- *Content:* Students will identify key details about their assigned topics through investigation.
- *Language:*

  1. Students will share the details they researched with their group members, and together they will organize them in a map.
  2. Students will orally share how they organized the details on their map.

Grouping Configuration: Small groups (4–5 students)

Directions:

1. Plan for heterogeneous groups of 4 to 6 students and assign each of the groups a topic to investigate related to the content you're teaching. You can assign a different topic to each group, or all groups can have the same topic to investigate.

2. Students are to scan the materials they have been given (research resources) or do a think-pair-share about a question related to the topic. This should take no more than 5–7 minutes.

3. Assign each student in a group an aspect or element of the topic to research and/or read about. Each student should discover 2 or 3 important details and write them down. *Note:* This is individual work and should take no longer than 15 minutes. This step is similar to a Jigsaw process because students work independently and then share their information with each other.

4. After all students have had a chance to research and write down the details, they re-join their preassigned groups at their posters.

5. In the groups, have students each share 1 or 2 ideas they researched about their assigned topic.

6. Using the chart paper, students work together to organize the information they each gathered into a map. Just provide a blank piece of chart paper, not a graphic organizer.

7. Group members decide where they want the various pieces of information to go on their poster—they can use circles, squares, lines, arrows, or any shape or organizational

structure they wish. The goal is for them to connect the pieces of information into a cohesive whole.

8. After students have completed their posters and you have reviewed and informally assessed each one, the posters can be posted on the walls around the room.

9. Group members then explain their maps and how they organized the information. Suggest that each student describe his or her own pieces of information so every member of the group has the opportunity to share researched details.

10. As an alternative to the group sharing, you can use the posters as a reference for discussing the content, or have the students visit each poster in a carousel, stay and stray, or gallery walk activity in order to take notes.

(i) Student-Generated PowerPoint® Slides

One of us (Amy) was working with a first-year teacher who had become frustrated with her middle school sheltered English classes. The teacher said of her students, "They don't know these concepts, but they won't spend any time learning them." The new teacher was pointing to the first chapter of the book where the students were to learn the English alphabet. Her newcomer students were recent immigrants who spoke little or no English, and as older students they didn't know the basics and weren't being motivated to learn simple skills. They also may have believed they didn't need to learn "school English" because they could easily and effectively communicate with their peers who spoke the same home language.

One way to provide older students with a challenge while allowing them to learn basic concepts is through technology. Students can create PowerPoint® slides about simple concepts like the suffix *-tion* or more complex concepts like the main idea of a story. By creating a title and incorporating slides that show examples with photos they have inserted, sentences they have written, and perhaps even sound, students will engage in learning simple or complex concepts for an extended amount of time.

SIOP Feature 25: Students engaged approximately 90% to 100% of the period

Additional SIOP Features: 20, 21, 22

Grade Level: 6–12

Materials: Computers or laptops; PowerPoint® software

Objectives:

- *Content:* Students will use technology, including the Internet, to create an original PowerPoint® presentation about [topic], in collaboration with other students.
- *Language:* Students will incorporate key vocabulary into the PowerPoint® presentation they created about [topic].

Grouping Configuration: Individuals, partners

Directions:

1. After introducing a concept, provide students with a rubric for a PowerPoint® presentation that you want them to create. The rubric should contain criteria for incorporating key vocabulary, providing examples and explanations about the key concepts, and using the features of PowerPoint®, like animation.

2. Model for students how to create a PowerPoint®. This works well on an interactive white board so that all of the students can see what you are doing.

3. If possible, walk students through the process as a whole group the first time you demonstrate the techniques for creating a presentation.

4. Model how to use notes and classroom artifacts to help students incorporate the features described on the rubric.

5. Model how to insert photos, text, and sound.

6. Students love to animate their slides. Be specific both in your directions and on the rubric about what can be animated:

   - Only animate key vocabulary and key concepts; animating everything can make the viewer dizzy!

   - Search, insert, and animate a picture or clip art that represents the key concepts.

   - Students can animate key vocabulary and explain how the words were animated; as students work with animation, they are repeatedly working with key vocabulary and concepts.

7. Allow students the opportunity to show their PowerPoint® slides to their peers. Ask students to show their PowerPoint® slides in small groups. During subsequent lessons, you can choose one or two of the students' PowerPoint® slides and present it to the entire class.

ⓐ Wave the Flag!

Even though most people agree that interacting with a peer can be very engaging, sometimes students need help interacting effectively. There are certain times during the day, after lunch for example, that students are unmotivated to discuss academic content. Wave the Flag provides movement, wait time, and structure for student-to-student interaction that engages all students. Allowing students to move around the room can stimulate the brain; it also combines thoughtful interaction with light-hearted fun.

SIOP Feature 25: Students engaged 90% to 100% of the time

Additional SIOP Features: 6, 16, and 17

Grade Level: K–8

Materials: Content material the students have prepared to share; 3" × 5" index cards

Objectives: Not applicable

Grouping Configuration: Pairs or triads

Directions:

1. Have students prepare something to share. This can be a journal entry from the day before, such as the completion of a sentence frame; explanation of a process; summary of a story; hypothesis; conclusion; sentences using key vocabulary; or almost anything that helps students practice both the lesson's content and language concepts.

2. Distribute 3" × 5" index cards, one per student, and ask them to write their ideas about the assigned topic on the card.

3. For young children, ask them to write their ideas on sticky note. Then ask the children to draw a flag on an index card and help them glue or tape a frozen treat stick to the short edge of the card. The children can use their "flags" for future games of Wave the Flag!

4. Depending on the age of your students, you might model the next steps with the help of a couple of volunteers.

5. On signal (bell, flash lights, train whistle, harmonica, or whatever you use), students are to begin walking around the room, waving their "flags" (index cards).

6. At the next signal, students freeze where they are and share with 1 or 2 other students who are nearest to them (not just with their best friends).

7. After all small group members have had a turn to share what's on their cards (or sticky notes), students end their conversation and start moving around again, waving their "flags" as they go, until they find another student who is waving his or her flag.

8. You can use a signal for movement, or just have students move and wave their flags when they've finished sharing and are ready to move and find another partner who is waving his or her flag.

9. Repeat the process until all students have had several times to share their information.

10. Other variations:

    • Use music to signal when students are to start or stop moving. They're to move while music is playing; they stop moving when the music goes silent and share their information.

    • A teacher we know asks students to hold up a hand to signal when they are ready to switch partners and share with another. After students find a partner, they smack hands, giving a High-Five. Then they share their information; and when finished, each holds up a hand to signal that he or she is looking again for another partner.

Feature 26 Pacing of the Lesson Appropriate to Students' Ability Levels

Personal Connection with MaryEllen Vogt

Sometimes I wish I could do a "do-over" with students that I taught during my first years in the classroom! Like many new teachers, I over-planned every lesson because I was afraid of running out of things to teach before the end of the period. I feared that chaos would ensue if I was "done" with my lesson ten minutes before the bell rang. Then, during my lessons, when I realized I had way more to teach than time allowed, I was on a race to the finish line to get it all "done," whether or not students were learning what I was teaching. What I didn't realize until some time later, is that it's not *how much* you teach that's important; what's more important is that *what* you teach is taught *well*.

Content and language objectives provide focus for the issue of *how much*; appropriate pacing helps you to teach to those objectives *well*: not too fast, not too slow, but just right for most of your students. Remember Goldilocks's visit to the bears' house? Also, consider that differentiation may be necessary for some, if not most lessons in order to achieve a balance of appropriate pacing for your students.

Ideas & Activities for Providing Appropriate Pacing

ⓘ Differentiate the Process

submitted by Donna Smeins Howard, Math Specialist, Port Towns Elementary School, Prince George's County, MD

While all of our students should be working toward meeting the lesson's objectives, it is not necessary or even possible that they all get there using the same techniques. So many teachers have asked us about how you achieve appropriate pacing with an academically diverse group of students. The answer is relatively simple; you can achieve effective pacing by differentiating the process. But learning to differentiate the process for an entire classroom of diverse learners is anything but simple. It is complex and requires practice, so we have asked Donna Howard, an elementary math interventionist, to share how she differentiates the process for her third grade class.

SIOP Feature 26: Pacing of the lesson appropriate to the students' English proficiency levels

Additional SIOP Features: 14, 17, 23, 24, 25

Grade Level: 3–10

Materials: Copies of small group and center materials; cubes of various colors, coins, and other sets of items; giant number line; journals; pencils; centers and books; word problems at various levels; sentence frames; markers; chart paper; blank number lines

Objectives: (Math examples)

- *Content:* I can read, write, and represent proper fractions of a set.
- *Language:* I can use the language of fractions to orally identify the denominator, numerator, and fraction of a set.

Grouping Configurations: Small groups (3–4)

Directions:

Small Group Rotations

1. Grouping configurations are determined through teacher observation during guided practice.
2. Students will rotate using an A-B-C pattern for small group instruction.

Teacher	A	B	C
Independent	C	A	B
Centers	B	C	A

3. There is a menu and a choice board in each center. Students are required to do activities listed on the menu, but they can choose from a list of activities posted on the choice board that they can complete over the course of the week.

Group A: Struggling with concepts; needs direct supervision

- *Teacher:* Provides direct instruction in determining fractional parts of a set using manipulatives and real-world problems.

- *Independent:* Continued practice with fractions of a set of word problems based on what was taught in direct instruction
- *Centers:* Fractions of sets

Group B: Having some difficulty but can work through it with the group

- *Centers:* Identifying fractions of a set; will do required assignments and choice assignments
- *Teacher:* Review center activity work product; students will present their answers to the group.
- *Independent:* Will complete word problems

Group C: Demonstrates understanding of concept; need less instruction and supervision

- *Independent:* Word problems with fractional parts of sets
- *Centers:* Will complete centers based on choice board requirements
- *Teacher:* Will present work product from independent and center activities

Thinking about Lesson Delivery

1. Which techniques do you find especially effective for keeping students highly engaged in your classroom? What things outside your control interfere with maintaining high engagement? Did you know there's research that correlates many classroom interruptions during an instructional period with lower student performance? If you are in a school that has many interruptions throughout the day, what might you do to reduce the number? You might need to enlist support from other teachers and administrators to reduce the number of intercom announcements, notes for students from the office, pull-outs of students, and so forth. It will be worth the effort!

2. How do classroom routines for attendance, transitions between activities, getting and returning supplies, ensuring all students have a chance to talk, closing out the period, and so forth contribute to student engagement in your classroom? If you don't have routines that students are aware of and participate in, what are some that you could incorporate into your teaching? What might be the outcome of establishing and maintaining classroom routines on your lesson delivery and student achievement?

9 Review & Assessment

Goodluz/Shutterstock

Teachers' Reflections

Review and Assessment benefits students because they need repeated exposure to concepts, words, and skills, and teachers need to continually check for understanding and make adjustments or reteach as necessary.

—Jody Conn, ESL Teacher, Silver Lake Elementary School, Washoe County Schools, Nevada >>>

Giving informative and timely feedback has increased the time my students are able to demonstrate knowledge of a concept. They are able to quickly fix their mistakes, and it allows us to maximize our class time.

—Molly Richardson, Resource Math Teacher, Grades 6–8,
Olympic Middle School, Auburn, Washington

W hile Review & Assessment is the final component listed in the SIOP® Model, it is certainly not the last component teachers should implement. In fact, within assessment driven instruction, we need to assess student needs first, even before writing objectives for the lesson. When you assess your students' needs, you can determine how familiar they are with the content concepts. Then you can create content objectives that are appropriate for the age and educational background of your students (Feature 3). If students have little knowledge of the concepts, you may at first use less rigorous verbs in your objectives, such as *label* and *define*. As students become more familiar with the content, your objectives can become more challenging with rigorous verbs like *compare* or *justify*. That said, be careful to foster higher-order thinking for all levels of students, not just those with lots of background knowledge about a topic.

Additionally, assessment of language learning needs is essential in order to write language objectives that target students' academic language proficiency. Remember the WIDA standards and the levels of language proficiency (see Feature 10)? By reviewing these levels for your students and assessing output when students read, write, listen, and speak in the classroom, you can determine the most appropriate language learning targets for them. What follows is a checklist of learner outcomes that you can use to assess your students' content and language learning needs. If students are unable to demonstrate that they understand the purpose or the objectives of the lesson (the first outcome), perhaps the objectives are not written at a level that students can comprehend, or they are not student friendly. Maybe students require more background information about the objectives, such as a review of key vocabulary. Look through the list of outcomes below and think about how each can help you develop a more effective SIOP lesson plan. Note that this list is derived from the SIOP protocol and essentially includes all of the features, stated a bit differently.

Checking Learner Outcomes in SIOP Lessons

After you have taught a SIOP lesson plan, check each of these outcomes to see if your students accomplished them. If not, what adjustments should you make to the lesson before you teach it another time?

During effective SIOP lessons with the SIOP® Model, students will:

- Demonstrate that they understood the purpose and objectives of the lesson.
- Use differentiated materials that are available and participate in meaningful activities.
- Actively make links between their own background and the lesson's concepts and activities.
- Have multiple opportunities to use new vocabulary in meaningful ways.
- Respond to your modified speech and comprehensible input techniques.
- Use learning strategies in completing tasks and assignments.
- Feel supported while completing tasks and assignments at their level of academic and language proficiency.
- Respond to a variety of questions including those that require higher-order thinking.
- Demonstrate that they can work both independently and collaboratively, using academic English.
- Participate in a variety of grouping configurations which facilitate interaction and discussion.
- Use their home language as needed to clarify key concepts.
- Contribute to the lesson by using hands-on materials and/or manipulatives to practice and apply their content knowledge.
- Engage in the lesson and work at their potential throughout the instructional period.
- Follow the pace of the lesson.

And, for Review & Assessment, your students will:

- Demonstrate understanding of the lesson's key vocabulary and content concepts.
- Receive appropriate and regular feedback on their output (e.g., language, content, work).
- Demonstrate awareness of their progress through assessment of the lesson's objectives.

Feature 27 Comprehensive Review of Key Vocabulary

Think back to when you were in elementary school. What was your vocabulary instruction like? Did your teacher give you a list of words? What did you and the other students do with this list of words? If you experienced what most of us did, you looked the words up in a dictionary, used them in a sentence, and had a quiz on Friday. Effective SIOP teachers have abandoned this ineffective practice, or at least made some major changes to it because we know that in order for students to *learn* new vocabulary, they need to *use* the vocabulary.

Students need to be active in developing their understanding of words, engage in techniques that help them to personalize word learning, be immersed in learning new words throughout a lesson—not just at the beginning—and develop word learning strategies. The dictionary is only one source of information, and given how difficult definitions are in some dictionaries, the one in your own classroom might be inappropriate for English learners unless you have one that provides picture support and modified definitions. As you look through the activities and techniques for reviewing key vocabulary, select those that provide active engagement, personalized practice, and repeated exposures that students need in order to develop academic vocabulary.

Ideas & Activities for Reviewing Key Vocabulary

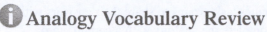 Analogy Vocabulary Review

submitted by Lynne Driscoll, Reading Consultant, Eden Park Elementary School, Cranston, RI

In this activity, Lynne Driscoll provides her students with opportunities to grapple with the meaning of new words and terms they are learning. Creating analogies is definitely a higher-order task because students must infer meaning in order to finish the analogy, by deciding how two words or concepts are similar. Lynne describes how she scaffolds this activity using a gradual release of responsibility approach (*I do; We do; You do*). Lynne states, "When I first start talking about using analogies there is a lot more matching analogies to pictures (*I do*). Then, once students understand what analogies are, in subsequent lessons I may move on to having them finish the analogies (*We do*). Finally, students write their own analogies (*You do*)." There is also specific language that must be taught in order for students to learn to write analogies, such as, *A fish is to water as a SIOP teacher is to scaffolding*. You get the analogy, right? Hopefully it makes you think, and that is the purpose of this activity—to help your students think about the meaning and relationship of words.

SIOP Feature 27: Comprehensive review of key vocabulary

Additional SIOP Features: 14, 15, 28

Grade Level: 2–8

Materials: Flashcards of vocabulary with a picture/word on one side of the card and just the word on other side of the card

Objectives:

- *Content:* Students will make logical inferences in order to complete analogies using key vocabulary.

- *Language:* Students will use the following sentence frame to complete analogies:

  - Cowboy is to ranch as _____ is to _____.

Grouping Configuration: Pairs and whole group

Directions:

1. Help students understand what an analogy is by providing an example, using key vocabulary and pictures to provide context.

2. Display the sentence, "Cowboy is to ranch as doctor is to _____." Show a picture of a cowboy riding his horse on a ranch, and then provide a picture of the doctor working at a hospital.

3. Explain that students are to look for the relationship between the two words and the two pictures. For example, cowboy ⟶ ranch; doctor ⟶ hospital. The relationship or similarity between the two pictures is where people work.

4. Show the word *cowboy* and the same picture of the ranch, but this time, provide the words *fireman* and a picture of a fire station.

5. Arrange students in pairs, and ask them to talk to their partners in order to determine what word goes in the blank.

6. After a few minutes, ask groups to share their answers with an explanation of why they chose to complete the analogy with a certain word.

7. For guided practice, provide each pair with flashcards with a word and picture on one side (*cowboy;* picture of ranch). On the other side of the card is a word (*doctor* or *fireman*). The students must determine the relationship between the person's role and the corresponding picture.

8. As students get better at analogies, you can provide new analogies or have students try to make up their own using the key vocabulary.

ⓐ Guess the Word/Draw the Word
submitted by Lynne Driscoll, Reading Consultant, Eden Park Elementary, Cranston, RI

Guess the Word/Draw the Word incorporates supplementary materials that allow students to review key vocabulary by personalizing it through drawings. Drawing a picture of a concept or a word requires analysis and interpretation, but not a lot of language.

SIOP Feature 27: Comprehensive review of key vocabulary

Additional SIOP Features: 5

Grade Level: K–12

Materials: Document camera; small dry-erase boards; dry-erase markers; wipes for cleaning the dry-erase boards; teacher-made index cards with vocabulary words on one side and pictures on the other, or commercial vocabulary flashcards

Objectives:

- *Content:* Students will infer the meaning of [key vocabulary words]. (Note: If vocabulary words are part of an objective, they should be listed individually).
- *Language:* Students will be able to define [key vocabulary words].
- *Student Friendly:*
  - I can use my "thinking cap" to figure out a word. (Again, the words should be listed for the students).
  - I can tell the meanings of my "thinking cap words."

Grouping Configuration: Individuals, whole group

Directions:

1. Use commercial or teacher-made flashcards that have pictures on one side and the vocabulary word on the other.

2. If using small flashcards, project the pictures, one card at a time, using a document camera. If using poster-sized vocabulary cards (K–2), show each card to the children.

3. Using small, dry-erase white boards, have students write down the vocabulary word they think the picture is showing and hold up the board with their answers for you to see. (Younger students can whisper to a partner what they think the word is, or you can provide index cards with the words written for them to choose from.)

4. Once all students have recorded their vocabulary word guesses, flip over the card showing the correct word.

5. Repeat this for all of the vocabulary words.

6. Now reverse the activity by showing students the words and having them draw a picture on their dry-erase boards. (For younger students, say the word as well as show the spelling of the word.)

7. Have students share their pictures with the group and vote on the best picture for each word.

8. Using the document camera, tablet, or smart phone, take a photo of each drawing to use for the class vocabulary word wall.

ⓐ Guesstimate Words from Context
submitted by Leslie Middleton, Instructional Coach, Rochester City School District, Rochester, NY

SIOP Feature 27: Comprehensive review of key vocabulary

Additional SIOP Features: 7, 8, 9, 13, 16

Grade Level: 1–10

Materials: White board or chart paper; students' journals or notebooks; vocabulary words; text to read that includes key vocabulary

Objectives: Not applicable

Grouping Configuration: Partners and whole group

Directions:

1. Display each key vocabulary word, one at a time, on an interactive white board, regular white board, or chart paper. The number of words you display depends on your students' ages, reading abilities, and language proficiencies.

2. Briefly talk about the definition of each word, but let students know that they will gain a deeper understanding of the vocabulary from reading the words in context. Review what "in context" means with as many examples as students need to understand the concept. For example:

   a. *The Era of Good Feelings began after the end of the War of 1812. People felt good because there was <u>prosperity,</u> a time when families had enough money for shelter, food, and clothing.* Ask students to identify the words and phrases that provide clues to the meaning of *prosperity.*

   b. *Andrew Jackson's presidential <u>campaign</u> was successful and he won the presidency. Voters believed his promises that he would support them if elected.* Again, ask students what they think *campaign* means, based on the context clues in the sentences.

3. Have students divide a page of their journals or notebooks into two columns. They should list the words in the left column. As students read text with the vocabulary words, have them use the context clues to "guesstimate" what they think the words mean.

4. Working with partners or small group members, students should share their guesstimates for word meanings, using evidence from the text to support their definitions.

5. After they discuss the words' possible meanings with peers, students can write their guestimates in the right column, leaving room for more complete definitions that they can add at a later date.

6. If relevant, students can sketch a quick picture of a word's meaning—something that will help them remember the word's meaning (prosperity: a dollar sign; campaign: picture of an Amerian flag or a campaign poster).

ⓐ Mystery Word

submitted by Pamela Dutter, Dodson Elementary School, Washoe County School District, Reno, NV

Students need continual exposure to vocabulary, even after it has been introduced and defined. Mystery Word is a fun way to keep students actively engaged in reviewing vocabulary terms from previous lessons.

SIOP Feature 27: Comprehensive review of key vocabulary

Additional Features: 4, 14, 25, 29, 30

Grade Level: K–8

Materials: A visible list of vocabulary words students have studied; teacher-created clues (it might be difficult to think of good clues during the game); small dry-erase boards (optional)

Objectives:

- *Content:* Students will determine the meaning of [vocabulary words].
- *Language:* Students will write their guesses to clues about the words' meanings.
- *Student Friendly:*
  - I can guess what a word means.
  - I can write the word I guessed.

Grouping Configuration: Whole group; partners can work together to guess the Mystery Word

Directions:

1. Review selected vocabulary words you have previously taught in a lesson or unit.

2. Explain to students that they will try to guess the Mystery Word by listening to clues.

3. Give clues, one at a time, for a vocabulary word.

4. As each clue is shared, students indicate when they have identified the Mystery Word through a signal (thumbs up, stand up, write the Mystery Word on small dry-erase boards, etc.)

5. Once the majority of students have indicated that they have guessed the word, call on specific students to check if it's correct.

6. You can award team or individual points for correct guesses; then move on and provide clues for the next Mystery Word.

7. Continue the activity so you can assess students' understandings of key vocabulary.

8. You may wish to have younger children and students with lower levels of English proficiency work with partners the first few times they play Mystery Word.

ⓐ Student-Created Cloze Sentences

submitted by Brooke Vecchio, 4th Grade Teacher, Woodridge Elementary School, Cranston, RI

Sentence frames and cloze sentences are an effective technique for scaffolding language for English learners. The teacher creates part of a sentence and the students fill in the missing words. Brooke Vecchio asks her students to create cloze sentences for the vocabulary words they are studying, a considerably more challenging task than just filling in the missing word. Brooke says, "This is a great review for tests, and I do use this method in all subject areas."

SIOP Feature 27: Comprehensive review of key vocabulary

Additional SIOP Features: 9, 15, 22

Grade Level: 3–12

Materials: Sentence strips or chart paper for students to post their cloze sentences

Objectives:

- *Content:* Write sentences describing key concepts using the vocabulary words.
- *Language:* Listen to cloze sentences to determine the missing vocabulary words.

Grouping Configuration: Small groups or partners

Directions:

1. Model how to write and use a cloze sentence. It is helpful if students are accustomed to using teacher-created cloze sentences. A cloze sentence has a missing word or words, with sufficient context so the reader can determine what goes in the blank(s): *A favorite pet of many people is a _____ because it likes to go on walks, fetches a ball, comes when you call its name, and is called "Man's Best _____."* Note that the sentence doesn't exactly define a dog, as much as it describes or characterizes it. The definition is embedded in the sentence.

2. Explain to students that they will create cloze sentences for vocabulary words that describe and characterize the word, while embedding its definition.

3. Ask students to choose one of the vocabulary words and work in cooperative groups to create a cloze sentence for their assigned word.

4. Members of each group share their cloze sentences with the class as the class tries to guess the missing word(s).

Feature 28 Comprehensive Review of Key Concepts

Most teachers provide their students with a review of the key concepts before a lesson ends and, traditionally, before students take *the test*. Since standards today focus less on memorized information and more on skills and strategies that students need to develop, we must do more than the typical test review. Review must take place throughout a lesson, and it needs to be *comprehensive,* covering all key concepts. If you're thinking you have too many concepts in the lesson to review, then you probably had too many concepts to teach in one lesson. The activities in this section provide students with opportunities to engage with and refocus on the key content concepts of the lesson.

Ideas & Activities for Reviewing Key Concepts

ⓐ All-American Baseball!

All students seem to enjoy classroom games, even when there's "work" involved. The All-American Baseball activity provides students with the opportunity to select the difficulty level of review questions that are asked prior to a chapter or unit test. It also provides you with assessment information about your students' understandings of the content concepts and vocabulary you've been teaching.

SIOP Feature 28: Comprehensive review of key content concepts

Additional SIOP Features: 6, 21, 23, 25

Grade Level: 2–10

Materials: Drawing of a baseball diamond on an interactive white board or large chart paper (see Figure 9.1); prepared questions on topic of your choice; markers for white board or chart paper

Objectives:

- *Content:* Students will analyze questions about (topic) to determine which are the most challenging.
- *Language:* Students will repeat the question that is asked and answer it in a complete sentence.

Grouping Configuration: Small groups and whole class

Directions:

1. Prepare a variety of questions at different levels of the Process Verbs and Products Matched to the Taxonomy for Learning, Teaching, and Assessing (see Appendix B). Easier questions are identified as "first base"; average questions are "second base"; and more challenging are "third base."

2. On game day, divide students into heterogenous groups of 3 to 4. It's important to select group members carefully, so that every group has a mix of student abilities and language proficiencies.

3. Younger students may enjoy naming their "teams" after Big League baseball teams.

4. You're the "pitcher" and you "throw out" questions as each team member "comes to bat."

5. If you have an interactive white board, students can trace their route around the baseball diamond. If not, you can mark four spots on the floor at the front of the room for each of the bases. If you're REALLY ambitious, students can move desks or tables to the sides of the room, and you can tape the classroom floor as a diamond with bases. Or students can just stay in their table groups while they do the activity.

6. One team at a time "goes to bat," with each student selecting the question of his or her choice, depending on difficulty level: first base, second base, or third base. Just let students choose what they want; sometimes your accelerated students want easier questions; sometimes struggling students choose more challenging questions. Try not to overly influence their choices.

7. It is your choice whether students can ask for help from their team members. If the game is for review, asking for help works well for students because they can work together to answer questions. If the game is right before a test, you may choose to have students bat by themselves and answer questions individually. If you choose the latter, be sure to have ground rules that forbid students from putting anyone down for failing to answer a question correctly. You can also have individual students answer questions while at bat, and then turn to their teammates for confirmation. If the team thinks the answer is wrong, the batter can take a "do-over" and try again. You may need to limit the number of do-overs for each team at bat.

8. On a regular white board, put an X on the corresponding base if the student answers the question correctly. Each time a student "runs" home (figuratively speaking, unless you've moved desks out of the way), the ball player's team earns a run (point).

9. There are no balls or strikes—unless you ask a question that no one can answer. Then it's the "pitcher's fault" (a ball) and every team gets a point. Students love it when this happens!

10. After one team strikes out (3 incorrect answers) or scores a predetermined number of points, then the other team comes to bat. Encourage students to develop strategies, such as, if the bases are loaded, the next one up to bat may wish to choose an easier question. Of if students are on 2nd and 3rd, the batter may wish to bring them home with a more challenging question.

11. Be sensitive to any students who may not know the American game of baseball. As needed, explaing how the game is played, show pictures of baseball players and a diamond, and/or watch a video clip of a professional game.

12. At the end of the period, total the team points to see who wins the game. Use what you've learned about questions that students have answered correctly and those that they have had difficulty with to plan re-teaching parts of lessons, test questions, and your lessons or unit that follows.

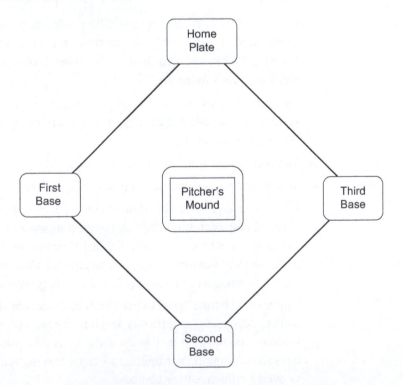

Figure 9.1 All-American Baseball Diamond

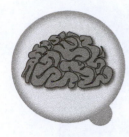

ⓐ Brain Dump!

submitted by Michaun Earhart, Teacher, Grade 4, Silver Lake Elementary School, Washoe County Schools, NV

A "brain dump" is the act of telling someone everything one knows about a particular topic or project. For years, we've called this *brainstorming*! When MaryEllen was working with teachers in Estonia in the mid-1990s, the interpreter she was working with said the closest translation of *brainstorming* in Estonian was *storm-braining* . . . and that works, too!

Michaun Earhart's fourth graders had a great time showing that they knew a lot about earthquakes and volcanoes when they participated in a review lesson that included three interactive activities: Brain Dump, Concept Ladder (p. 96), and Colored Cards for Review & Assessment (p. 174).

SIOP Feature 28: Comprehensive review of key content concepts

Additional SIOP Features: 6, 7, 9, 12, 15, 16, 17

Grade Level: 3–10

Materials: Chart or construction paper; markers, one for each student; a copy of the Concept Ladder (see p. X) for each student

Objectives: These are the objectives that Ms. Earhart had on her Prometheus white board at the beginning of the lesson that reviewed earthquakes and volcanoes:

- *Content:* I can integrate information from several texts on the same topic in order to speak about the subject intelligently.
- *Language:* I can apply what I learned about earthquakes and volcanoes by discussing with my team and completing a concept ladder.

Grouping Configuration: Small groups of 4–6

Directions:

1. Following are the actual directions depicted on Ms. Earhart's Prometheus white board:

   a. Brain Dump!

   b. In the center of your table, you have a large green paper. Everyone is to contribute to this project.

   c. We have learned a lot about volcanoes and earthquakes. Take a moment and collect all of that information in your mind.

   d. Write down anything and everything that comes to your mind about what we've learned about volcanoes and earthquakes. Don't worry about the spelling of your words at this time. (Everyone wrote their thoughts at the same time on the green sheets of paper.)

   e. Discuss what your group members have written down. Is there anything that can go together? Is there anything that would make a great question for your concept ladder?

2. After they had covered their papers with their thoughts and ideas students then began discussing how they would complete their concept ladders.

3. After the concept ladders were completed as a group, Ms. Earhart distributed small (2" × 4") laminated pieces of colored construction paper. Each student in the small

Marilyn Amy Washam

group had a different color. The groups' colors were the same; for example, every group had blue, green, red, yellow, and orange strips. These were distributed, one per child.

4. During the work on the concept ladder, Ms. Earhart told students they would be using questions from their concept ladders during a game. Of course, that spurred on competition.

5. Similar to Numbered Heads Together with a Review Sheet (Vogt & Echevarria, 2008, p. 183), the colored cards were used in place of numbers (see next activity, Colored Cards for Review and Assessment).

6. Ms. Earhart called on a group and indicated a color (blue). The student with the blue card stood and answered the question; he then picked another group and color (red), asked a question from his group's concept ladder, and the student who held the color answered the question. This process continued until the end of the instructional period.

ⓐ Colored Cards for Review & Assessment
submitted by Kimberly Howland, SIOP Trainer; Washoe County School District, NV

Kimberly uses this activity to review material and says that everyone always loves it! Colored Cards for Review and Assessment allow students to work in teams to compete against their classmates for points. Students get to choose which teams they want to challenge with their prepared questions, and there is a chance to steal points. Also, this activity asks students to read the text closely in order to write higher-order questions, provide textual evidence to support their answers to the questions, and collaborate with other students on the quality and justifiability of the questions. This activity provides necessary practice for students to meet the Common Core State Standards for reading.

SIOP Feature 28: Comprehensive review of key content concepts

Additional SIOP Features: 6, 12, 15, 16, 21, 22, 25, 30

Grade Level: 2–12

Materials: Text for students to read; colored cards (construction paper or tag board, laminated); Review and Assessment Half Sheet Template

Objectives:

- *Content:* You will cite specific textual evidence to support the answers to questions you wrote about the text.

- *Language:* You will collaborate to determine the quality of the questions and answers your team members created by using the following sentence frames:

  - "I can tell your questions are high quality because _____."
  - "The answers you provided are justifiable because _____."
  - "One question I have about your questions is _____."
  - "One question I have about your answers is _____."

Grouping Configuration: Individual, small groups, whole group

Directions:

1. Students work in groups of 4 or 5 to read a text and create questions about it. Since this activity is a competition to see which team can score the most points, give each group a team name or ask students to create their own.

2. Assign a chapter, portion of text, or whole text for students to read independently with a partner, or with teacher support. You can differentiate the reading assignment for students with less English proficiency by highlighting passages within the text for them to read, instead of the entire reading assignment.

3. Give each student a half-sheet template to write a question and answer based on his or her assigned text. The goal is for each team to create 4 questions (5 if there are 5 team members) about the text and to provide a justifiable answer to each question created.

4. Once teams have written their questions and answers, they check in with each other to make sure that the questions are high quality and the answers can be justified with evidence from the text.

5. The teams number off 1 to 4, (or 1 to 5), and begin asking and answering each other's questions.

6. Designate a starting place for the game, such as Team A with the person who holds the yellow card; that person decides which group and team member will answer one of Team A's questions.

7. Even though Team B gets to answer the question first, all teams put heads together to determine the answer to the question. If Team B's answer is correct, they win a point, but if the answer is incorrect, another team can try and win the point. Points are given to the team that answers correctly.

8. The team that gets the point by answering the question correctly poses a new question to another team. The person chosen to answer the question always consults with his or her team first and then poses the question to the team and team member of his or her choice.

9. Points are awarded to each team for correct answers to the questions until all students have had the opportunity to pose their questions.

10. The team with the most points wins!

Figure 9.2 Colored Cards Review and Assessment Student Question Sheet

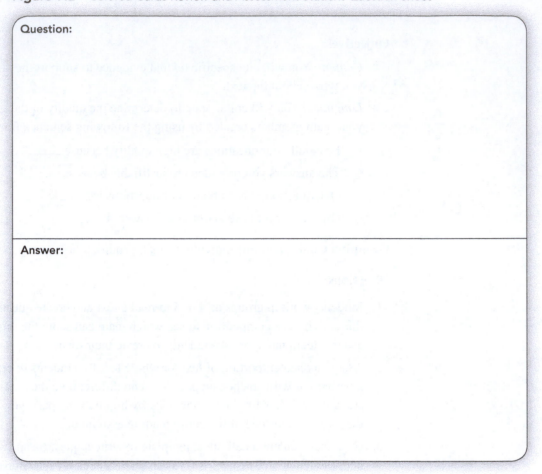

Question:

Answer:

ⓐ Learning Journals for Review

submitted by Leslie M. Middleton, Instructional Coach, Rochester City School District, Rochester, NY

It is common practice for secondary students to write class notes in journals or notebooks, electronic tablets, or laptops. This practice of note-taking has probably existed since schools began, with the exception of tablets and laptops, of course. Some teachers have students submit their notes, and they read and grade them. Other teachers believe that notebooks or journals are the students' business and they never look in them. Leslie Middleton uses students' journals or notebooks to review lessons' content and language concepts in tandem with the respective content and language objectives. Students sometimes believe that writing content and language objectives in their journals or notebooks is just one more teacher requirement. With Leslie Middleton's idea, however, students begin to realize that content and language objectives are cumulative, and when reviewed along with a unit's content and language concepts, students are directed to material that is most important and will undoubtedly be the focus of a unit exam.

SIOP Feature 28: Comprehensive review of key concepts

Additional SIOP Features: 6, 8, 23, 24, 27

Grade Level: 6–12

Materials: Student journals, notebooks, or tablets

Objectives: Not applicable

Grouping Configuration: Individual and partners

Directions:

1. After students have been reading, writing, and talking about a particular lesson topic with partners and/or small groups, reassemble the class (whole group) to discuss the key concepts and key vocabulary studied in the lesson.

2. Refer students to their learning journals or notebooks, tablets, or laptops.

3. Ask students to read through their notes and review the content and language concepts, as well as key vocabulary terms that were taught and practiced in a previous lesson or during multiple lessons. Have students highlight these, either with highlighter pens or electronically with the highlighter function.

4. Have students compare what they have highlighted with the lessons' content and language objectives.

5. In small groups, ask students to share their highlights, referring back regularly to the content and language objectives. Students can make suggestions and revisions based on classmates' ideas.

6. Ask groups to share out with the whole class some of the observations that occurred during the small group sharing. As students share, be sure to correct, scaffold, and redirect as necessary.

7. Read the objectives students wrote in their learning journals and have them give thumbs up if you believe they have met them.

8. If this activity takes place prior to an exam, clarify any misconceptions, misunderstandings, and incorrect information.

ⓐ Row Races

submitted by Andrea Rients, Social Studies Teacher, Shakopee High School, Shakopee, MN

This is a very engaging activity in which students compete in large groups to answer questions about previously learned content and language concepts. It provides a great review opportunity for students and an equally beneficial chance for teachers to assess students' understandings.

SIOP Feature 28: Comprehensive review of key content concepts

Additional SIOP Features: 25, 27, 29, 30

Grade Level: 3–12

Materials: Prepared worksheet with questions or statements about the content (one worksheet for each row), such as:

Heat 1: The Depression

1. This agency regulates the Stock Market.

2. This company helped provide cheap electricity.

3. This paid farmers not to grow certain crops.

4. Purchasing stock without paying for it in full called _____.

5. Hoover believed that government's role in solving the Depression was _____.

Objectives:

- *Content:* Students will analyze and determine the correctness of answers written by classmates.
- *Language:* Students will write answers to questions about [topic]

Grouping Configuration: Groups of 6 to 8 students

Directions:

1. Divide the class into groups of 6 to 8 and have each group form a row.

2. Give the first student in each row a prepared worksheet and one pencil.

3. Have the first students in the rows answer question 1 on the prepared worksheet.

4. After the first student has answered the first question, he/she passes the worksheet to the student behind him/her.

5. The second student checks answer 1 and revises it, if necessary, and then answers question 2.

6. Continue until the worksheet is completed.

7. The first row to bring up a complete worksheet with the most correct answers wins!

ⓐ Script a Simile

submitted by Andrea Rients, Social Studies Teacher, Shakopee High School, Shakopee, MN

SIOP teachers help their students review content concepts while developing academic language. In addition to learning new vocabulary words, language instruction should include the use of complex sentences. The Script a Simile activity provides students with a complex sentence frame that enables students to articulate comparisons in the form of a simile.

SIOP Feature 28: Comprehensive review of key content concepts

Additional SIOP Features: 27, 29, 30

Grade Level: K–12

Materials: Sentence frame written clearly for students to view; various objects that are associated with the lesson placed on a table

Objectives:

- *Content:* Students will identify characteristics and make comparisons of (topic).
- *Language:* Students will use the following sentence frame to create similes about (a lesson's topic):

"(Yesterday's topic) is like (object from table) because of _____, _____, and _____."

Grouping Configuration: Partners, whole group

Directions:

1. As a review activity, place items on the front table and ask students to complete the following simile. Review the definition of a simile (comparison using *like* or *as*). Model with another example, if needed:

   A violin is like a viola because of its strings, shape, and bow.

   "(Yesterday's topic) is like (object from table) because of _____, _____, and _____."

2. Encourage students to use words on a word wall to complete their simile.

3. Provide students time to think and write possible answers.

4. Before sharing with the whole group, students can share their answers with a partner.

a Twenty Seconds to Think

submitted by Charlotte Daniel, Education Specialist-Pearson, Kansas City, MO

In addition to listening, speaking, reading, and writing, students need time to simply think. This activity reminds students to do so, and it gives them the opportunity to reflect on previously studied topics. In addition to reviewing content and language, this technique can be used to exercise students' memory, help them build connections, and provide them time to work through mental maps.

SIOP Feature 28: Comprehensive review of key content concepts

Additional SIOP Features: 18, 27

Grade Level: 2–8

Materials: Charts, pages from textbook, classroom notes

Objectives:

- *Content:* Students will review information and identify remembered facts and concepts.

- *Language:* Students will recall information and facts and will silently complete the following sentence frames:
  - Some details I remember from this page are _____
  - Some details I do not remember from these pages are _____

Grouping Configuration: Individual, whole class

Directions:

1. Show students artifacts from a previous lesson (e.g., map, PowerPoint® slides, realia, graphic organizer, etc.).

2. Ask them to think about what they learned in the previous lesson by silently reflecting about the classroom artifacts.

3. Explain with a think-aloud what a "silent reflection" might sound like in your head. For example, ask students to think about the facts they remember, and then try to remember some they forgot.

4. Direct students to scan charts, pertinent pages from a textbook, or classroom notes and explain that they should silently review these for about 20–30 seconds.

5. As a class, have students select several charts, textbook pages, or notes for further review.

6. Point to or call out a chart or page and count to 20 slowly (whispering).

7. Direct students to think about the topic on the given chart or page during the 20-second count.

8. At the end of the time, ask students to identify what they now remember, and, if there were any facts they had forgotten that they recall now.

9. Remind students that periodic review of facts and concepts from previous lessons is critical for remembering them.

Feature 29 Regular Feedback Provided to Students on Their Output (e.g., Language, Content, Work)

Personal Connection with Marilyn Amy Washam

As any teacher who is also a parent will do, I go through all the papers my children bring home from school, looking at both their work and the comments and grades given by the teacher. When my son was in kindergarten, his teacher used smiley faces as a form of feedback. Of course, I interpreted these smiley faces as an indication that my son was making good progress and assumed that his understanding of the smiley faces was similar to my own. But one day, my son brought home a paper that had a face with a frown on it. After pulling him off the trampoline, I sat him down on the stairs, showed him the paper, pointed to the face with a frown, and asked, "What does this mean?" He looked up at me and said, "The teacher had a bad day!" My first thoughts were that my son was simply too young to understand the significance of grades, but then I remembered conversations I had with my students when I taught high school sheltered English Language Arts. I would ask a student why he was able to make an A in math but was making a D in science, and he would respond, "The science teacher hates me."

So how do we provide feedback that students will take ownership of and understand? Rick Stiggins reminds us that, "for students to be able to improve, they must have the capacity to monitor the quality of their own work during actual production" (Stiggins, Arter, Chappuis, & Chappuis, 2006, p. 34). Students must understand the performance criteria that will be used to assess their learning. The problem with traditional letter and number grades, and yes smiley faces, is that they do not provide students with any specific performance criteria. The reason a student receives either a smiley face or a frown seems totally subjective, depending on the mood of the person giving the grade. By providing students with specific performance criteria, we can help them assess where they are, how far they have come, and how far they have to go toward meeting the objectives. The following activities are designed to make feedback more comprehensible and meaningful to students, and eventually, put the students in charge of assessing their own learning of the objectives.

Ideas & Activities for Providing Appropriate Feedback to Students

ℹ Captain of the Day

submitted by Donna Smeins Howard, Math Specialist, Port Towns Elementary School, Prince George's County Public Schools, MD

In order to effectively differentiate instruction, it is necessary for students to learn to work independently for short periods of time while you work more closely with a small group of students. There should be clear classroom rules established so that students know not to interrupt you when you are working with a group of students. Assigning a Captain of the Day is a technique that provides students with a resource, besides the teacher, for questions they have.

Donna Howard explains, "My students know who in the room is "Captain of the Day," and this person is a resource if they get stuck. The Captain is trained not to give out answers; sometimes this backfires but for the most part, it works. Instead, he or she is to help the student by asking questions or making statements, such as, 'What do you notice? What part do you understand?'"

SIOP Feature 29: Regular feedback provided to students on their output

Additional SIOP Features: 13, 14, 15

Grade Level: K–6

Materials: A poster or paper reference to the questions or statements the Captain of the Day should use to help other students; an official Captain of the Day clipboard; a standardized Captain of the Day evaluation rubric

Objectives:

- *Content:* Students will adapt their speech to combine academic phrases with appropriate tone for classroom collaboration with peers.

- *Language:* Students will ask and answer appropriate clarifying questions using the following sentence frames:

  - What part do you understand? I understand _____.

  - What part do you not understand? I do not understand _____.

  - What do you notice about _____? I noticed that _____.

- *Student Friendly:*

  - I can use words and sentences to talk about (topic) with my classmates.

  - I can ask and answer questions with these sentence frames (see above).

Grouping Configuration: Independent or small group work

Directions:

1. At the beginning of the year, explain the concept of Captain of the Day.

2. Tell students that the Captain of the Day is a resource for them while they are participating in centers.

3. Explain that you will be unavailable because you are working with students in one of the centers. Instead, students will ask the Captain of the Day for assistance when they get stuck.

4. Further, explain that the Captain of the Day does not have the answers, but will use a list of suggestions and questions to help struggling students.

5. Go over the list of questions and statements that the Captain of the Day is allowed to use when students ask him or her for help.

   a. What part do you understand?

   b. What part do you not understand?

   c. What do you notice about . . .?

   d. Read this sentence again.

   e. Try looking over this part again.

   f. Let's read the directions again.

6. Depending on the age of your students, generate with students a list of unacceptable statements that the Captain of the Day should *not* use. For young students, create the list and model the "do's" and "don't."

   a. The answer is . . .

   b. I can't believe you don't know the answer to that!

   c. Didn't you read the directions?

   d. This is wrong.

7. Model both the acceptable and the unacceptable statements and questions, and discuss the rationale behind each.

8. Hand out a list, or post a list of acceptable statements.

9. Allow students to role-play Captain of the Day in their small groups as you walk around to assess how well they understand the concept.

10. Provide a space on the wall or board to write the name of the Captain of the Day. You could also provide an official clipboard that the Captain of the Day carries during his or her tenure in office.

11. Finally, create a rubric for assessing the Captain of the Day's performance. Some ideas for the rubric could be:

    a. Only uses allowable statements and questions

    b. Friendly and understanding

    c. Pays attention to his or her responsibilities

    d. Helpful and responsive to classmates

ℹ Rubrics for Self-Assessment of Group Discussions
submitted by Kelly LaLonde, Cranston, MD

As mentioned previously, many students may struggle to understand the feedback they receive on their work. They may even feel disconnected from the grades they receive, as if they had nothing to do with the grade the teacher *decided* to *give* them. One way teachers can help students comprehend what is expected of them and understand the feedback they receive on their work is through the use of rubrics. Kelly LaLonde provides her students with self-assessment rubrics designed to help them monitor their own progress while they are learning to participate in group discussions. Kelly has shared one of the self-assessment rubrics she uses (see Figure 9.3).

Learning to write effective rubrics is much like learning to write effective objectives—it takes practice and time. To help you design assessment rubrics and facilitate student talk about their descriptions, see Stiggins, Arter, Chappuis, and Chappuis (2006), pp. 214–215.

SIOP Feature 29: Regular feedback provided to students on their output

Additional SIOP Features: 12, 13, 30

Materials: Rubrics with clearly defined expectations that show performance tasks and levels of performance criteria

Objectives:

- *Content:* Participate effectively in an academic conversation about (topic).
- *Language:* Self-assess your participation in the conversation about (topic) by indicating the criteria that best describe your performance.
- *Student Friendly:*
  - *Content:* I can talk to my friends about (topic).
  - *Language:* I can explain how I talked to my friends about (topics) using the following sentence frames:
    a. I felt comfortable talking about (topic), and had more than three interesting things to say.
    b. I was not really comfortable, but I was prepared to talk about (topic) and had exactly three important things to say.
    c. I was able to say at least one thing about (topic), but I did not feel comfortable or prepared for the conversation.

Grouping Configuration: Individuals; whole class

Directions:

1. Create a rubric that includes categories for academic conversations and descriptions of what student performance looks like for each level. See Figure 9.3 for the categories and descriptions that Kelly LaLonde uses in her academic conversation rubric.

2. Introduce the rubric to the students by explaining both the categories and the various descriptions of performance at each level for each task.

3. One way to help students learn the rubric is to model how to use it. For example, show students a short video of a discussion and then model how to use the rubric to analyze it.

4. All students should be allowed to discuss the tasks in the rubric along with the criteria for each level of performance before they begin the conversation.

5. The rubric should be available for the students before, during, and after the group discussion that is being rated.

6. After completing the group discussion, students self-assess by choosing the descriptions under each category that best describes how they think they performed on each task.

Figure 9.3 Self-Assessment of Group Discussion

Expectations:

✔ Should work toward making (at the minimum) three comments or responses

✔ Should work toward becoming prepared with all literature circle materials and prepared to talk

✔ Should work toward using at least three accountable talk phrases during discussion

	3- Excelling	3- Proficient	2- Making Progress	1- Emerging
Comments/ Responses	I had more than three unique things to say and positively contributed to the discussion.	I had exactly three things to say and contributed to the conversation.	I was able to say at least one or two things during the conversation.	I did not talk during the discussion, but I listened to others and recognized some of what they were saying.
Preparation	I completed all of my literature circle prep materials and knew the information so well that I didn't have to look at my notes!	I completed all of my literature circle prep materials and was prepared for the discussion.	I completed some of my literature circle prep materials and had to look at my notes a lot during the discussion.	I brought my uncompleted work to literature circle.
Accountable Talk Phrases	I used more than three accountable talk phrases during the discussion and talked to my peers and not through my teacher.	I used exactly three accountable talk phrases during the discussion and mostly talked to my peers and not through my teacher.	I used at least two accountable talk phrases. I mostly talked to my teacher.	I listened to others use accountable talk phrases during the discussion.
Comfort Level	I loved this discussion and felt like my peers really understood what I was trying to tell them. I wasn't worried about my English at all!	I felt fine during the discussion and felt like my peers understood what I was saying. I did not feel too worried about my English.	Even though I felt nervous during the discussion, I tried to participate. Sometimes my peers understood what I was saying.	I didn't talk a lot because I was very nervous about my English, but I listened to my peers.

Name: _____   Date: _____

7. Go over the rubric with your students, either whole class or one on one, as long as each student has an opportunity to compare and discuss the scores they gave themselves with those you assigned.

8. Students also can use the scored rubrics to discuss or journal about the steps they can take to improve their overall score in each category.

9. As students become more proficient at using rubrics, the class can generate their own rubrics for discussions.

ⓘ Video Feedback

You can use your computer web cams to videotape feedback to student work. This feedback can be emailed to the students who have access to a computer or tablet and the Internet, or students can view the feedback on classroom computers or tablets in school.

SIOP Feature 29: Regular feedback provided to students on their output

Additional SIOP Features: 27, 28

Grade Level: K–12

Materials: Computer or laptop with a web cam; students need access to email.

Objectives: Not applicable

Grouping Configuration: Individual or groups

Directions:

1. Record on the web cam specific academic feedback to individual students based on assignments, projects, tests, and so forth.

2. The feedback will be more effective if students have been introduced to a rubric for the assignment prior to its completion. Discuss evaluation of the work in terms of the rubric, adding context to the feedback.

3. Email the video feedback to students.

4. Have students view the feedback at home or in school the next day.

Feature 30 Assessment of Student Comprehension and Learning of All Lesson Objectives (e.g., Spot Checking, Group Response) throughout the Lesson

Assessment Driven Instruction

Imagine if you could see what your students were thinking. You would be able to assess whether they really understood the key vocabulary or content concepts you just introduced. You would also see their questions and be able to address them quickly. If they were off-task and daydreaming, you would be able to redirect them immediately. While there isn't a gadget out yet that allows this kind of insight, teachers can incorporate activities and techniques that allow them to assess how well their students are progressing in their comprehension of key content and language concepts. As you read through the activities, notice how they require a great deal of student engagement and interaction. The key to assessment driven instruction is that we are able to determine whether students are making progress in meeting objectives at nearly any point in a lesson. In contrast, when students are just passively listening to a lengthy lecture, it's very difficult to assess what they're learning.

Ideas & Activities for Assessing Student Comprehension and Learning of All Objectives

ⓘ Exit Tickets

Exit Tickets (sometimes called Tickets Out) are a terrific way to have students sum up what they have learned throughout a lesson. At the end of class, post an open-ended question about the lesson(s) you have taught. For example, you can ask students to complete a simple sentence starter such as: *Today I learned _____*. To help students keep their comments on topic, you can have them incorporate key vocabulary into their Exit Tickets. Not only do the Exit Tickets allow you to assess what students learned, but their comments can be used to begin the lesson the next day, providing a link to past learning.

SIOP Feature 30: Assessment of student comprehension and learning of all lesson objectives (e.g., spot checking, group response) throughout the lesson

Additional SIOP Features: 8, 23, 24, 27, 28

Grade Level: 2–12

Materials: Prepared questions posted in the room for all students to see; sticky notes; index cards or small squares of paper for students to write their responses to Exit Ticket prompts

Objectives: Not applicable

Grouping Configuration: Individual

Directions:

1. At the end of class, post a prompt for students to answer or a sentence starter for them to finish. Here are some starters that we like to use:

   During class today . . .

   - I thought about _____.
   - I wondered _____.
   - I realized _____.
   - I learned that _____.
   - I was excited about _____.
   - I felt _____.
   - One question I still have is _____.

2. Provide small squares of paper for students to use to write their answers. These will become their Exit Tickets out the door.

3. Read the question or sentence starter to the students and model some ways you might answer or complete it.

4. You can choose to have each student write his or her name on the Exit Ticket or answers can be anonymous. Sometimes students will feel more comfortable writing something if they don't have to put their names on the Tickets.

5. Provide students time to complete the Exit Tickets, and when the bell rings, ask students to bring their Exit Tickets to you as they leave the room.

6. After the students have left, read through the Exit Tickets and choose a few to read to the class at the beginning of the period the next day. You might consider choosing an assortment of thoughtful insights, questions, and misunderstandings. The misunderstandings can be the source of re-teaching and thoughtful conversations about the lesson's objectives.

ⓘ Private Eyes

submitted by Lindsay Young, Pearson SIOP Consultant; former middle school teacher, instructional coach and certified SEI trainer; Creighton School District, AZ

It is critical for students to assess their level of understanding throughout a lesson and be able to communicate this to their teachers. Many students are self-conscious about openly displaying their understanding of new concepts. Using the Private Eyes activity allows students to share a quick response with the teacher while hiding their response from others.

SIOP Feature 30: Assessment of student comprehension and learning of all lesson objectives throughout the lesson

Additional SIOP Features: 28

Grade Level: All levels, especially if your students have lower levels of English proficiency

Materials: None

Objectives: Not applicable

Grouping Configuration: Whole group

Directions:

1. For a quick spot check for understanding, model for students and tell them to wait to show you a response until you say:

   a. *Show me Private Eyes.*

   b. *If you are very confident in your understanding, show me both eyes wide open.*

   c. *If you are somewhat confident but have a question or comment for clarification, wink at me.*

   d. *If you need a lot of support because you don't understand right now, show me both eyes closed.*

2. When you give the prompt, *"Show me Private Eyes,"* students can hold both hands to their temples, palms facing in, to hide their response from anyone but you. You then scan the room to see the students' responses.

ⓐ Text Sort

submitted by Jaclyn McKinney, ELD Teacher, Horizon Middle School, Falcon School District 49, Colorado Springs, CO

This activity for a summative assessment requires students to recall important information from the lesson by reading short passages from the text they are studying. Text Sort utilizes hands-on manipulatives—strips of text in a baggie—to help students practice their knowledge of the content. Jaclyn McKinney uses Text Sort in her classroom with middle school students, and says, "I have noticed that this has helped with comprehension, and after they do it a few times, [students] get familiar with clues and key words that help them identify the passage and major details."

SIOP Feature 30: Assessment of student comprehension and learning of all lesson objectives throughout the lesson

Additional SIOP Features: 4, 27, 28

Grade Level: K–12

Materials: Copies of pages from a textbook, zippered plastic bags

Objectives:

- *Content:* Determine central ideas or themes of a text.
- *Language:* Use context clues to infer the meaning of a text.

Grouping Configuration: Groups of four

Directions:

1. Copy random pages from the text students are studying.
2. Cut the copied pages into strips and put a code on the back of each strip that will help you identify the origin of the text.
3. Put the strips of text into zippered plastic bags.
4. Have students pull a strip from the bag.
5. It is the students' job to know the origin of the strip of text. For language arts, students can tell the title of the story or poem and recall some important details from the piece they selected. For social studies, students can indicate a particular theme or event in history that the text is referring to. For science and math, students can indicate the concept the text is related to.
6. Students continue pulling strips of text from the bag. After they do this a few times, they become familiar with clues and key words that help them identify the passage and major details.

Thinking about Review & Assessment

1. Review the objectives, both content and language, throughout a lesson. How will you ensure that students have repeated exposures to the content and language they are learning? What activities or techniques will you incorporate in order to help your students engage in learning academic vocabulary? Choose activities that allow students to experience the vocabulary repeatedly in different modalities, if possible, and from various sources.

2. How will you provide feedback that is specific, academic, and meaningful to your students? How will you help your students learn to self-assess their own progress toward meeting the objectives? Set a goal to learn more about creating effective rubrics that provide students with specific feedback.

10 Creating SIOP Lessons

Kzenon/Fotolia

A Teacher's Reflection

Lesson preparation helps me process ways to best communicate what I want students to know and be able to do. Differentiated instruction usually occurs in my head rather than on paper, but this is where I think about it. My process assures a lesson suitable for all learning levels.

—Rosemarie Olheiser, Art Teacher, Grade 7–8, O'Brien STEM Academy,
Washoe County School District, NV

Getting Started with SIOP

In some ways, this chapter section could have been the first one in the book so that lesson planning would be the focus of the text, rather than instructional ideas and activities. Instead, we've placed this chapter on creating SIOP lessons as the conclusion, so that you can pull all the bits and pieces of what you know about the SIOP® Model together in a cohesive instructional plan. We hope that you now see that we start with content and language standards that lead to content and language objectives that lead to effective content and academic language instruction. Once your objectives are determined, you are ready to make decisions about the rest of the lesson, using the SIOP features as your guide.

If *creating* a lesson plan from scratch seems too demanding for where you are in your SIOP learning curve, start with a less challenging task and follow these steps:

- Use the verb *label* to begin the SIOP lesson planning process.

- *Label* a lesson plan you have previously taught with any of the features of the SIOP® Model that you recognize. See Figure 10.1 for an example of what we're suggesting.

- In Figure 10.1, *examine* the SIOP features that are labeled in the arrow-shaped boxes that point to parts of the lesson plan.

- Now, *determine* which SIOP features are missing. Use the SIOP protocol to help you do this (see Appendix A).

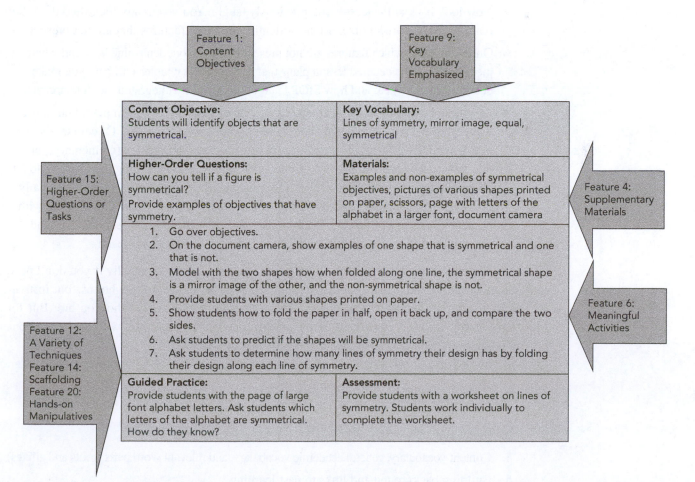

Figure 10.1 Label a Lesson Plan

- In the lesson in Figure 10.1, you may notice that the features of Building Background and Interaction are not present.

- Additionally, there are no language objectives. A good place to start, then, might be to ascertain the language students would need to know and use in order to talk about the concept of symmetry. You might write a language objective such as, "Using the following vocabulary words, predict if shapes will be symmetrical: *equal, not equal, symmetrical, mirror image, lines of symmetry.*"

- Next you might need to incorporate the three features of Building Background, especially if students don't know the word or concept *symmetry,* and need some background building with commonplace examples (Feature 7), such as, "Are you ears symmetrical?" "Are your eyes symmetrical?" "Are leaves on a tulip symmetrical?" If you've previously explored symmetry, then an explicit, but brief review will get everyone on the same page (Feature 8). The vocabulary listed in the language objective will need to be taught and reviewed (Feature 9) if students are to meet the objective. To assist you further, review Chapter 3 on Building Background (p. 37). You can look through the activities and ideas for incorporating Features 7, 8, and 9, until you find something that will work for your students and the content and language concepts you are teaching. You may also decide that you already know a few activities that will help incorporate the features, or you can consult with a colleague who teaches the same content and the two of you can provide each other with an idea or two.

- Now look back at the lesson you previously taught. You've already identified the SIOP features that you recognize. So, now identify the SIOP features that are not present.

- Once you know which features are not present in the lesson, determine how and where to include them. The detailed lesson plans that follow in this chapter will help you make decisions about where and how SIOP features are logically integrated into a lesson plan.

- As you're beginning to think about creating an original SIOP lesson plan, you may be wondering which features you should incorporate into your lesson. Of course, the goal is to eventually have all thirty features in lessons that span the day (elementary), or that last for two or three periods (secondary). While you're learning the SIOP® Model, choose components that you feel comfortable incorporating, knowing that eventually, you will need to attend to all of them. For example, if you are quite comfortable with the three features of Building Background, start by incorporating features 7, 8, and 9 into a lesson plan for one of the subjects or preparations that you teach.

This sequence for creating a SIOP lesson plan works well, especially if you don't need too much guidance. If that sounds like you, you may be one of those who toss out instructions when purchasing furniture that needs assembling. You know who you are. But for those of you who feel more comfortable putting together the bookshelf with the instructions in hand, in the next section we offer some more support.

In the beginning of planning SIOP lessons, it may be helpful to plan your lessons in this order:

1. Content standards

2. Content objectives

3. Language objectives

4. Content vocabulary, general academic vocabulary, and relevant word parts (roots and affixes)

5. Building background and links to past learning

6. HOTS: Higher-Order Thinking Skills (although these questions and/or tasks may change as your lesson plays out)

7. Meaningful activities: lesson sequence

8. Ideas for review and assessment

9. Supplementary materials

Of course, after you've planned your lesson sequence, you may need to go back and adjust it as necessary. A description of each of these elements is found in Figure 10.2. The lesson plan format is similar to or the same as the plans SIOP teachers used to create the lesson plans you'll find later in this chapter.

Figure 10.2 Writing a SIOP Lesson Plan

Key: SW = Students will;	TW = Teacher will;	HOTS: Higher-Order Thinking Skills

SIOP Lesson: Indicate your specific lesson topic.   **Subject:**   **Grade level:**

Content Standard: Indicate the content standard(s) that guide the writing of your content objective(s).	**WIDA or ELD Standard (Language Focus):** Indicate the language standard(s) that guide the writing of your language objective(s).

Key Vocabulary: List the content words and terms; also list general academic (cross-curricular) words or terms that students need to use or know to meet lesson objectives.

Supplementary Materials: List any resources you will include in the lesson to scaffold students' understanding and that provide opportunities for students to practice and apply content and language concepts.

HOTS (Higher-Order Thinking Skills): Write higher-order questions or tasks requiring critical thinking. Make sure English learners have the language to be able to respond fully.

Connections to Students' Background Experiences and Past Learning: Indicate how you will activate students' prior knowledge and build background where gaps exist. Indicate how you will explicitly link to previous lesson concepts and academic vocabulary.

Content Objective(s): Write content objective(s) that can be taught, practiced and applied, and assessed during this particular lesson. **Language Objective(s):** Write language objective(s) that can be taught, practiced, and assessed within this particular lesson.	**Meaningful Activities/Lesson Sequence:** Write the sequential steps of the lesson, beginning with sharing the content and language objectives with students. Include opportunities for student-to-student interaction (with varied grouping configurations) and activities for practice and application of key content and language concepts, including vocabulary. Consider if each step of the lesson will be comprehensible to students, and include content and language scaffolds where necessary.	**Review & Assessment:** As you are writing the lesson sequence, indicate where you will review, spot-check, and assess students' comprehension of key content and language concepts. You should be able to informally assess through the lesson's meaningful activities, while students are engaged in interactions with classmates.

Grouping Configurations: 1. Whole class 2. Small groups 3. Partners 4. Independent
Identify in Lesson Sequence which grouping configurations will be used, by marking G1, G2, G3, or G4.

Wrap Up/Review/Assessment: Write a quick wrap-up activity for reviewing key content and language concepts. Include how you will review with students the content and language objectives at the end of the lesson.

"*This* lesson plan and others are available electronically on the PDToolkit for SIOP. If you do not already have access to the PDToolkit for SIOP, visit http://pdtoolkit.pearson.com to purchase a subscription to the website."

Adding SIOP Components

We always suggest that you slowly and purposefully add SIOP components to your lessons as you become more knowledgeable about and comfortable with them. In order to be prepared to add components, we suggest that you carefully read and internalize one of the core SIOP books (Echevarria, Vogt, & Short, 2013; 2014a; or 2014b), if you haven't already done so. It's also helpful to engage in discussion with colleagues about each of the components, so that you begin to see the Model as a "whole" rather than eight (or even thirty) disparate parts.

After you have read one of the core SIOP books, you may wish to consider one of the following implementation schedules that schools and districts have found to be workable:

1. Teachers incorporate one SIOP component each month, beginning in September. We have found that this schedule is workable IF you have sufficient support that includes:

   a. Professional development on implementing the SIOP® Model.

   b. Coaching by experienced SIOP coaches.

   c. Observations using the SIOP protocol (Appendix A) with pre- and post-conferences led by an experienced SIOP coach, mentor, or other trainer.

   d. Pupil-free time each week for collegial planning. Our research findings have shown that this schedule, with ample support, can bring about significant academic gains for English learners and other students.

2. Here's another option that has worked well:

   a. Implement one component in one subject area (elementary) or one preparation (secondary) every nine weeks.

   b. Add another component and strive to implement both for nine weeks; and so forth.

      By the end of the first year, you'll be implementing four components; by the end of the second year, you'll be on your way to becoming a high-implementing SIOP teacher if you're consistently incorporating all of the features in lessons. Of course, developing consistency is more likely with periodic SIOP professional development opportunities, and occasional observations by a peer, coach, or administrator using the SIOP protocol. (For more information on how to use the protocol ratings for observations, see Chapter 11 in Echevarria, Vogt, & Short, 2013; 2014a; or 2014b.) The least effective schedule that we have seen is really no schedule at all, but is the expectation that teachers will begin using all thirty SIOP features at once, with minimal professional development or other support, such as coaching. We're sure you realize by now that the SIOP® Model is complex, and even though many of the features are familiar instructional methods you've known about for some time, implementing all of them consistently and systematically takes time, patience, and practice.

Whatever implementation plan you and your school (and/or district) decide on, we strongly recommend that you begin incorporating the six features of Lesson Preparation sooner, rather than later. This is because many of SIOP's features can't be incorporated without content and language objectives. Much like the lesson on mitosis, once you have had some time to practice, creating SIOP lessons will far less time consuming.

Regardless of whether you're a newbie or a veteran SIOPer, please remember this important point. Be consistent in using the SIOP protocol to remind yourself of the thirty features that need to be included in lessons, and then be consistent in how the SIOP features are implemented. Teachers who are consistent in their implementation of SIOP features in their lessons are the same teachers whose English learners and other students demonstrate measurable academic gains. Those teachers who are inconsistent with SIOP implementation are the ones whose students plug along, but often without the measurable academic gains.

Sample SIOP Lesson Plans

Modeling is a terrific way to ensure that content concepts are clear, so we're including several lesson plans that have been shared by SIOP teachers. Most of the plans follow the lesson plan template in Figure 10.2, so you might find it helpful to read through the explanations provided earlier in the chapter if you have not already done so. For those of you who toss the instruction manual before opening up the appliance, you can move on to the lesson plans on the following pages.

The preceding lesson plans utilize many of the activities in this book so that you can get an idea of how activities can help you incorporate SIOP's features. Additionally, we chose some plans that provided guidance on how to scaffold rigorous lessons for students who are not yet proficient in English. When we showed the objectives from these lesson plans to a group of teachers in Washington, they told us it would take a couple of days for students to meet these objectives. We agree. Some of the lessons span over several days, each day filled with scaffolding and language instruction that English learners, and indeed all students, need in order to meet the challenging objectives. **We acknowledge that it's not practical to write daily lesson plans with the level of detail you will find in the sample lesson plans. The details are necessary here so that you can easily follow the plan sequence.** In addition, you may find that when you begin writing SIOP lesson plans, they will be more detailed until incorporating the features becomes automatic. Note that the activities and ideas from this book are not explained in depth in the lesson plans because you can refer back to the activity page for more information on how to incorporate it into your lessons.

If you are interested in learning more about the SIOP lesson and unit planning process, we have four other books that target lesson and unit planning specifically for teachers of mathematics, science, history/social studies, and English/language arts. These books are each divided into K–2, 3–6, 6–8, and 9–12, and they include many more ideas and activities (for more information, see Echevarria, Vogt, & Short, 2010 ; Short, Vogt, & Echevarria, 2011a; Short, Vogt, & Echevarria, 2011b; and Vogt, Echevarria, & Short, 2010).

LESSON PLAN Drawing Inferences
(Joli Butler, Reading and Social Studies Teacher, Rogers Heights Elementary School, MD)

Teacher: Jolie Butler

SIOP Lesson: Drawing Inferences	**Subject:** Reading	**Grade Level:** 5th

Content Standard:	**ELD Standard (Language Focus):**
Review the key ideas expressed and draw conclusions in light of information and knowledge gained from the discussions.	Writing a summary.
Quote accurately from a text when explaining what the text says explicitly and when drawing inferences from the text.	

Key Vocabulary:	**Supplementary Materials:**
Context Clues, Background Knowledge, Inference (infer; inferring), professions, summary	PowerPoint®, Inferring Professions, Graphic Organizer, Pencils, Working Groups

HOTS (Higher-Order Questions and Tasks):

Connections to Students' Background Experiences and Past Learning:

- Introduce the objectives and discuss what it means to make an inference (Text Clues + Background Knowledge = Inference)
- Tell the students that to practice making inferences, we are going to solve riddles. In order to be successful at solving riddles, you need to WRITE down any context clues you find on your graphic organizer. We are going to read riddles on the PowerPoint . . . you will need to find context clues in order to figure out the answer to the riddles.

Content Objective:	**Meaningful Activities (Lesson Sequence):**	**Review & Assessment:**
Students will use context clues and background knowledge to make inferences (or to infer).	Riddle #1 Teacher Models (show the first riddle on the PowerPoint slide).	
	Because I stop by your house, you won't have to leave home. You may think I am wrong when you see me on the road, but your packages won't be delivered without me. While you may be excited by what I bring you, remember that I am not excited about your dog. Who am I?	
Language Objective:	Read the riddle aloud and use a think-aloud technique to model the thought process for solving the riddle.	
Students will write a summary to describe their inferences.	"Now, I'm thinking that this is describing a mail man. I used several context clues in this poem. I used: stop by my house, deliver packages, on the wrong side of the road, and that he doesn't care for dogs. All of these context clues made me think of my mailman.	

Continued.

They drive on the opposite side of the road when delivering the mail, they come by my house, and they deliver things to me. In some movies, I have seen dogs chasing mailmen. I think it's because they seem like strangers, so I infer mailmen don't like them."

Pass out the graphic organizer and refer students to the section marked, Riddle #1. Show students how you have written your Think Aloud comments about Riddle #1 and say, "Now you have my thinking right in front of you." Explain that your thinking is a summary of the inference you made about Riddle #1.

Students can use the teacher's sentences as a guide for creating their own.

Listen to student responses; note how they vote; note the evidence that students find in the text.

Riddle #2 Together. When you think you know the answer, raise your hand. After we have a couple of answers, we will vote and use evidence from the text to support our answers.

Show the second riddle on the PowerPoint® slide.

Circulate and read answers to the riddle and evidence students have recorded.

I really like apples, numbers, and books. But chewing gum is not on my list of favorite things. I have lots of lists and stick to a strict schedule. I have to be organized in order to keep track of my 32 kids. Time for a test!

Students to talk with their group members to come up with their own answers to the riddle. Remind students to record the evidence from the riddle in the graphic organizer, which is the summary. They can use the teacher's notes from Riddle #1 as a guide. You can also provide the following sentence frames on the graphic organizer for students who need more language support.

- I infer the riddle is about ___

- In the riddle, it says, ___ just like ___

- It also says ___, which means ___

- The ___ line of the riddle really tells me that ___ is ___ because it says, ___

Go over sentence frames with students who need them. Students should orally read sentence frames and suggest possible words and phrases for the blanks

- Ask several of the groups to share their solutions to the riddle and their evidence from the text to support their answers. Remind students that these are their summaries of the riddle.

- Have the class vote on the best answer.

- Riddle #3 Independent

While the answer to the riddle is teacher, make sure to listen to all of the students' guesses, and ask students to provide evidence from the text to support their guesses. Students may make some logical inferences which will provide rich classroom discussion.

(continued)

Continued.

For our final task, you will work on your own to solve a riddle. Remember to use your background knowledge + evidence from the text to infer the solution to the riddle. You will be summarizing your inferences on the graphic organizer in the Riddle #3 space provided.

I deliver people and animals from danger. I fight the enemy with ladders, axes, and hoses, but sometimes my weapons come in handy when kittens climb too high. I keep my head protected at all times, and my best friend is covered with spots.

- Some students might need to work with the teacher to make inferences about the third riddle while other students can make the inferences on their own without the sentence frames.

Based on student understanding and language proficiency, determine who needs additional support.

Students who are ready to move on can practice their inferences skills using appropriate texts. Be sure to remind students to use their background knowledge along with clues from the text to make their inferences.

Differentiate for more accelerated students.

Lesson Wrap Up:

Ask students to share with a partner what they did when they made inferences about the answers to the riddles. Ask them to include their key vocabulary in their explanations. Go over the content and language objectives with the students.

LESSON PLAN   Photosynthesis
(Dorothea Bell, Grade 4 Intervention Teacher, Winters Elementary School (Rominger Campus), Winters, CA

SIOP Lesson Plan

Teacher: Dorothea Bell

Grade/Class/Subject: Grade 4 Science; Photosynthesis

Unit/Theme: Life Science

Standards: Life Science 2.a: Students know plants are the primary source of matter and energy entering most food chains.

Content Objective: We will compare and contrast two plants and relate their similarities and differences to the process of photosynthesis.

Language Objective: We will explain the process of photosynthesis using a diagram labeled with the words *sunlight, photosynthesis, oxygen, carbon dioxide, stomata, chlorophyll,* and *nutrients.*

Key Vocabulary:

photosynthesis, solar energy, oxygen, carbon dioxide, stomata, chlorophyl.

Review: *compare, contrast*

Supplementary Materials:

For the experiment: Two (or more) plants, aluminum foil, magnifying glasses, assorted green leaves, microscope, prepared slides, plant observation graphic organizer.

For today's follow-up lesson: Venn diagram, drawing materials, chart paper/sticky notes, video clips from United Streaming, animated clip accompanying science text, adapted passage of text from student science book, photo cards with pictures of different types of green plants and leaves, Four Corner Vocabulary Chart, interactive science notebooks, glue.

SIOP Features

Preparation		Scaffolding		Grouping Options	
X	Adaptation of content	X	Modeling	X	Whole class
X	Links to background	X	Guided practice	X	Small groups
X	Links to past learning	X	Independent practice	X	Partners
X	Strategies incorporated	X	Comprehensible input	X	Independent

Integration of Processes		Application		Assessment	
X	Reading	X	Hands-on	X	Individual
X	Writing	X	Meaningful	X	Group
X	Speaking	X	Linked to objectives	X	Written
X	Listening	X	Promotes engagement	X	Oral

Lesson Sequence:

NOTE: This lesson is part of a class structured into work stations. Students move through these stations after a brief introduction to the objectives. The class of 19 is divided into groups of 4 and 5. Stations are as follows:

(continued)

Continued.

1. <u>Small Group Working with the Teacher</u>: Students create a Venn diagram of the experiment results and use this information to explain the role photosynthesis played in the similarities and differences between the two plants.

2. <u>Science Technology Station</u>: Students view videos related to photosynthesis. Students work individually.

3. <u>Science Writing</u>: Students create the labeled diagram and write a summary paragraph. Students work either independently or with a partner, depending upon their language and content proficiency.

4. <u>Science Reading</u>: Students reread the adapted text related to the subject matter, highlight the vocabulary words and context clues, and fill in the vocabulary graphic organizer in their interactive notebooks. Students work either independently or with a partner, depending upon their language and content proficiency.

Content and Language Objectives:

● Read content and language objectives to students. Students repeat them chorally. Clarify meaning of objectives, if needed.

Building Background:

● Students are asked what they know about the needs of plants. Students work with their table group (each has 3–4 students) to write what they know on sticky notes, which they place on a KWL (Ogle, 1986) chart at the front of the room. Results are shared. Picture cards are reviewed, and live plants/leaves shown to make certain that students know language required prior to this lesson: *leaf, stem, top, bottom, grow, dark, light*. Since school is in an agricultural region and many students' parents are farm workers, this link is also made. Connections are also made with gardens.

● Students are briefly introduced to the photosynthesis diagram in the textbook, shown with document camera (with the vocabulary word labels missing). Their general knowledge from previous lessons is assessed through questioning. Students think-pair-share to arrive at the missing words and the labels are filled in with student input.

Guided Practice:

● Brief instructions are given for each work station. Students are already familiar with the routine, and written directions are posted at each station, with illustrations. Groups are formed heterogeneously so all students will have access to the information needed to proceed.

● *Small Group Working with the Teacher:* Students observe the experiment that was begun a week ago—two similar plants have been growing under different conditions. One has the leaves covered with aluminum foil; the other does not. At this time, students take foil from one leaf, observe the changes, and then discuss the differences within the small group and with the teacher. Observations are recorded on a Venn diagram—the teacher models and students copy the information. Students are questioned regarding the results—mostly why these changes have occurred. Students think-pair-share to respond, and then share with the small group. Students are led to make connections to the process of photosynthesis. They complete a sentence frame at the bottom of the graphic organizer:

The uncovered leaves looked _____, *but the covered leaves looked* _____.

This happened because _____.

Practice & Application:

● *Science Technology:* Students watch short video clips on photosynthesis. They complete short answer cloze questions prepared to accompany the videos. Students are allowed to compare responses after they view the videos and make necessary corrections.

Continued.

- *Science Writing:* Students will label diagrams similar to those reviewed at the beginning of the lesson. They will have a word bank available for reference. After completing the diagram, they will use a sentence frame organizer to review the process of photosynthesis orally with the group. For example:

  - *First, the sun shines on the* _____

  - *Next, plants take in* _____.

  - *They also take in* _____ *from the air, and* _____ *and* _____ *from the soil.*

  - *Finally, plants give off* _____.

Students will glue this organizer with the completed diagram and paragraph into their interactive science notebooks.

- *Science Reading:* Students will reread a passage of adapted text taken from their science books titled, "How do plants get energy?" They will highlight the vocabulary words (as shown in the word bank and on the diagram accompanying the passage), as well as the context words that help them understand the vocabulary. Students will use a Four Corner Vocabulary Chart (includes an illustration, a student-created definition, a sentence using the word, and the word) to review and practice the words, and will glue this in their interactive science notebook. Students will be accountable for varying numbers of words—depending upon their levels. (Groups will have differentiated product instructions at each station.) Students will orally read with a partner or small group.

Review & Assessment:

- After the rotation time has been completed, students will work independently to complete their choice of assessment: a summary paragraph and illustration, a labeled diagram, or a completed cloze paragraph using a word bank.

- As time allows, various student products are displayed using the document camera, with positive comments or questions from the class.

Wrap Up:

- Students again read the content and language objectives chorally.

- Teacher selects random students to briefly review the process of photosynthesis using the poster.

- Tickets Out: Students do a stand-up, hands-up, pair-up activity using a blank diagram of the process of photosynthesis (arrows, but no words are on the diagram). Their assignment: Explain what you have learned about this diagram today. Pretend that your partner has never seen the diagram before.

- Students give thumbs up if they met the objective and thumbs level if they think more time is needed before they really understand the objectives.

LESSON PLAN   Major Contributions to the Scientific Revolution

(Todd Ferguson, Social Studies Teacher, Mabelvale Magnet Middle School, Little Rock School District, AR)

SIOP Lesson Title: Major Contributors to the Scientific Revolution	**Teacher:** Todd Ferguson	**Grade:** 8

Content Standards:

H.6.8.9: Identify major contributors of the Scientific Revolution (e.g., Muhammed Al-Khwarizmi, Francis Bacon, Nicholas Copernicus, Galileo, Johannes Kepler, Isaac Newton, Zhang Heng.).

H.6.8.12: Investigate influences on modern society of Enlightenment thinkers including but not limited to John Locke, Baron de Monte, Jacques Rousseau.

RH KID 1- Cite specific textual evidence to support analysis of primary and secondary sources.

Key Vocabulary:

Copernicus, Kepler, Galileo, Newton, Descartes, Thomas Hobbes, Montesquieu, Voltaire, Diderot

Visuals/Resources/Supplementary Materials:

Students will use textbook and primary/secondary source documents to determine the significant accomplishments of their assigned major contributor. Dictionaries, thesaurus (both online and hard copy), and a list of online sites will be used by students to find synonyms and figurative language.

Content Objective:

Day 1

Students will determine three significant accomplishments of one major contributor of the Scientific Revolution.

Language Objective:

Day 1

Students will build on the ideas of others in their group and express their own ideas clearly using the following sentence frame:

The accomplishments of (name of major contributor) are significant because ___

Day 1

Introduce the content and language objectives for the day.

Building Background:

Help students think about how we learn about historical figures and place that knowledge in our long-term working memory.

- Arrange students into groups of three. Students will remain in these triads throughout the lesson.

- Display photos, no names, of recognizable figures on the interactive white board. Examples of recognizable figures might be Benjamin Franklin, Abraham Lincoln, Martin Luther King Jr., or even Michael Jordan.

- Ask groups to discuss the recognizable figures using the following questions:

  1. Who is this person?

  2. What are two major contributions this person is known for?

- Allow 2–3 minutes for students to discuss the questions with their table partners.

- Allow each group to share their answers with the whole class.

Visit each group to determine if their discussions are appropriate and on topic. Also help students who have trouble identifying the recognizable figures.

Continued.

- Use one of the Think Before You Answer (p. 115) techniques to ask the following questions:

    1. What do you know about this person?

    2. Do you remember when you first learned about this person?

    3. How do we learn about people we may not be interested in so that we can remember them and their accomplishments beyond the test?

- Title a large piece of chart paper "Ways to Remember" and chart the students' answers. (See sample chart.)

> This whole class discussion should help the teacher assess how aware the students are of their own learning.

Ways to Remember
  1. Find something you have in common with this person.
  2. _____
  3. _____
  4. _____
  5. _____
  One thing I have in common with _____
  is _____

Introduce the concept of a significant contribution.

Teacher asks - Who is Michael Jordan?

Student answers - A basketball player.

Teacher asks - So What? What makes Michael Jordan more important than other basketball players?

> Circulate and listen to students' discussions to determine how well they understand the concept of *significant*.

- Use one of the Think Before You Answer Techniques (p. 115) for the following:

    1. Compare a significant accomplishment—one that will probably be remembered for years or centuries—to an accomplishment or detail that only close friends and family will remember.

    2. Call on several students to share their discussions.

    3. Title a chart, "Characteristics of Significant Accomplishments" and chart student answers. (See sample below.)

Characteristics of Significant Accomplishments	
Not Significant	**Significant**
Had five children.	Discovered the solar system is heliocentric.
The accomplishments of ___ are significant because ___	

(continued)

Continued.

● Write the following sentence frame at the bottom of the poster, "The accomplishments of ___ are significant because ___"

Meaningful Activities:

● Tell students that today they will be looking for significant accomplishments of major contributors of the Scientific Revolution. They are looking for what Todd Ferguson calls the *So What Factor* or the bigger purpose for learning.

● Ask students to look at the Time Lines on the Ceiling (p. 74) and locate the Scientific Revolution.

● Assign one of the following significant contributors to each of the groups: Copernicus, Kepler, Galileo, Newton, Descartes, Thomas Hobbes, Montesquieu, Voltaire, Diderot.

Visit each group to make sure they understand how to use their resources and if they are selecting significant accomplishments.

● Each group member will use his or her resources to determine one significant accomplishment for the assigned contributor.

● Go over the resources students will use to research their significant accomplishments.

● Remind students to refer to the poster they charted—"Characteristics of Significant Accomplishments."

● Point to the sentence frame at the bottom of the poster.

● Tell students to complete the sentence frames about their assigned contributor. The first blank is for the name of their assigned contributor.

The accomplishments of (name of major contributor) are significant because ___

● Students should share their sentence frame with the other two group members.

Visit each group and provide feedback on the significant accomplishments they recorded.

● Tell students to use the "Characteristics of Significant Accomplishments" poster to decide if the accomplishments chosen by the group members are significant. The teacher can model how to use the poster as a checklist.

● Have students share their sentence frames in a Pairs Squared (p. 110) activity.

● For tickets out the door, students should complete this sentence frame on their own:

  • One thing I have in common with (name of the major contributor) is ___

Continued.

Content Objective:

Day 2

Students will develop three clues about the significant accomplishments of one major contributor of the Scientific Revolution.

Language Objective:

Day 2

Students will use and pronounce correctly the names of major contributors of the Scientific Revolution to discuss their significant contributions.

Day 2

Building Background:

Go over the content and language objectives.

● Have students share the sentence frames they wrote for their Tickets In in a Pairs Squared activity (p. 110).

● After the activity, have students look over the "Ways to Remember" poster they created on Day 1 and share with their table partners how they remembered certain significant contributors of the Scientific Revolution. Ask: What makes it easy to remember this person? What makes it difficult to remember this person?

● Arrange students in their original groups from Day 1.

● Help the whole class with the pronunciation of each major contributor.

● Post the stressed syllable within the name using all capitalized letters written phonetically for each major contributor. Most textbooks provide this when introducing the name or a key term.

● Model pronouncing each name while pointing to the phonetic spelling.

● Tell students to practice pronouncing the name of their major contributor in their group. They can reread their sentence frames to practice pronouncing the names.

Meaningful Activities:

● The groups will Riddle Brainteaser (p. 137) about their major contributor by turning the three significant accomplishments they researched on Day 1 into clues.

● Model this process by providing a sample riddle for students to solve.

Sample Riddles:

(Ptolemy)   *I am a self-centered astronomer from Egypt; I see the universe only from my perspective. While others thought I might be eccentric; I was really just geocentric.*

(Copernicus)   *Though from Poland, my mind lived in space. The universe was not yet metric, but at least I knew it was heliocentric.*

Visit each group to help with pronouncing the names.

Visit each group to assess their writing of the clues and provide help when needed.

(continued)

Continued.

(Kepler)   *There are so many smart people who talk about the universe and their words abound. But the planets move more like a serving platter than a pizza pan, which is round.*

- The groups can work in class to write the three clues.
- Students can find synonyms for the clues for homework.

Content Objective:

Day 3

Students will infer the answers to the riddles written by their peers by reading the clues, referring to their resources, and collaborating with their group members.

Language Objective:

Day 3

Students will use figurative language to describe the major contributions of their assigned significant contributor.

Day 3

Meaningful Activities:

- Students continue to work in their original groups of three.
- Students share their synonyms with their groups.
- Work with students on how to write similes and metaphors and allow time for students to add figurative language to their clues. (Some groups might be able to write one simile for one of their clues, while other groups might use figurative language in all three of their clues.)
- Students write their completed riddles on chart paper without the answers.
- Post the riddles around the room.
- Students move from poster to poster, with their assigned group, to guess the answer to each riddle. Students are encouraged to use their resources to help them guess the riddles.
- Each group posts a sticky note with their guess and why they think their guess is the right answer to the riddle using the following sentence frame:

  - We think the answer to this riddle is ___ because the riddle says ___

- After all of the groups have posted a sticky note guess on each riddle poster, the class reviews each riddle and their sticky note guesses with the teacher using Verbal Scaffolding for Higher-Order Questions (p. 99).

Review the content and language objectives.

Tickets out: Students complete the following sentence frames:

- The contributions of ___ are the most significant to me because ___

- The contributions of ___ are the most significant to society because ___

Visit each group and read each riddle. Help correct errors or misconceptions before providing chart paper to the group.

Walk around and listen to the groups discuss their guesses to the riddles to assess student comprehension.

Continued.

Students from one class can try and solve the riddles from other classes throughout the week. At the end of the week the teacher can post the riddles for each major contributor all together on the same wall space and ask students to identify common themes used in each riddle.

LESSON PLAN   A Zentangled Self-Portrait

(Rosemarie Olheiser, Grade 7–8 Art Teacher, O'Brien STEM Academy, Washoe County School District, NV)

Key: SW = Students will;	TW = Teacher will;	HOTS: Higher-Order Thinking Skills

SIOP Lesson: Zentangled Faces   **Subject:** Art   **Grade level:** 7–8

Content Standard:

Visual Arts: Interpret artwork based on various characteristics such as themes, styles, purposes, and subject matter.

WIDA or ELD Standard (Language Focus):

ELA: Acquire and use accurately grade-appropriate general academic and domain-specific words and phrases; gather vocabulary when considering a word or phrase important to comprehension expression.

Key Vocabulary:

abstract art, counter drawings, Zentangling (like doodling, it is a creative form of self-expression), string line, positive space, negative space.

HOTS (Higher-Order Thinking Skills):

How do I organize my learning into a set of steps for drawing people that works for me?

Supplementary Materials:

5" × 11" paper—anatomy proportioning; 8.5" × 11" sheet of copy paper per student; gesture drawing warm-up; pencils; Zentangle pattern folders; PowerPoint® slides with objectives and Zentangle examples

Connections to Students' Background Experiences and Past Learning:

Previous lesson: Explain to students that before they can be expected to draw a person, they need to have a general idea of anatomical structure. People, in general, are better looking if their body proportions are symmetrical (review symmetrical and asymmetrical). Monsters or cartoon characters are more interesting, if not better looking, when their proportions are not.

Links to Past Learning:

Remind students that as in earlier lessons they cannot contort human features until they know the general structure of human anatomy. Remind students to remember that the basic unit in figure drawing is the model's head, from top to chin.

Content Objective(s):	**Meaningful Activities/ Lesson Sequence:**	**Review & Assessment:**
Students will explain how one's own artwork employs various visual characteristics to communicate.	TW go over content and language objectives on PowerPoint® slides. (G1)	Ask if there are questions about the objectives; clarify, if needed.
Language Objective(s):	TW review key vocabulary. Ask students to add words to their note sheets, if necessary (for new students). (G1)	
Students will define "Zentangling" to a partner and explain why they think it's an interesting technique to use; or if they don't care for it, explain why.	TW have students examine the examples of pervious students' and other artists' Zentangle creations. (G1)	
Students will participate in the Zentangle discussion.		

Continued.

Students will write an explanation about how realistic and abstract self-portraits tell the viewer something about you.

SW share with partners if they like Zengangle, and if so why. If students don't like it, why? (G3)

SW trace the contour lines of students' previously drawn self-portrait. (G4)

SW add unusual shapes to the facial features of the drawings. (G4)

SW draw a string line in the negative space of the portrait. (G4)

Observe and listen to student responses about Zentangle.

Model and project how to do this; observe students as they trace the contours on their self-portraits.

Ms. Olheiser's example of Zentangling portrait.

Rosemarie Olheiser

TW tell students they are to Zentangle 99–100% of the composition. Show an example of a Zentangle with about 100% covered; show example with much less. (G1)

With a partner, SW talk about and then write an explanation of how Zentangle portraits (abstract) and self-portraits (realistic) tell the viewer something about you. (G3)

Remind students, as needed, about how to draw the string line, and then observe.

Circulate and help, as needed.

Have partners share their writings with other table group members. Assess understanding with the written explanation.

Grouping Configurations: 1. Whole class 2. Small groups 3. Partners 4. Independent

Identify in Lesson Sequence which grouping configurations will be used, by marking G1, G2, G3, or G4.

Wrap Up/Review/Assessment: If time, ask one or two students to share with the class how their abstract and realistic art tells about them as individuals. Review content and language objectives.

LESSON PLAN   Introduction to Solids and Surface Area
(Stephen Lanford, Math Teacher, Mabelvale Magnet Middle School, Little Rock School District, AR)

Teacher: Stephen Lanford

SIOP Lesson: Introduction to Solids and Surface Area	**Subject:** Math	**Grade Level:** 7th

Content Standards:	**ELD Standard (Language Focus):**
G.8.7.1 - Identify, draw, classify, and compare geometric figures using models and real world examples	Content vocabulary and plurals
G.10.7.2 - Plot points that form the vertices of a geometric figure and draw, identify, and classify the figure	
G.11.7.1 - Build three-dimensional solids from two-dimensional patterns (nets)	
M.13.7.4 - Derive and use formulas for surface area and volume of prisms and cylinders and justify them using geometric models and common materials	

Key Vocabulary:	**Supplementary Materials:**
Three-dimensional shapes, solid, face–faces, edge–edges, vertex–vertices	Locate images to represent math vocabulary words, main concepts, and other vocabulary words that might be unfamiliar to English learners.
HOTS (Higher-Order Questions and Tasks): The students will be asked to work in pairs to answer 6 questions about three-dimensional shapes	Geometry Block manipulatives, Khan Academy website, iPads, Mangaghigh website

Connections to Students' Background Experiences and Past Learning:

Introduce the lesson's vocabulary words using the following sentence frame:

"Three-dimensional shapes are made up of _____" and showing the following images on the smart board:

1. a lot of faces
2. present being wrapped
3. net of cube and cylinder
4. solid with parts labeled: faces, edges, verteces
5. web chart of solids
6. cube, pyramid, cylinder, prism

Content Objective:	**Meaningful Activities/Lesson Sequence:**	**Review & Assessment:**
You will be able to identify solids by their base.	Discuss content and language objectives.	
You will solve real-world problems related to the concept of surface area.	Introduce content by introducing vocabulary (See Building Background).	

Continued.

Language Objective:

You will describe a three-dimensional shape (solid) using either the singular or the plural of the following vocabulary words: *face*, *edge*, and *vertex*.

Pair students heterogeneously by putting higher functioning students with lower functioning students. Think about all kinds of skills such as language proficiency, math ability, or ability to work with others. Even though the students are functioning at different ability levels, make sure the groups are compatible by pairing students that are only a little above or below the level of the other students.

The pairs will work to answer the following questions:

1. What is the difference between 2D and 3D shapes?

2. What is the name of the shape of your desk?

3. Create at least two rules to name or label any solid.

4. How would you describe surface area?

5. How would you find the surface area of this cube?

6. Would the same rules work to find the surface area of a cylinder?

Provide a visual for each question. Then, one question at a time, have students work in pairs to answer the question using the Talking Tokens Activity (p. 146)

After the groups have been able to discuss each question, the teacher leads the class in discussion. The teacher can put the visual that has been used throughout the lesson on an interactive white board or a document camera so that the class will have context for their discussions. The students will practice and apply the content and language using one of the following differentiated products:

Activity #1: Divide students into groups of three. The group will build and calculate three different solids—a type of pyramid, a type of prism, and the third choice is up to the group. Since there are three students, each student can take the lead on one of the shapes, essentially jigsawing the process. Using construction paper, the group will make a template or "net" of each solid. They will calculate the area of each section of the net, and write this on the net before taping it together. Students must be able to identify each solid, calculate its surface area, and label the faces, edges, and verteces.

Activity #2 - Students will work on their own to play a Math Prodigi game on Mangahigh. Students should select 3-D Shapes. This game asks students to compete against the clock to identify types of solids. There are

The teacher should monitor the groups carefully. It may be necessary to adjust if the students are not engaging in the activity. Some adjustments might be to discuss one of the questions in the whole group before having students work in pairs, model with another student how pair work would look and sound, or change up some of the groups if some of the students are not working well together.

The teacher should not rush to answer these questions for the students. Instead, the teacher should encourage students to try and answer the questions even if they are unsure of their answers.

The teacher monitors the students to make sure they understand the concepts.

(continued)

Continued.

three levels students can achieve—bronze, silver, or gold. At the end of the game the students should record their score in their journal and explain the concepts they used to reach the level in the game and what they would need to do in order to reach a higher level. Students should incorporate the terms *surface area, face, edge, vertex,* and *calculate.* You could ask students to complete the following sentence frames:

I used ___ in order to reach level ___

In order to reach a higher level I would need to ___

Activity #3 - Students work individually to match Geoblock manipulatives to their corresponding net and identify each solid by its base. Pair up students to share their results. Students can use sentence frames like:

I think this base corresponds to the ___ because ___
What do you think?

Then students choose three of the solids and calculate the surface area of each. This can be done the same way individually and then the students pair up to check their answers.

Meaningful Activities/Lesson Sequence:

Teach a mini-lesson on plurals by holding up one book and asking students what the name of this is. When students say, "a book," write the word *book* on the board. Then hold up two books and ask, "What do you call these?" When students say, "books" or "two books," write the word *books* on the board.

Ask students to talk to their partner about the different ways we make words plural in English. They may come up with "add *-es* to the end of the word," or they may remember that some words are irregular like fish and geese.

Using visuals from the building background lesson, teach the students the plural of the words: *face, edge* and *vertex.* Vertex will be the challenging word.

Ask students to listen for the words *face, edge,* and *vertex,* and their plural forms as they watch a video on surface area. (Khan Academy)

Have students work in pairs to summarize the video using the words *face, edge, vertex,* and/or their plural forms.

Review & Assessment:

The teacher should monitor student conversations to assess their understanding of the concepts and how to use the vocabulary.

Continued.

Students with less English can be given the following cloze sentences to complete:

The sides of any three-dimensional shape are called ___

Where the ___ meet, ___ are formed.

The point where ___ meet is called a ___

English learners in the beginning stages of learning English could benefit from visuals that are labeled to help them complete the cloze activity.

Wrap-up:

After reviewing the objectives, have students complete Exit Tickets using the following sentence frames:

Today I learned _____

Today I had questions about _____

LESSON PLAN   "A Rose for Emily"

(Lois Hardaway and Isabel Ramirez, Grade 11 Sheltered ELA Teachers, Lewisville High School, Lewisville, TX)

Teachers: Lois Hardaway and Isabel Ramirez

SIOP Lesson Title: "A Rose for Emily" by William Faulkner   **Grade:** 11   **Subject:** ELA

Content Standards:

TEKS110.31(b),(2),(5) Reading/Comprehension of Literary Text/Fiction. Students understand, make inferences and draw conclusion about the structure and elements of fiction and provide evidence from text to support their understanding. Students are expected to analyze non-linear plot development (foreshadowing) and compare it to linear plot development.

Key Vocabulary:	**Visuals/Resources/Supplementary Materials:**
lime (not the fruit, but the mineral), day laborer, cling, indentation, chronology phrases such as: thirty years before, two years after, a short time after	copy of Faulkner's short story, "A Rose for Emily," guided reading questions for "A Rose for Emily," quizzes, teacher made timeline, large butcher paper or large dry erase boards, dictionaries

---

Content Objective:	**Day 1**	**Review/Assessment:**
Day 1 Discuss the characteristics of the literary device flashback.	Introduce the content and language objectives for the day.	
Language Objective:	**Building Background:**	
Day 1 Students will use the following phrases to tell their memories in chronological order: . . . years ago . . . years before . . . years after . . . a short time after	Introduce the concept of flashback. "A Rose for Emily" by William Faulkner can be difficult for students to comprehend because it is not told in chronological order. Before reading the text, help students think about the connection between our memories and the literary device flashback. Tell students to write down two or three of their favorite memories, and allow time for them to share with another student.	As the students write down their memories, the teacher walks around the room to monitor their answers, checking to see if the memories were recorded in chronological order or not.

Students will read closely to determine what the text says explicitly and to make logical inferences from it.	Talk about the memories students wrote down in a whole group discussion and connect memories to the concept of chronology. The students may not have shared their memories in chronological order; point that out.
	
	Ask:
	
	    Can we remember things out of order?
	
	    Do we always have to go back to the beginning to remember?	

Continued.

Introduce the chronology phrases:

... years ago

... years before

... years after

... a short time after

Tell students to rewrite the memories they recorded in chronological order using the chronology phrases. The teacher can model this by using a list of his/her own memories. Students work on their own to rewrite their memories.	The teacher walks around the room to monitor students' use of the chronolgy phrases.

Allow students time to share the memories they recorded in chronological order.

Introduce the idea of flashback by verbally scaffolding the conversation.

Meaningful Activities:

Read the first two or three paragraphs of the short story "A Rose for Emily" in class.

The teacher can read the passage or call on individual students to read.

Isabel Ramirez says, "My English students can't always get the phrasing right, and so I read the passages aloud so the students can concentrate on the meaning."

Point out the chronology phrases used in the text, and verbally scaffold the conversation* to draw students' attention to how Faulkner uses the literary device of flashback to construct the chronology of the short story.	As students answer the guided reading questions, the teacher circulates to assess student answers.

Hand out the Adapted Text Guided Reading Questions for "A Rose for Emily."

Model how to answer the first question. Provide time for students to answer the second question on their own, and ask for volunteers to share their answers. Provide feedback to their answers.

Explain and model turning a question into a sentence.	When students share their answers to the first couple of questions, the teacher monitors their responses and provides feedback.
Students read the first two sections of "A Rose for Emily" and answer the Adapted Text Guided Reading Questions, 3–26. (The first two questions were answered in class.)	

(continued)

Continued.

See Adapted Text Guided Reading Questions for "A Rose for Emily."

Review the content and language objectives.

Content Objective:

Day 2

Students will determine the central themes in "A Rose for Emily" by analyzing the flashbacks and foreshadowing used in the text.

Language Objective:

Day 2

Students will read closely to determine what the text says explicitly and to make logical inferences from it.

Students will predict and discuss the outcome of "A Rose for Emily."

Day 2

Meaningful Activities:

Go over the content and language objectives.

Discuss the homework—answers to the Adapted Text Guided Reading Questions—in class using Verbal Scaffolding for Higher-Order Questions. See a sample of student answers to the Adapted Text Guided Reading. Questions for "A Rose for Emily."

After the discussion over the guided reading questions, students take a quiz over sections 1 and 2 using their guided reading questions.

The students are allowed to use their guided reading questions on the quiz.

After the quiz, engage in whole class discussion over the chronology of the first two sections focusing on paragraphs 25 and 28 using Verbal Scaffolding for Questioning.

The teacher goes over passages from the text and creates a timeline of the chronology.

| Miss Emily's father dies and she refuses to allow people in the in the house | Two years later Miss Emily's sweetheart deserts her. | A short time after Miss Emily's sweetheart leaves, a bad smell comes from her house. |

After discussing the timeline, lead the students to the conclusion that the smell can't be coming from the dad using the following questions:

- Why were the men sent to sprinkle lime on Emily's property?

- Why wasn't Emily married before she was thirty?

- Why do you think that Emily won't allow the townspeople to take her dad's body right away?

Help students understand what post-Civil War southern society was like for women by asking the following questions:

As students discuss their answers to the guided reading questions, the teacher assesses student comprehension of the text as well as their English usage.

The teacher engages students in discussion and explanation of their answers as well as provides feedback to any errors in English usage.

The students are reviewing key content and vocabulary as they reread their answers on the guided reading questions in order to complete their quiz.

Assess student comprehension by listening to the students' responses to the questions. If students are discussing the questions in small groups or pairs, the teacher should walk around the room to assess student understanding of the text.

Continued.

- What was a woman's job at this time?

- What was she supposed to do?

- Why would the Grierson family not want Emily to marry a day laborer?

Ask students to focus on paragraph 28, which is one of the quotes on the guided reading questions, and have students complete the following sentence frame on dry erase boards:

I predict the smell is coming from ___ because ___

Students first share their predictions with a partner, and then the teacher calls on individual students to share their predictions.

For homework, students read sections 3, 4, and 5 and answer the Adapted Text Guided Reading Questions 27–44.

Remind students how to turn a question into an answer by asking students, "What are some things to keep in mind when you answer these questions for homework?" Allow students to discuss what they learned about turning questions into statements.

Review the content and language objectives.

The teacher assesses student comprehension by reading and listening to their sentences. Students receive feedback by sharing their sentences with their peers.

If students are not able to verbalize how to turn a question into a statement, model the process again.

Content Objective:	Day 3	
Day 3	**Meaningful Activities:**	
Students will determine the central themes in "A Rose for Emily" by analyzing the flashbacks and foreshadowing used in the text.	Introduce the content and language objectives.	As students discuss their answers to the guided reading questions, the teacher assesses student comprehension of the text as well as their English usage.
	Go over the homework—Adapted Text Guided Reading Questions 27–44 using Verbal Scaffolding of Higher-Order Questions.	
Language Objective:		
Day 3		
Students will participate effectively in a conversation with their peers by building on others' ideas and expressing their own ideas using the following sentence frames:		The teacher engages students in discussion and explanation of their answers as well as provides feedback to any errors in English usage.
We agree with ___ because ___	Students use their answers to the Adapted Text Guided Reading Questions to take a quiz on sections 3, 4, and 5 of "A Rose for Emily."	The students are reviewing key content and vocabulary as they reread their answers on the guided reading questions in order to complete their quiz.
In addition to ___ we think ___		

(continued)

Continued.

Links to Past Learning:

Show the timeline the teacher created yesterday, and ask students to consider what the timeline indicates about the origin of the smell.

Continue to engage students in academic conversation by verbally scaffolding the following questions:

- What does Faulkner mean when he describes the past as, [Teachers should insert a quote from the text for students to interpret.]?

- Think about your childhood. Do your memories of your childhood change?

- So what is a meadow that no winter has touched?

- What is the significance of the word, "indentation" in the very last paragraph?

- Why do they keep sending the ministers to talk to Emily about her behavior?

Use the Chart and Share activity to help students explore the question, *Why is Homer dead?* Require that students record at least two quotes from the text as textual evidence for their answer. Ask students to use one of the following sentence frames when sharing their ideas with the group:

We agree with _____ because _____

In addition to _____ we think _____

For homework, students prepare for engaging in the Pick Ten Words activity. (p. 53). At home, students look for ten words in the text that they think are important for understanding the story. The words must reflect the tone and major themes in "A Rose for Emily." Students provide a definition of each word using a dictionary and must be able to justify why the word they chose is significant to the tone and major themes in the story.

Review the content and language objectives.

The teacher visits the groups as they chart their answers in order to assess student comprehension and help the students with any English usage errors on the posters.

Students both assess and receive feedback on their answers as other students defend their own answers.

Content Objective:	**Day 4**
Day 4	**Meaningful Activities:**
Students will determine the tone and major themes in "A Rose for Emily" using textual evidence to support their answers.	Introduce the content and language objectives. Links to past learning

Continued.

Language Objective:

Day 4

Students will analyze how Faulkner's specific word choices shape the meaning and tone of "A Rose for Emily."

Students have read "The Lottery" and talked about tone. Ask students what they remember about the tone in "The Lottery." Discuss the tone in "A Rose for Emily."

Using their homework as a jumping off point, students engage with their table groups in the Pick Ten Words activity to determine specific words that shape the tone and the most important themes in "A Rose for Emily." Individual students share the words they picked for homework, and then the table comes to consensus on the final ten words and their best definitions. Each group presents the words to the whole class, and then the class chooses ten important words and the best definitions.

These words and definitions will be on the final test.

Review the content and language objectives.

Students will both assess and receive feedback from their peers as they work to come to consensus on which ten words should end up on their group's poster. The teacher should visit each group to assess their progress in choosing the best ten words to represent the themes in "A Rose for Emily" as well as the definitions.

During the whole class share, the students will assess and receive feedback from their peers as they defend their vocabulary choices.

"A Rose for Emily" Study Questions   **Lois Hardaway**

1. Who went to Miss Emily's funeral?

2. What did the women want to see?

3. Who were the only people to see it in the past ten years?

4. What surrounded Miss Emily's house?

5. What does Faulkner mean when he says, [Teachers should insert a quote from the text for students to interpret.]?

6. Why did Colonel Sartoris remit Miss Emily's taxes?

7. What happened when the next generation mailed her tax notices?

8. When the men went to her house to discuss the taxes,

    a. how did the house smell?

    b. how did the house look?

9. Describe Emily at this point in her life (when the men come to visit).

10. What do the words [Teachers should insert a quote from the text for students to interpret.] suggest?

11. How does she react to their questions about her taxes?

12. What is the name of her servant?

13. What did the fathers of these men come to ask her about thirty years before?

14. What does *vanquish* mean?

15. What caused Emily to go out very little?

16. What caused her to become even more reclusive?

17. Why were the women of the town not surprised when the smell developed?

18. Who complained first about the smell?

19. What did the mayor think was causing the smell?

20. What did four men do to help with the smell?

21. What is lime? (Hint: it's not the fruit.)

22. What did people in the town think about the Grierson family?

23. Why was Emily thirty years old and still single?

24. How did the death of her father change the town's opinion of Emily?

25. How did Emily react when the ladies came to offer condolences?

26. For how long did she fight to keep her father?

27. What does Faulkner mean when he writes, [Teachers should insert a quote from the text for students to interpret.]?

28. After her father's burial, how did Emily's appearance change?

29. Describe Homer Baron.

30. Why didn't the public take their relationship seriously?

31. Why does the public call her "poor Emily"?

32. The public says this about her "behind their hands." What does this mean?

33. What does Emily buy from the druggist?

Continued.

34. What does she let him believe it is for?

35. What does the town believe she is going to do with it?

36. What did the Baptist minister go to Emily's house to talk to her about?

37. How does the town feel about the cousins who come from Alabama?

38. What convinces the town that Emily and Homer are married?

39. Where was the last place Homer Baron is seen?

40. What color is Emily's hair when the public next sees her?

41. What kind of lessons did she give for extra money for a short while?

42. What part of the house did she shut up?

43. What does Faulkner mean when he describes [Teachers should insert a quote from the text for students to interpret.]?

44. What was in the room that no one had seen in forty years?

45. What was on the pillow?

Final Thoughts

While we hope that you find the activities in this book helpful, what is most important is that you incorporate consistently SIOP's thirty instructional features in whatever way works best for you and your students. The activities you select and use are always negotiable and dependent on your students' strengths and needs and the content and language you are teaching. We hope you will enjoy using and adapting some or all of the 99 ideas and activities, and that they will serve as a springboard for new activities that will enhance your lessons and enrich the academic lives of your English learners . . . as well as all your other students!

Appendix A: SIOP Protocol (Abbreviated)

The Sheltered Instruction Observation Protocol (SIOP)®
(Echevarria, Vogt, & Short, 2000, 2004, 2008, 2013, 2014a, 2014b)

Observer(s): _____

Date: _____

Grade: _____

ESL Level: _____

School: _____

Teacher: _____

Class/Topic: _____

Lesson: Multi-day Single-day (circle one)

Total Points Possible: 120 (Subtract 4 points for each NA given) _____

Total Points Earned: _____   Percentage Score: _____

Directions: Circle the number that best reflects what you observe in a sheltered lesson. You may give a score from 0–4 (or NA on selected items). Cite under "Comments" specific examples of the behaviors observed.

	Highly Evident		Somewhat Evident		Not Evident	
Lesson Preparation	4	3	2	1	0	
1. **Content objectives** clearly defined, displayed, and reviewed with students	☐	☐	☐	☐	☐	
2. **Language objectives** clearly defined, displayed, and reviewed with students	☐	☐	☐	☐	☐	
3. **Content concepts** appropriate for age and educational background level of students	☐	☐	☐	☐	☐	
4. **Supplementary materials** used to a high degree, making the lesson clear and meaningful (e.g., computer programs, graphs, models, visuals)	☐	☐	☐	☐	☐	N/A
5. **Adaptation of content** (e.g., text, assignment) to all levels of student proficiency	☐	☐	☐	☐	☐	☐
6. **Meaningful activities** that integrate lesson concepts (e.g., surveys, letter writing, simulations, constructing models) with language practice opportunities for reading, writing, listening, and/or speaking	☐	☐	☐	☐	☐	

Comments:

	4	3	2	1	0	N/A
Building Background						
7. **Concepts explicitly linked** to students' background experiences	☐	☐	☐	☐	☐	☐
8. **Links explicitly made** between past learning and new concepts	☐	☐	☐	☐	☐	
9. **Key vocabulary** emphasized (e.g., introduced, written, repeated, and highlighted for students to see)	☐	☐	☐	☐	☐	

Comments:

	4	3	2	1	0
Comprehensible Input					
10. **Speech** appropriate for students' proficiency level (e.g., slower rate, enunciation, and simple sentence structure for beginners)	☐	☐	☐	☐	☐
11. **Clear explanation** of academic tasks	☐	☐	☐	☐	☐
12. **A variety of techniques** used to make content concepts clear (e.g., modeling, visuals, hands-on activities, demonstrations, gestures, body language)	☐	☐	☐	☐	☐

Comments:

(continued)

SIOP Protocol Continued.

	Highly Evident	Somewhat Evident			Not Evident
Strategies	4	3	2	1	0
13. Ample opportunities provided for students to use **learning strategies**	☐	☐	☐	☐	☐
14. **Scaffolding techniques** consistently used assisting and supporting student understanding (e.g., think-alouds)	☐	☐	☐	☐	☐
15. A variety of **questions or tasks that promote higher-order thinking skills** (e.g., literal, analytical, and interpretive questions)	☐	☐	☐	☐	☐

Comments:

	Highly Evident	Somewhat Evident			Not Evident	N/A
Interaction	4	3	2	1	0	
16. Frequent opportunities for **interaction** and discussion between teacher/student and among students, which encourage elaborated responses about lesson concepts	☐	☐	☐	☐	☐	
17. **Grouping configurations** support language and content objectives of the lesson	☐	☐	☐	☐	☐	
18. Sufficient **wait time for student** responses consistently provided	☐	☐	☐	☐	☐	
19. Ample opportunities for students to **clarify key concepts in L1** as needed with aide, peer, or L1 text	☐	☐	☐	☐	☐	☐

Comments:

	Highly Evident	Somewhat Evident			Not Evident	N/A
Practice & Application	4	3	2	1	0	
20. **Hands-on materials and/or manipulatives** provided for students to practice using new content knowledge	☐	☐	☐	☐	☐	☐
21. Activities provided for students to **apply content and language knowledge** in the classroom	☐	☐	☐	☐	☐	☐
22. Activities integrate all **language skills** (i.e., reading, writing, listening, and speaking)	☐	☐	☐	☐	☐	

Comments:

	Highly Evident	Somewhat Evident			Not Evident
Lesson Delivery	4	3	2	1	0
23. **Content objectives** clearly supported by lesson delivery	☐	☐	☐	☐	☐
24. **Language objectives** clearly supported by lesson delivery	☐	☐	☐	☐	☐
25. **Students engaged** approximately 90% to 100% of the period	☐	☐	☐	☐	☐
26. **Pacing** of the lesson appropriate to students' ability level	☐	☐	☐	☐	☐

Comments:

	Highly Evident	Somewhat Evident			Not Evident
Review & Assessment	4	3	2	1	0
27. Comprehensive **review of key vocabulary**	☐	☐	☐	☐	☐
28. Comprehensive **review of key content concepts**	☐	☐	☐	☐	☐
29. Regular **feedback** provided to students on their output (e.g., language, content, work)	☐	☐	☐	☐	☐
30. **Assessment of student comprehension and learning** of all lesson objectives (e.g., spot checking, group response) throughout the lesson	☐	☐	☐	☐	☐

Comments:

Appendix B: Process Verbs and Products Matched to the Taxonomy for Learning, Teaching, and Assessing

Level	Process Verbs	Products
Create	compose, propose, formulate, assemble, construct, set up, manage, plan, design, pretend, revise, blend, arrange, collect, create, invent, develop, hypothesize, generalize, originate, derive, compile, predict, act, modify, suppose, reorganize	film, poem, story, formula, machine, design, blueprint, goal, plan, play, solution, cartoon, new game, invention, video, event, newspaper
Evaluate	judge, evaluate, appraise, rate, compare, value, validate, defend, probe, assess, measure, decide, revise, conclude, evaluate, determine, justify, support, prioritize, recommend, reject, referee, debate, award, score, choose estimate	investigation, opinion, report, survey, editorial, debate, scale, conclusion, review, recommendation, critique, verdict, estimation
Analyze	distinguish, calculate, test, question, solve, analyze, research, question, characterize, appraise, interpret, diagram, experiment, compare, contrast, examine, scrutinize, dissect, probe, discover, categorize, investigate, order, differentiate, sift, sort, deduce	diagram, checklist, investigation, chart, graph, outline, conclusion, list, category, plan, illustration, survey, inventory, database, graphic organizer, rubric, matrix
Apply	teach, apply, employ, adapt, show, manipulate, exhibit, relate, solve illustrate, operate, schedule, calculate, interview, collect, interpret, change, dramatize, prepare, record, construct, make, translate, use	puzzle, prediction, scrapbook, drawing, demonstration, diary, photograph, report, illustration, diorama, simulation, poster, sculpture, experiment, lesson
Understand	restate, describe, explain, paraphrase, report, tell, discuss, recognize, summarize, locate, review, list, research, locate, calculate, convert, outline, expand upon, annotate, give example, give main idea	recitation, example, summary, definition, reproduction, quiz, collection, list, explanation, test, dramatization, label, show & tell, outline
Remember	define, repeat, list, name, label, memorize, record, recall, match, locate, show, select, group, quote, underline, recite, distinguish, cite, choose, give example, sort, describe, reproduce	quiz, label, definition, list, test, worksheet, workbook.

Based on Anderson, L. W., & Krathwohl, D. R. (Eds.). (2001). *Taxonomy for learning, teaching, and assessing: A revision of Bloom's Taxonomy of Educational Objectives.* Boston, MA: Longman as cited in *Making Content Comprehensible for English Learners: The SIOP® Model,* 4th ed.; pp. 124-125

References

Allen, J. (2007). *Inside words: Tools for teaching academic vocabulary, grades 4-12.* Portland, ME: Stenhouse Publishers.

Anderson, L. W., & Krathwohl, D. R. (Eds.). (2001). *Taxonomy for learning, teaching, and assessing: A revision of Bloom's Taxonomy of Educational Objectives.* Boston, MA: Longman.

Bear, D. R., Helman, L., Invernizzi, M., Templeton, S., & Johnston, F. (2011). *Words their way with English learners: Word study for spelling, phonics, and vocabulary instruction.* (2nd ed.). Boston, MA: Pearson.

Bloom, B., Engelhart, M., Furst, E., Hill, W., & Krathwohl D. (Eds.). (1956). *Taxonomy of educational objectives: The classification of educational goals. Handbook I: Cognitive domain.* New York, NY: David McKay Co.

Common Core State Standards. (2010). Retrieved from www.doe.in.gov/commoncore

Echevarría, J. (2012). *Effective practices for increasing the achievement of English learners.* Washington, DC: Center for Research on the Educational Achievement and Teaching of English Language Learners. Retrieved from http://www.cal.org/create/resources/pubs/

Echevarría, J., Richards-Tutor, C., Canges, R., & Francis, D. (2011). Using the SIOP Model to promote the acquisition of language and science concepts with English learners. *Bilingual Research Journal, 34*(3), 334–351.

Echevarría, J., Richards-Tutor, C., Chinn, V., & Ratleff, P. (2011). Did they get it? The role of fidelity in teaching English learners. *Journal of Adolescent and Adult Literacy, 54*(6), 425–434.

Echevarría, J., & Short, D. (2010). Programs and practices for effective sheltered content instruction. In California Department of Education (Ed.), *Improving education for English learners: Research-based approaches* (pp. 250–321). Sacramento, CA: CDE Press.

Echevarría, J., & Short, D. (2011). *The SIOP Model: A professional development framework for comprehensive schoolwide intervention.* Washington, DC: Center for Research on the Educational Achievement and Teaching of English Language Learners. Retrieved from http://www.cal.org/create/resources/pubs/professional-development-framework.html

Echevarría, J., Short, D., & Peterson, C. (2012). *Using the SIOP Model with Pre-K and kindergarten English learners.* Boston, MA: Pearson.

Echevarría, J., Short, D., Richards-Tutor, C., & Himmel, J. (in press). Using the SIOP Model as a professional development framework for comprehensive schoolwide intervention. In J. Echevarría, S. Vaughn, & D. Francis (Eds.), *English learners in content area classes: Teaching for achievement in the middle grades.* Boston, MA: Pearson.

Echevarría, J., Vogt, M.E., & Short, D. (2010). *The SIOP Model for teaching mathematics to English learners.* Boston, MA: Pearson.

Echevarría, J., Vogt, M.E., & Short, D. (2013). *Making content comprehensible for English learners: The SIOP Model* (4th ed.). Boston, MA: Pearson.

Echevarría, J., Vogt, M.E., & Short, D. (2014a). *Making content comprehensible for elementary English learners: The SIOP Model* (2nd ed.). Boston, MA: Pearson.

Echevarría, J., Vogt, M.E., & Short, D. (2014b). *Making content comprehensible for English learners: The SIOP Model* (2nd ed.). Boston, MA: Pearson.

Gillet, J. W., & Temple, C. (1998). *Understanding reading problems: Assessment and Instruction* (2nd ed.). Boston, MA: Allyn & Bacon.

Hunter, M. (1982). *Mastery teaching: Increasing instructional effectiveness in secondary schools, college, and universities.* El Segundo, CA: TIP Publications.

Marzano, Robert J. (2007). *The art and science of teaching. A comprehensive framework for effective instruction.* Alexandria, VA: Association for Supervision and Curriculum Development.

Ogle, D. (1986). K-W-L: A teaching model that develops active reading of expository text. *The Reading Teacher, 39,* 564–570.

Pearson, P. D. (2013, January 25). *Research and the Common Core: Can the romance survive?* Webinar sponsored by TextProject. Retrieved from www.textproject.org.

Raphael, T. E., Highfield, K., & Au, K. H. (2006). *QAR now: A powerful and practical framework that develops comprehension and higher-level thinking skills.* New York, NY: Scholastic.

Readence, J., Bean, T., & Baldwin, R. (2012). *Content area reading: An integrated approach* (12th ed.). Dubuque, IA: Kendall Hunt.

Ruddell, M. R. (2007). *Teaching content reading and writing* (5th ed.). Hoboken, NJ: John Wiley & Sons, Inc.

Shanahan, T. (2011, August 21). *Rejecting instructional level theory* [Web log post]. Retrieved from www.shanahanliteracy.com/search/label/text%20difficulty

Short, D., Echevarría, J., & Richards-Tutor, C. (2011). Research on academic literacy development in sheltered instruction classrooms. *Language Teaching Research, 15*(3), 363–380.

Short, D., Fidelman, C., & Louguit, M. (2012). Developing academic language in English language learners through sheltered instruction. *TESOL Quarterly, 46*(2), 333–360.

Short, D. J., Vogt, M.E., & Echevarría, J. (2011a). *The SIOP Model for teaching history/social studies to English learners*. Boston, MA: Pearson.

Short, D. J., Vogt, M.E., & Echevarría, J. (2011b). *The SIOP Model for teaching science to English learners*. Boston, MA: Pearson.

Stiggins, R. J., Arter, J. A., Chappuis, J., & Chappuis, S. (2006). *Classroom assessment for student learning: Doing it right—using it well*. Portland, ME: Educational Testing Service.

Tovani, C. (2000). *I read it, but I don't get it. Comprehension strategies for adolescent readers*. Portland, ME: Stenhouse Publishers.

Vogt, M.E., & Echevarría, J. (2008). *99 ideas and activities for teaching English learners with the SIOP Model*. Boston, MA: Pearson Allyn & Bacon.

Vogt, M.E., Echevarría, J., & Short, D. (2010). *The SIOP Model for teaching English language arts to English learners*. Boston, MA: Pearson.

Watson, K., & Young, B. (1986). Discourse for learning in the classroom. *Language Arts, 63*(2), 126–133.

WIDA Consortium. (2007). *English language proficiency standards and resource guide, 2007 edition, prekindergarten through grade 12*. Madison, WI: The Board of Regents of the University of Wisconsin System.